# CiTY·SMaRT™
## GUIDEBOOK

# Tucson

### by James Reel

John Muir Publications
Santa Fe, New Mexico

John Muir Publications, P. O. Box 613, Santa Fe, New Mexico 87504

Printed in the United States of America.
First edition. First printing September 1998

ISBN 1-56261-368-5
ISSN 1099-2502

Editors: Sarah Baldwin, Elizabeth Wolf
Graphics Editors: Heather Pool, Stephen Dietz
Production: Janine Lehmann
Design: Janine Lehmann
Cover Design: Suzanne Rush
Typesetter: Melissa Tandysh
Map Production: Julie Felton
Printer: Publishers Press
Front Cover Photo: © Leo de Wys, Inc./Fridmar Damm—San Xavier del Bac Mission
Back Cover Photo: © Leo de Wys, Inc./Masa Uemara—Organ Pipe Cactus National
Monument

Parts of this book originally appeared in the *Arizona Daily Star* and are used here with
permission.

Distributed to the book trade by
Publishers Group West
Berkeley, California

# CONTENTS

# MAP CONTENTS

# HOW TO USE THIS BOOK

Whether you're a visitor, a new resident, or a Tucson native, you'll find *City•Smart Guidebook: Tucson* indispensable. Author James Reel brings you an insider's view of the best Tucson has to offer.

   *City•Smart Guidebook: Tucson* presents the Tucson metropolitan area in five geographic zones. The zone divisions are listed below and are shown on the map on the following pages. Look for a zone designation in parentheses at the end of each listing. You'll also find maps of downtown Tucson and the greater Tucson area in chapters 3, 4, and 5 to help you locate the accomodations, restaurants, and sights covered in those chapters. Wheelchair accessibility is indicated in chapters 3 through 7 by the ⅄ symbol.

## Tucson Zones

### Downtown (DT)
*Bounded on the west by the Santa Cruz River (just west of I-10), on the east by Park Avenue/Euclid, on the north by St. Mary's Road/Sixth Street, and on the south by 22nd Street.* Includes the government offices and main library; the Downtown Arts District; and Tucson's oldest neighborhoods, including Snob Hollow, Armory Park, and the largely gentrified barrio.

### Central-North (CN)
*Bounded on the west by First Avenue, on the east by Wilmot Road, on the north by the Santa Catalina Mountains and Coronado National Forest, and on the south by 22nd Street.* Includes the University of Arizona, the city's main shopping and business corridors, and much of the tony foothills residential district.

### East Side (ES)
*Bounded on the west by Wilmot Road, on the east by the Pima/Cochise county line, on the north by the Santa Catalina Mountains and Coronado National Forest , and on the south by I-10.* Encompasses Sabino Canyon, the most easily accessible portions of the Catalinas (including Mount Lemmon and its town of Summerhaven), the eastern unit of Saguaro National Park, Colossal Cave, and a huge residential area.

### South Side (SS)
*Bounded on the north by 22nd Street, on the south by the Tohono O'odham Reservation and Mission San Xavier, on the west by I-10/I-19, and on the east by Wilmot Road.* Includes the little embedded municipality of South Tucson, Davis-Monthan Air Force Base, Tucson International Airport, Desert Diamond Casino and the aforementioned mission.

### West Side (WS)
*Includes everything west of the already-mentioned zones: from First Avenue/ Downtown/I-19 west to Sandario Road, with the southern line at the Tohono O'odham Reservation.* Herein lie the major north-south artery Oracle Road and the sprawling northwest developments, the Pima Community College west campus (with its Center for the Arts), the Tucson Mountains, Old Tucson theme park, the Arizona-Sonora Desert Museum, the western unit of Saguaro National Park, and Casino in the Sun.

# TUCSON ZONES

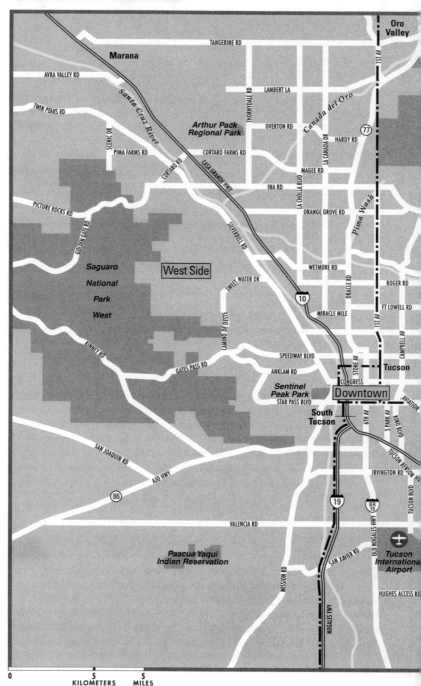

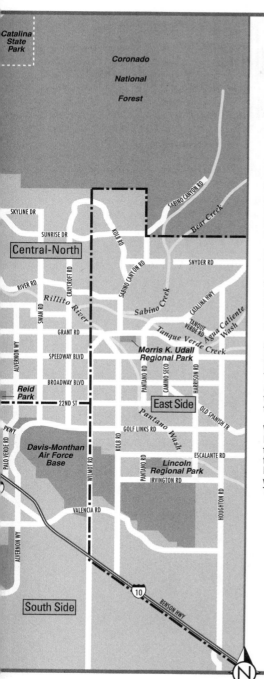

## TUCSON ZONES

**Downtown (DT)**
Bounded on the west by the Santa Cruz River (just west of I-10), on the east by Park Avenue/Euclid, on the north by St. Mary's Road/Sixth Street, and on the south by 22nd Street.

**Central-North (CN)**
Bounded on the west by First Avenue, on the east by Wilmot Road, on the north by the Santa Catalina Mountains and Coronado National Forest, and on the south by 22nd Street.

**East Side (ES)**
Bounded on the west by Wilmot Road, on the east by the Pima/Cochise county line, on the north by the Santa Catalina Mountains and Coronado National Forest, and on the south by I-10.

**South Side (SS)**
Bounded on the north by 22nd Street, on the south by the Tohono O'odham Reservation and Mission San Xavier, on the west by I-10/I-19, and on the east by Wilmot Road.

**West Side (WS)**
Includes everything west of the already-mentioned zones: from First Avenue/Downtown/I-19 west to Sandario Road, with the southern line at the Tohono O'odham Reservation.

© Metro Tucson CVB

# 1

## WELCOME TO TUCSON

*'Desert' is an unfortunate word all around and most of its usual associations are inaccurate as well as unfavorable. In the first place the word doesn't even mean 'dry,' but simply uninhabited or deserted—like Robinson Crusoe's island. In that sense, the expanse about me is far from being a desert, for it is teeming with live things very glad indeed to be right there.*
— Joseph Wood Krutch, *The Desert Year* (1952)

Some people plant lawns. Many huddle under the chill draft of air conditioners. But, try as they may, there's no escaping the fact that Tucson, Arizona, is a desert city. The temperature begins creeping toward 100 degrees in May and hovers there into September. The riverbeds run with dry sand most of the year. The underground water table gradually withdraws from the surface. People sweat, their unprotected skin turns brown and splotchy, and if they wander too far into the wild without provisions, they may soon die. Yet Tucson's residents and visitors do not languish, weak and cotton-mouthed, in what little shade is afforded by the spindly trees and slim cacti. Rather, they thrive here, and in fact Tucson is a fast-growing city whose economy greatly depends on tourism.

Tucson sprawls at the northernmost edge of the Sonoran Desert, that forest of saguaro cactus that casts scant shade and where other vegetation seldom grows more than thigh-high. The land's vastness is sobering—look out across the glare of the rolling valley and you recognize what a small space you occupy in a wide world. Yet you can also find a place for yourself here. The space is open, ringed with landmark mountain ranges, so you can always get your bearings. And such a stern landscape is just intimidating enough to inspire a sense of communal isolation. Tucson's inhabitants are not anonymous individuals cowering in cramped urban cubbyholes; rather, we're out on the frontier together, both self-sufficient and, when necessary, cooperative.

The city's current nickname, "the Old Pueblo," was more florid a hundred years ago. Back then the editor of the *Arizona Daily Star* referred to the town as "this ancient and honorable pueblo." He used the term so often that he came to abbreviate it "the a. and h. p.," as if it were the name of a railroad. It was all exaggeration, of course. "Ancient"? Not by the standards of the pioneers; Europeans didn't establish a permanent settlement on the spot until 1775. "Pueblo"? The indigenous people didn't build pueblo-style multiple dwellings. And "honorable"? Well. . . . Yet deep cultural truths lurked within that nickname. People had lived by Sentinel Peak, at "the foot of the black mountain" (*Chuk Shon*, in the O'odham language), since well before the time of Christ. Though the practical, heat-resistant adobe homes that the Mexican settlers built were not pueblos, the word *pueblo* (Spanish for "town") nevertheless accurately describes the sense of community these settlers helped to create. And despite the undercurrent of individualistic opportunism that characterized westward expansion, there's always been a sense here that we're all in this together.

# A Brief History of Tucson

## The Early Years

Tucson's earliest village people farmed corn, used tobacco, and shot one another in the back as early as 760 B.C. These would remain common local pursuits for the next 2,500 years, through successive waves of new settlers. The earliest Tucsonans, archaeologists have recently learned, occupied several sites along the Santa Cruz River, which flowed during most of the year until the end of the nineteenth century. One settlement, now designated Santa Cruz Bend, thrived between the eighth and third centuries B.C.; it contained at least 176 pit dwellings, storehouses, and communal structures. Its people foraged for food and cultivated corn with some of the earliest irrigation ditches in the Southwest. They were the original Marlboro men, too; the site has provided evidence of the earliest use of tobacco in North America. Santa Cruz Bend also boasted the earliest known formal cemetery in Southern Arizona; in it was found the skeleton of one of the

## TRIVIA

Plenty of rough customers passed through territorial Tucson, but guns were rarely fired in the streets except in celebration, and the town recorded only one lynching—of four murderers at once, in 1873.

# Name That Town

*When, in 1698, the Jesuit missionary Father Kino stumbled upon an Indian village called Chuk Shon, he dubbed the place San Cosme del Tucson. During the next 70 years, Spanish colonial administrators would rename the settlement San José and then San Agustín del Tucson, in each case pronouncing the hard "c" in the middle of "Tucson." Both "San Agustín" and the hard "c" were eventually stripped away, but Augustine remained the town's patron saint. San Agustín Cathedral downtown is now the sole reminder that a smaller Tucson once boasted grander names.*

region's first victims of violent crime—three arrowheads were lodged in its back. Excavated in the mid-1990s, the site has now been built over, sitting unmarked just southwest of the Miracle Mile interchange on Interstate 10.

These Late Archaic people were succeeded by the Mogollon, Anasazi, and Hohokam cultures. The first two groups were seminomadic—Tucsonans have always been wanderers—but the Hohokam were farmers and traders. All along, a favorite settlement site lay on the west bank of the Santa Cruz by a massive hill of black volcanic rock. This location gave Tucson its name: *Chuk Shon*, which the Spaniards later rendered as Tuc-son. Anglos would retain the Spanish spelling but allow the central "c" to fall silent. The hill itself is now officially known as Sentinel Peak, because it is an excellent lookout point commanding a view of the entire valley to the east. More recently it has been nicknamed "A" Mountain, for the large, sloppily whitewashed "A" (for University of Arizona) swelling like a goiter on the hillside.

In 1698 the Jesuit missionary and explorer Father Eusebio Francisco Kino stopped at the foot of the black mountain and rested at a large village of Sobaipuri-Piman Indians—there were perhaps 750 of them, living in small, dome-shaped brush huts (the Hohokam had disappeared mysteriously some 200 years before). Kino and his fellow Jesuits were building a system of missions through what are now Mexico, Arizona, and California, and Tucson became a way station for soul-savers, a Pima village administered by a priest who usually worked out of the nearby village of Bac. (Today Bac is the site of the lovely Mission San Xavier del Bac, known as the "White Dove of the Desert.") Spanish influence in the area was feeble, and Apache raiders were beginning to move west into the Tucson basin. Their assaults lessened Piman resentment of the Spaniards; as Tucson and Bac began to seem more like refugee camps than villages, the Pimans—and a newly arrived tribe, today called Tohono O'odham—pressed the Spaniards for military assistance.

Franciscans replaced the disgraced Jesuits in 1768. The new priest assigned to Bac, Francisco Garcés, understood Tucson's strategic position and began to build a large fortified residence in 1771. Previously, Captain Juan Bautista de Anza had helped Tucson's Indians fortify the center of their village. In 1775 Hugo O'Conor, an Irish mercenary in Spanish employ, arrived to establish a presidio, or military fort, across the river from Garcés' civilian fortifications. Because timber-worthy trees were miles away, all this construction was done with adobe—a mixture of mud, clay, and straw. Over time the Piman population declined, the Apaches agreed to a period of peace, colonial New Spain became independent Mexico, and the frontier mission system was squelched by the new government. In the course of all this change, the mission settlement west of the river, at the foot of the black mountain, began literally to melt into the earth. By 1950 a commercial brickyard had taken over the site. Next came a landfill. Today a flat, barren field off Mission Road bears poor witness to the 2,700 years of life and strife at this spot.

## Modern Times
East of the river, the Spanish presidio became the nucleus of a little Mexican village, which, after the 1854 Gadsden Purchase, gradually grew into an American frontier town. It served as capital of the Arizona Territory from 1867 to 1877. Cattle ranchers began to take over much of the valley; farmers warily tilled the desert soil within reach of the Santa Cruz; gold

---

# The Pope Blesses Tucson

*In March 1880 Mayor Bob Leatherwood had so swollen with civic pride over the arrival of the railroad that he telegraphed every dignitary he could think of with the news. He even wired an announcement to the Pope, requesting his benediction. The telegraph clerks decided to have a bit of fun at the mayor's expense. During the festivities surrounding the arrival of the first train in Tucson, the clerks delivered to Leatherwood the following message: "His Holiness the Pope acknowledges with appreciation receipt of your telegram informing him that the ancient city of Tucson at last has been connected with the outside world and sends his benediction but for his own satisfaction would ask, where in hell is Tucson?"*

*Hunters and trappers in Arizona, c. 1908*

and copper miners headed for the hills. The railroad arrived in 1880, and with the surrender of Geronimo in 1886—the Apaches had become aggressive again as the area boomed—Tucson began to shake off its dust and stretch.

The railroad allowed fine goods and raw materials to be imported at dramatically reduced costs—a half-cent per pound per 100 miles, compared to the five and a half cents charged by the stage services. Now Anglos from the east—another booming import—could afford to turn up their noses at the "primitive" (but cool, sturdy, and practical) Mexican adobe houses. They began to build with imported wood and brick and to quarry the foot of Sentinel Peak for big black stones to use in foundations and garden walls. Gas lighting, a municipal water system, and the city's first bathtub all appeared during the early 1880s.

Anglo men initially married Mexican American women without hesitation, but the arrival of the railroad allowed an easier influx of Anglo brides, and by the 1890s the Hispanics found themselves outnumbered. Throughout its modern history, Tucson has drawn many leading citizens from its Mexican American population, but it was clear during the first two-thirds of the twentieth century that the Anglos wielded greater public influence. That meant making way for progress and development, with comparatively small regard for the preservation of the city's heritage.

The city's idea of progress has at times been rather odd. In 1885 enraged citizens nearly lynched the lobbyist who came back from the territorial legislature not with the coveted prison or insane asylum, but with the promise of a university—in a territory where secondary schools were almost nonexistent. Two gamblers and a saloon keeper grudgingly donated 40 acres of useless land far beyond the city limits, and the University of Arizona opened in 1891; most of its 32-member class enrolled in the high

# TUCSON TIMELINE

**600–1450** Hohokam culture flourishes but mysteriously disappears by the fifteenth century.

**1774** Juan Bautista de Anza begins to forge his route from Sonora to California, stopping in Tucson along the way.

**1775** Irish-born Spanish soldier Hugo O'Conor surveys the site of the Spanish presidio in what will eventually become downtown Tucson.

**1797** Mission San Xavier del Bac is completed.

**1821** Mexico wins independence from Spain; Tucson becomes a northern frontier town.

**1854** Gadsden Purchase brings Tucson under U.S. jurisdiction.

**1862** The Confederates briefly occupy Tucson under Sherod Hunter.

**1870** The weekly *Arizona Citizen*, the city's oldest continuously published newspaper (now the daily *Tucson Citizen*), is founded.

**1877** The newspaper that would become the *Arizona Daily Star* is established as a triweekly publication; two years later it becomes the city's first daily.

**1880s** Mexican persecution drives Yaquis into Arizona in an exodus that will last 40 years.

**1880** The railroad arrives and transforms local lifestyles.

**1886** Geronimo's final surrender brings peace to southern Arizona.

**1889** Fred Ronstadt founds the 40-piece band Club Filarmónico Tucsonense.

**1891** The U.S. Army's Fort Lowell closes; Mexican families settle into that area, which becomes known as El Fuerte.

The University of Arizona opens.

**1897** Downtown's San Agustín Cathedral is built; it is remodeled in Mission style in 1929.

**1907** Despite strenuous objections from saloon owners and many leading citizens with vested interests, gambling is outlawed in Arizona.

**1912** Arizona becomes the 48th state on February 14.

**1915** The Spanish-language Teatro Carmen opens.

**1916** The Papago (later renamed Tohono O'odham) Reservation is established near Tucson.

**1926** Construction begins on the Temple of Music and Art.

**1927** Charles Lindbergh flies in to dedicate Davis-Monthan Air Field, at the time the largest municipal airport in the United States. D-M would become a military base during World War II.

| | |
|---|---|
| Tucson Symphony Orchestra is founded. | 1928 |
| Isabella Greenway opens the Arizona Inn, ostensibly to house extra furniture produced in her workshop for disabled World War I veterans. | 1930 |
| Evaporative coolers are invented; summer becomes almost tolerable. | 1934 |
| Tucson singer Lalo Guerrero and Los Carlistas appear on the New York–based radio show *Major Bowes and His Original Amateur Hour*. In 1997 Guerrero will be awarded the National Medal of Arts by President Clinton. | 1938 |
| Broadway Village, the city's first modern-style shopping center, opens. | 1939 |
| Tucson's first drive-in movie theater opens with *Golden Boy*, starring Barbara Stanwick and William Holden. | 1940 |
| The paved road from Tucson up the south side of the Catalinas is completed after 18 years of work by federal prisoners. | 1951 |
| Civil defense authorities blanket the city with 20 air-raid sirens. Within a year, the Air Force announces that 18 Titan missiles will soon ring Tucson. | 1959 |
| Urban renewal destroys ravaged Territorial-period neighborhoods, making way for the Tucson Convention Center, La Placita Plaza, and a complex of government offices. | 1960s–1970s |
| The landmark El Conquistador Hotel is demolished to allow expansion of El Con Mall. | 1968 |
| A municipal ordinance permits the creation of historic zones, helping protect old buildings from demolition. | 1974 |
| The Tucson Museum of Art opens. | 1975 |
| After lengthy legal haggling, desegregation begins in the Tucson Unified School District. | 1978 |
| The Fiesta de San Agustín, a local celebration dating to the early nineteenth century, is revived as a mainly secular festival after several decades of dormancy. | 1983 |
| Revival of Hotel Congress is the first recent sign of life downtown; during the next ten years, downtown Tucson will be transformed into a modestly successful arts district. | 1985 |
| The Federal Indian Gaming Regulatory Act is passed; after several years and much harassment from the state government, casinos are opened and flourish on the reservations. | 1988 |
| The University of Arizona Wildcats win the NCAA basketball championship. | 1997 |

school division. Over the decades the UA came to sharpen Tucson's character, giving it an intellectual and technological component even more highly developed than in other Southwestern college towns. Thanks in part to the presence of the university, Tucson is now home to many high-tech industries and is also one of the world's astronomy capitals.

The railroad brought literally hundreds of health-seeking tuberculosis patients to town as the nineteenth century concluded. Until the development of good hospitals between 1910 and 1928, most of these people lived in a squalid tent city. Tourists in good health began flocking to the city around that time, lounging at dude ranches and shopping for indigenous goods. World War II siphoned off many of the city's young men but blessed Tucson economically with the establishment of Davis-Monthan Air Force Base, which remains one of the city's major employers. Beginning in the 1950s city development sprawled out of control. Tacky strip malls lined the major east-west streets, unappreciated desert vegetation was bladed away to accommodate cheap tract homes, and in the late '60s a good chunk of the old barrio was destroyed to make way for government offices and a performing arts and convention center.

During the 1970s Tucsonans began to understand what they were losing. By the early '90s what remained of the barrio had been gentrified and the decaying downtown business area had been transformed into an arts district. Developers had to maneuver around the interests of environmentalists and historical preservationists. Bulldozers still scrape the edges of Tucson, some old buildings are allowed to rot, and a vast economic disparity exists between the residents of the posh North Side foothills and the working-class South Side neighborhoods. But Tucsonans in general have developed a greater appreciation for their surroundings and pride in Tucson's heritage, as evidenced by the popularity of the city's outdoor spaces and its many botanical fairs and multicultural festivals.

## Getting to Know Tucson

In 1997 a change in state law made it easier for areas near cities to become independent municipalities. Incorporation mania hit Tucson sud-

## TRIVIA

Tucson flew the Confederate flag during the Civil War—for about three months in 1862. A minor skirmish between small Union and Confederate forces took place in April of that year at Picacho Peak, 40 miles northwest of Tucson, representing the Civil War's westernmost battle.

denly and hard. The residents of some areas mainly wanted to avoid city taxes. Others were determined to preserve the rural nature of their neighborhoods and avoid high-density development. How things will turn out is uncertain at this writing, but it seems likely that at least a few townlets will assert their independence along Tucson's northern and northwestern edges. Already well established are, in the north, the towns of Oro Valley and Marana—the latter an aggressive land-grabber—and, well to the south, Sahuarita. There's also a curious, one-square-mile municipality called South Tucson long embedded in the city a bit south of downtown.

*Rose Canyon on Mount Lemmon*

Whatever its various components are called, metropolitan Tucson stretches across a gently rolling desert valley ringed by mountains. The tall range to the north, which supports forests of pines and aspens and other trees you wouldn't expect in desert lands, is the Santa Catalinas, often called simply the Catalinas. Its high point is Mount Lemmon (when locals talk about going to Mount Lemmon, they sometimes mean any spot along the main highway that snakes into the Catalinas). The jagged brown peaks to the west are the Tucson Mountains. To the east, more distant from the central city, are the high but rounded Rincons. State and federal lands in all these areas limit Tucson's expansion; Saguaro National Park has units in both the east and west, and most of the Catalinas fall into the domain of Coronado National Forest. The city's southern boundaries are man-made: Davis-Monthan Air Force Base, Tucson International Airport, and San Xavier Indian Reservation. Yet another coniferous mountain range, the Santa Ritas, lies about 45 minutes further south.

Straddling the city's tidy street-grid system are a great many districts that are, frankly, nondescript. Much of the housing and commercial construction since World War II has been generic—single-story strip malls and subdivisions of squat tract homes. Many of the newest midpriced subdivisions are particularly offensive to the desert aesthetic; they're packed tight with the same one- and two-story wood-frame-and-stucco houses that infest the nation from California to Pennsylvania. The more interesting neighborhoods tend to be, on one hand, the oldest, and on the other, the toniest. Downtown offers the most variety: century-old adobe dwellings, Victorian brick structures, a few fine old mansions. Immediately east of the University of Arizona is the Sam Hughes neighborhood, with its lovely variety of mid-twentieth-century upper-middle-class

In 1885 Tucsonans saw no practical benefit in establishing a university in their town. One bartender offered this economics-based argument against the school, giving new meaning to the term *dry academics*: "What good will it do us? Who in hell ever heard of a university professor buying a drink?"

homes. Still further east and a few blocks to the south, in the vicinity of Country Club Road and Broadway Boulevard, are the grandest central-city residences, particularly in the El Encanto neighborhood. The most fashionable area for well-heeled newcomers is the foothills, specifically the lower part of the Catalinas. Here sprout arresting new mansions—or at least conspicuously spacious houses—surrounded by desert acreage. This is also the one district of Tucson where all the streets twist confusingly; if you go on a driving tour, take a map.

The foothills are home primarily to wealthy Anglos. The city's East Side is also mainly white man's land, although more middle class. The South Side is where poor families tend to wind up, especially Hispanics. The rest of the city's neighborhoods, though, are very well integrated ethnically; these areas are distinguished from one another by real estate value, not race.

## The People of Tucson

Tucson is a city of transients. Young people attend the University of Arizona, then move on. Midlife workers arrive on corporate assignment or looking for a new opportunity, then mosey along after five years or so. Retirees come to spend their final years under the sun, near a golf course and good medical care. Only 26 percent of metro householders have lived in their present homes more than ten years. But ever since the end of a business slump way back in 1896, more people have stayed than left. Right now, about 50,000 folks move to Tucson each year—mainly from the upper Midwest and California—and 30,000 move out. The metro population, meaning the inhabitants of all of Pima County, currently stands at 806,000. Within the 194 square miles of Tucson itself dwell 462,000 sweltering souls. Despite the constant influx of retirees, the median age in the city is only 34.

Until the very end of the nineteenth century, Tucson's leading citizens were mainly Mexican American. For the past hundred years, the power brokers have tended to be Anglo, although not exclusively. Hispanics have been outnumbered since the 1890s and still constitute only 24.5 percent of the population (compared to the Anglos' 68.2 percent). Even so, Hispanics are rapidly regaining cultural parity and are the source of the city's richest and most-celebrated civic and social traditions. Most governmental agencies offer assistance in both English and Spanish; at voting time, ballots are bilingual; and on Tucson's West and South Sides, the billboards are likely to be in Spanish.

Another important ethnic group, but one that takes a less active role in formal civic affairs, is Chinese. Their ancestors came to construct the railroad in the late 1870s and stayed on to build a solid if sometimes barely visible corner of Tucson society. Also reticent are the Native Americans, whose cultures do not suffuse public life in Arizona to the extent that they do in, for example, New Mexico. The Tohono O'odham and Yaqui peoples living at Tucson's edge are, however, newly asserting their presences, largely through their casino-based economies. They also allow glimpses of their cultural traditions during powwows, rodeos, and Easter celebrations, as well as at the city's annual multicultural festivals like the Fiesta de San Agustín and the Tucson Heritage Experience (T.H.E.) festival.

African Americans constitute a curiously small portion of Tucson's population, considering their important but ignored work as cowboys a century ago and their special "Buffalo Soldier" unit at nearby Fort Huachuca during the same period. The highest-profile African American contribution to life in Tucson is the annual Juneteenth celebration, commemorating the

## Second City

*Tucson takes pride in its "second city" status, which allows it to cultivate an individualistic, somewhat contrarian character. Any local will tell you that Tucson is the heart and soul of Arizona; in their view the state capital, Phoenix, is an unfortunate blight, a smoggy sacrificial area where the state politicians can be quarantined. Tucsonans will tell you that they have a superior appreciation of the desert and its peculiar demands, whereas Phoenicians are interested primarily in asphalt and Bermuda grass. The big corporations and wealthiest retirees are centered in Phoenix, but Tucson is the state's cultural capital, where the statewide theater and opera companies originated (never mind that Phoenix has three times as many small theater groups, and is home to the state's primary ballet troupe). Phoenix is slick, shallow, and pretentious—or so Tucsonans will tell you. They are, of course, correct.*

In 1887 Mexican-born carriage maker Fred Ronstadt formed Tucson's first substantial (10-piece) concert band; two years later he founded a 40-piece ensemble. He also established a hardware store that lasted a century and a family dynasty that produced, in the current generation, a police chief, a parks director, and several more musicians—including singer Linda Ronstadt.

Emancipation Proclamation. Tucson has welcomed a strong Jewish presence since Territorial days; synagogues for every Judaic branch dot the city, and an impressive, well-equipped Jewish Community Center also exists. The *Arizona Jewish Post* is the weekly newspaper especially geared to that community. The University of Arizona has drawn a great variety of scholars and students from around the world, many of whom have put down roots here. Muslim, Indian, and Southeast Asian populations, in particular, are beginning to flourish, thanks to the university. And socially, Tucsonans stretch across the rainbow, from rednecks to blue-haired opera dames.

## When to Visit

Summer reveals the true Tucson, climatically. If you have what it takes to survive June, July, and August in the Old Pueblo, you can pride yourself on being no mere tourist, but a sturdy traveler. For obvious reasons, hotel rates

*Laying railroad track through Arizona Territory, c. 1898*

National Archives & Records Admin.

plummet in the hot months. But, frankly, there's less to do in the summer than during the rest of the year. The greatest variety of special events and ongoing cultural attractions may be found in late fall, winter, and early spring.

One drawback to visiting Tucson in the winter is traffic congestion. These mild months draw thousands of "snowbirds," part-time residents from colder climes. From December through March, traffic on the major thoroughfares can be slow, although Tucson is almost never subject to true gridlock, except occasionally between 5 and 5:45 p.m. on eastbound Interstate 10. Also, if your visit coincides with the Gem and Mineral Show in February, UA Homecoming weekend in November, or the Copper Bowl in December, be sure to make room reservations well in advance.

Spring is wildflower season, but only if the autumn and winter rains have come at the right time in the right amount. The spring air is dry and temperatures are mild, although the heat does begin building quickly from the beginning of May. Summer can be miserable for heat-sensitive visitors. By June, the afternoon temperature frequently peaks between 100 and 110, and it can reach even higher from time to time. (Tucsonans are baffled by U.S. Weather Bureau figures that place the "average" maximum temperature in June and July at a mere 99.) But, as the residents point out, it's a dry heat—until the summer rainy season begins around the Fourth of July. Sometimes pompously referred to as the "monsoon season," this time of year brings heavy cloud buildup most afternoons, with sudden—and brief—thunderstorms common from midafternoon to

## Tucson's Climate

|  | High | Low | Precipitation |
|---|---|---|---|
| January | 63 | 39 | 0.87 |
| February | 68 | 41 | 0.70 |
| March | 73 | 45 | 0.72 |
| April | 81 | 50 | 0.30 |
| May | 90 | 58 | 0.18 |
| June | 100 | 68 | 0.20 |
| July | 99 | 74 | 2.37 |
| August | 97 | 72 | 2.19 |
| September | 95 | 68 | 1.67 |
| October | 84 | 57 | 1.06 |
| November | 73 | 46 | 0.67 |
| December | 64 | 40 | 1.07 |

Source: National Weather Service

early evening. Twenty years ago, these storms could be spectacular, with heavy lightning and pelting hail, all dissipating in half an hour. Recently the summer rains have been disappointing—all muggy promise and little action. By Labor Day, the rainy season is officially over, but it's usually petered out sometime in late August.

Things don't cool off until October, when the days turn mild and slightly breezy. There may be a brief cold snap between Thanksgiving and Christmas, but it's usually possible to lunch outdoors in total comfort through January. February can be windy and cold (by Tucson standards, meaning highs in the 60s), although the weather has been less bitter in the 1990s. During winter nights, the mercury dips into the high 30s, and exposed water pipes and delicate plants do need periodic protection from freezing.

# Calendar of Events

### January
Northern Telecom Open, Doubletree Copperbowl Adult Tennis Open, Southern Arizona Square and Round Dance and Clogging Festival, Tucson Quilters Guild Show

### February
Tucson Gem and Mineral Show, World of Wheels Car Show, La Reunion de El Fuerte, La Fiesta de los Vaqueros and Rodeo Parade

### March
Wa:k Pow Wow, AZ Jazz Week, Tucson Winter Chamber Music Festival, PING/Welch's Championship (golf), Fourth Avenue Street Fair

### April
Spring Fling (UA carnival), Cigna Beau Bridges Celebrity Tennis Classic, Pima County Fair, Tucson International Mariachi Conference, Waila Festival (polka-inspired Native American music), Ft. Lowell Pioneer Days, Yaqui Easter Ceremony, Tour of the Tucson Mountains (biking; Sunday after Easter)

### May
Cinco de Mayo

### June
Juneteenth

### July
Independence Day, Fiesta de San Agustín

### September
Mexican Independence Day, Muscular Dystrophy Association Oktoberfest

### October

Jazz Sundae, Fiesta de los Chiles, T.H.E. (Tucson Heritage Experience) Festival (formerly Tucson Meet Yourself), Tucson Blues Festival, DeAnza Days (in Tubac)

### November

Michelob Rugby Classic, Western Music Festival, Downtown Holiday in Lights, Southwestern Rockhound Roundup and Lapidary Weekend, El Tour de Tucson (bicycling)

### December

Balloon Glo, Fourth Avenue Street Fair, Tucson Marathon (Boston qualifier), Copper Bowl, Las Posadas, Winterhaven Festival of Lights

*Snacking at the Fourth Avenue Street Fair*

## Surviving the Summer

All public buildings, motels, and hotels in Tucson pump cooled air onto their patrons. Usually it's dehumidified and refrigerated. Some smaller establishments, and many private homes, rely on swamp coolers, which blow moist air around and are least effective on especially hot or humid days. Once you venture outside, you will do fine as long as you remember the essentials: sunscreen with an SPF of at least 15 on all exposed skin, light clothing to reduce skin exposure, sunglasses that block ultraviolet radiation, and a fairly wide-brimmed hat to protect your face and neck and to keep the sun from baking your brain. Also, even if you're just tooling around in the car, it's a very good idea to carry water or some fluid replacement beverage like Gatorade. Dehydration happens fast; if you start to feel thirsty, dehydration has already begun, and it can lead to headache, nausea, cramps, and fatigue. If you're doing a fair amount of sweaty exerting, don't rely on sodas, fruit juices, or caffeinated or alcoholic beverages, which act as diuretics and exacerbate dehydration. Scared yet? Good. That means you'll be careful to prepare and then can go out and have fun with confidence, even if you can't raise your arms because of the perspiration stains.

In any desert the air is dry, clouds don't form in the daytime to protect the ground and the creatures on it from heat and radiation, and the sun bakes the earth. In the evening there are no clouds to keep down the heat that rises from the ground. So, except in the hot and fairly humid July and August, you could wind up sweating by day and shivering by night. Carry along a light layer or two of clothing in case you need it after sunset.

One more note, and an ominous one. Every summer and winter during the rainy seasons, a few people in Tucson nearly drown. They try to cross a flowing wash on foot or in a vehicle—many roads just dip into little washes rather than bridge them—and are swept away. Even if no raindrops are falling on your head, if it's been raining upstream recently, the moisture may be collecting into a flash flood, a wall of water rushing through the arroyos. Once the flow has arrived, it tends to be fast—there's little vegetation holding it back, after all—and deeper than it looks. Unless you see several vehicles with local license plates passing through water that is obviously little more than ankle-deep, don't chance it. At the very least, your car will probably stall out. And at worst you could, ironically, drown in the desert.

## Dressing in Tucson

The essential hot-weather tips are covered in Surviving the Summer, above. Remember that the evening low temperature will likely be 20 to 30 degrees lower than the daytime high, so have a little something to throw on at night, unless the daytime high is 100.

Tucson accommodates a wide variety of fashion aesthetics. If you're interviewing for a job, go ahead and put on a nice suit or dress; the rest of the time, if you look too formal, people will know you're either a lawyer or an out-of-towner. Shorts are acceptable in any informal situation, even in most low- to medium-priced restaurants. Just be sure to wear a shirt and shoes, too. In the fanciest restaurants it's a good idea to spruce up a bit. A jacket and tie for men are advisable only in the ultra-high-end establishments and are not generally expected during hot weather. Going to the symphony or opera? The only thing likely to draw stares is a tux. Although grunge may not be appropriate for an evening of Mozart—that look is on its way out even in alternative circles, anyway—Tucson is emphatically not a fashion-conscious city like Dallas.

## Business and Economy

During its first century of U.S. attachment, Arizona's economy was built on the "Three Cs"—copper, cattle, and cotton. Little more than vestiges of that economy remain in the Tucson area. The mining industry took a dive in the 1980s, and although BHP Copper is one of Pima County's top ten employers, copper has lost much of its clout. Cattle ranching tends to be a family affair and is practiced many miles from the city limits. Cotton has maintained some presence, but the farms and orchards in Tucson's outlying areas are just as likely to grow hardy vegetables, citrus, dates, or pecans.

Ranked by number of full-time employees (or full-time equivalents), Pima County's top ten employers are the University of Arizona, the state government, Tucson Unified School District, Davis-Monthan Air Force Base, the county government, Hughes Missile Systems, the city government, BHP Copper, HealthPartners of Southern Arizona, and Carondelet Health Care. Additional government, educational, and healthcare agencies dominate the next ten positions on the list, too. Otherwise, the big employers fall into a very few categories: mining, high-tech manufacturing and research (Burr-Brown, IBM, Learjet), transportation and utilities (Tucson Electric Power, US West Communications), trade (supermarkets, Wal-Mart, fast food joints), and services ranging from healthcare providers and resort hotels to—and this, disturbingly, is a biggie—warrens of telephone solicitors.

Arizona is a "right to work" state, meaning that unions are weak. Because of that, and because of the preponderance of service jobs, wages are fairly low. The average per capita income in 1997 was $20,838; according to HUD estimates, a family of four averaged a household income of $37,800. Still, Pima County enjoys a mere 3 percent unemployment rate, its lowest since labor force statistics have been kept.

## Cost of Living

In most respects Tucson falls just a bit below the national cost-of-living average. A few things, however, are comparatively pricey, for reasons nobody, not even investigating state legislators, can explain. Gasoline, for example, costs more in Arizona than in many other states. Tucson stations do underprice their counterparts elsewhere in the state by a few cents; a gallon of regular unleaded gas averages $1.27 in town. Cab fare, while not exorbitant, is hardly a bargain at $8.75 for a five-mile ride. The cost of your daily news fix depends on what time of day you read the paper; it's 50 cents for the morning *Arizona Daily Star*, 35 cents for the declining afternoon *Tucson Citizen*. Otherwise, visitors can expect few surprises. The average dinner for two runs about $25. A hotel double room will probably coax $65 from your suitcase, less if you choose a modest motel. Movie admission is the now-standard $7, with twilight shows running around $4 and discount houses charging $1.50. Need milk? A gallon costs $2.65.

*El Presidio adobe*

© Metro Tucson CVB/Gill Kenny

## Taxes

A state sales tax of 5 percent is applied to everything *except* real estate, prescriptions, and groceries for home consumption. An additional 2 percent tax is imposed in Tucson, Oro Valley, and Marana on goods

## Top Ten Things I Like about Tucson
By George Miller, Tucson mayor 1991–99

1. The people—friendly and active
2. The weather
3. The University of Arizona
4. Pima Community College
5. The four school districts that are inside the city limits: Tucson Unified School District, Sunnyside, Amphitheater, and Flowing Wells
6. Sabino Canyon
7. The air quality
8. The Arizona Inn
9. The rodeo
10. The arts—the various museums, theater, dance, symphony, and opera

taxed by the state. The state personal income tax ranges from 3.25 to 7 percent, based on income. Property owners fork over the dough under a number of tax assessments—Arizona, Pima County, Tucson, the local school district, Pima Community College, the city-county library system, the Central Arizona Conservation District, and Pima County Flood Control District.

## Housing
Sixty percent of Tucsonans own their homes, but with the price of new construction rising, more and more people are purchasing older houses or renting. In 1990 the median value of all owner-occupied homes in Tucson was $76,500. By August 1997, the average sales price of all single-family housing—new and old—was $128,852; the median price for previously owned homes was $107,000, a figure that's been rising by about $10,000 per year. The average house sat on the market for 71 days. As an indication of where prices are going, *construction* costs—materials and labor, not land—for new single-family homes were $48 per square foot in the second quarter of 1997, and these units averaged 2,594 square feet; that means these houses will sell for well above $130,000 if builders are going to make even a minimal profit. As for rentals, in the fourth quarter of 1996, RealData, Inc., reported average rents of unfurnished multifamily units, excluding utilities, at $480 per month. Typical rents in 1996 were $318 for a studio apartment, $413 for one bedroom, $611 for two, and $714 for three.

# Schools

Tucson Unified School District sprawls across the valley, with 73 elementary, 19 middle, 11 high, and nine alternative education campuses. A few of these are "magnet" schools, campuses with a specialized curriculum (science, arts) that draw students from all over the city rather than from local neighborhoods. Some schools are bilingual, which means that Spanish-speaking kids are eased into the educational mainstream, not that all children are brought to fluency in both English and Spanish. TUSD schools are neither ghastly nor, on the whole, outstanding.

Ten other school districts encircle TUSD, providing a total of 45 elementary, 15 junior high, nine high, and five other campuses. According to standardized test scores—which, of course, tell only part of the story— the greatest academic distinction goes to the Catalina foothills district, which benefits from a solid tax base of privileged neighborhoods. More than 100 private and parochial schools have also set up shop in Tucson, including a number of "charter" schools that receive a chunk of funds otherwise earmarked for public schools, allowing students to enroll without tuition.

The University of Arizona consists of 14 colleges, eight schools, 95 doctoral programs, and the state's only medical school. Pima Community College, offering two-year programs, scatters five campuses across the city and also holds night classes in high school facilities. Private colleges include the University of Phoenix, Prescott College, and Tucson University.

Sun Tran

# 2

# GETTING AROUND TUCSON

Truly a city of the West, Tucson was developed largely by contrarian individuals starting fresh. Partly because of the settlers' independent natures and partly because of the initial lack of reliable materials for multistory buildings, Tucson has always been a low-slung, spread-out city. Unlike eastern cities, which were developed on European models a good century or two before Tucsonans erected anything halfway permanent, Tucson and other Western towns tend to segregate business, residential, and recreational areas. Except on a couple of streets downtown, you don't see three or four floors of apartments above rows of street-level shops. And because the city's density is low, you can forget about getting around on foot—again, except downtown. The frontier independence mentality lives on in a general resistance to big mass-transit projects. At the same time, Tucsonans oppose the spread of freeways, realizing how they can destroy or isolate neighborhoods and natural areas. So, unless you want to wait 20 minutes or so for a city bus to pick you up and poke its way across town, or unless you're a hardy bicyclist, you're probably better off in your own car.

## Tucson Layout

The city streets follow a clean grid system, with most avenues running north and south and most streets running east and west. Don't be confused by all the street names that begin with *Calle* or *Camino*; these are simply the Spanish words for "street" and "road," respectively. Remember that you can always get your bearings from the mountains. The Catalinas—the

Lost? Tucson's street-naming rules can at least help you narrow your direction down to two compass points. Avenues and Avenidas run north and south. Streets and Calles run east and west. "Stravenues," as you might guess from the hybrid term, run diagonally. Places or Courts are cul-de-sacs or dead-end roads. But if you're on a Drive, Lane, Road, or Camino, you could be heading in any direction.

big, tall range with greenery toward the top—are to the north. The Tucson Mountains—a lower, ragged, all-brown range—mark the west. The more distant Rincons lie in the east. And don't forget that in this sunniest of cities you can try solar navigation, too. Broadway Boulevard, which runs laterally through the city's middle, is the "zero point" for north-south street numbers. However, the east-west dividing line, Stone Avenue, is skewed far to the west. This means that a 2500 west address is likely at the western city limit, but a 2500 east address is barely at Tucson's longitudinal center.

As mentioned, Tucson has resisted elaborate freeway systems; only two full-scale freeways skirt the city. Interstate 10 comes down from the north (Phoenix) along Tucson's west side, then curves east to follow the city's southern boundary and shoot off toward New Mexico. At the curve, I-19 takes off to the south, and the Mexican border. A couple of "parkways"—fairly high-speed divided streets impeded by only a few stoplights—have been developed recently. Kino Parkway is actually the southern extension of Campbell Avenue; it's the fastest way to get to and from the airport, even though the street that actually leads into the terminal is the more leisurely Tucson Boulevard. Aviation Parkway cuts diagonally from Davis-Monthan Air Force Base up to the downtown area. It moves some commuters around efficiently, but because it was built mostly through an undeveloped no man's land, it's of little use to visitors and does nothing to relieve congestion on the major east-west streets to the north.

Toll roads and toll bridges are unknown in Arizona, except when you're being charged to enter public lands. A small fee has been announced for access to Coronado National Forest via Catalina Highway, but that charge has raised such an outcry from residents that it remains to be seen whether the little toll booth will stay up much longer.

## Driving in Tucson

Sitting behind the wheel is relatively easy on the nerves in Tucson, except perhaps during afternoon rush hour and the December shopping/snowbird season. Traffic on westbound I-10 can slow to 25 miles an hour right after

## TIP

It rains so infrequently in Tucson that many of the older streets were designed to double as temporary aqueducts. To avoid driving through deep water during a rainstorm, stay in the inside lane and approach low-lying intersections with caution.

work, and on the surface streets cars can back up at some midtown intersections for a couple of traffic light cycles. Otherwise, no problem, unless the street you want happens to be under construction, which is often the case in this bond-happy city.

Not many years ago, the middle turn lane in each major east-west street would convert to a regular traffic lane during rush hours—westbound in the morning, eastbound in the evening. These "suicide lanes" are being phased out as the streets are widened, but watch for overhead signage, especially on Grant Road, for restrictions.

Some general tips: Unless told otherwise, you may turn right on a red light. Left-turn signals have been installed at the busiest intersections, so don't give up when the general light turns red; a green arrow may point the way for you. If you're in a hurry, do not drive behind buses, pickups, or RVs; if you're driving an RV, keep right and remember to signal before you turn, and the locals will accept you.

Parking poses problems only downtown and on the University of Arizona campus. Almost everywhere else it's free and convenient. Downtown, the streets are metered during weekday business hours, and open spaces are hard to come by. Several lots and a couple of garages are scattered around the area, and, despite the yelping of the locals, the rates are not prohibitive by national standards. You do get gouged, though, at the UA. And that's only if you can find a metered space or a garage. Most of the lots are restricted to UA permit-holders, and the school's parking and transportation experts have never provided enough spaces to accommodate students, staff, and visitors

*Control Tower at the Tucson International Airport*

Steven Meckler

adequately. Residents of the surrounding neighborhoods got so fed up with the situation, they banned all parking from their streets except for holders of residential permits. (A few such restrictions are also enforced just north and south of downtown). Read the signage carefully before you park.

## Public Transportation

### Bus

There's been idle chatter for years about a light rail system similar to Portland's, but nothing has come of it. Meanwhile, Sun Tran, the city bus system, is adequate but not entirely convenient, because ridership isn't what it could be, and doesn't support much service expansion, because the bus system is not entirely convenient. . . . Still, it's a responsible way to travel if you're in no hurry and you're not worried about sitting at a bus stop in the hot summer sun for a good quarter-hour or more. In Sun Tran's defense, it must be said that the buses do run on schedule, the drivers are helpful, all

---

# Famous Tucsonans

*Tucson is a city of transients—not just those homeless folks you see downtown, but others who pause here a few years and then move on. Here are some famous one-time or sometime Tucsonans: writer Edward Abbey (spent his final decade or more in Tucson, where he died), astronaut Frank Borman (a Tucson High School graduate), writer Ray Bradbury (during junior high), actor Ted Danson (as a preschooler), singer John Denver (half his childhood, including a stint in the Tucson Boys Chorus), former senator Bob Dole (two semesters at the UA), actress Barbara Eden (born in Tucson but moved when she was 3), comic actor Don Knotts (UA alum), rocker Paul McCartney (his wife, Linda, was from Tucson; he owns a home and about 200 acres on the city's east side), actress Valerie Perrine (UA alum), tabloid TV czar Geraldo Rivera (attended the UA under the name Jerry Rivers), singer Linda Ronstadt (born, bred, and again residing in Tucson), jazz singer Diane Schuur (about four years at the beginning of her career), and comedian Garry Shandling (graduate of Palo Verde High School and the UA).*

---

## Silly Spanish Street Names in Tucson

*Calle Sin Vacas (Street Without Cows)*
*Calle Zafiro (Crazy Street)*
*Camino Llanta de la Ponchada (Flat-Tire Road)*
*Granito (Pimple Face) Vista*
*No Le Hace (It Doesn't Matter) Street*
*Placita Taza (Toilet Bowl Place)*

buses have bike racks on the front bumpers, many are equipped with wheelchair lifts, and transfers are free. Maps and schedules are available once you get on a bus, not at the stops, but you don't need to board in ignorance; schedule information is available in English and Spanish by calling 520/792-9222. The standard fare is 85 cents, and exact change is required. There's no further charge for venturing from one end of the city to the other.

### Taxi

You can find taxis and similar transport at the airport and bus terminals, but from any other location you'll have to call, and wait. Some residents have complained that it can take 45 minutes for a cab to show up, and if the driver doesn't immediately see you where you've promised to be, he'll zip off. This is not a consistent problem, but don't schedule yourself too tightly just in case. Typically, the privilege of entering a Tucson taxi costs $1.25, and the meter adds another $1.50 per mile. The leading cab companies are Allstate (520/798-1111), Yellow Cab (520/624-6611), Fiesta Taxi (520/622-7777; Spanish-language service a specialty), and Checker (520/623-1133).

Unless you're splitting cab fare with a couple of strangers, a more economical way for a solo traveler to get from the airport into town, or vice versa, is Arizona Stagecoach. The rate varies with distance but always beats the cab; the drawback is that, because it's a shuttle, several other people are likely to be picked up or dropped off before you reach your destination. For shuttle information, call 520/889-1000.

### Trolley

A historic trolley runs from the Fourth Avenue shopping district to the University of Arizona, but it's more of a pleasant diversion than a meaningful mode of transportation. Trolleys were the principal form of mass transit in Tucson during the first third of this century, but by World War II the lines were closed and the tracks were being paved over. Just a few years ago, the rails were uncovered along Fourth Avenue and University Boulevard, and one of Tucson's last trolley cars was located in Japan and brought home for new service. The route is so short that this qualifies as a fun thing to do, rather than a significant reduction of smog and fatigue. The price of pleasure: $1 each way (50 cents for seniors and kids under 12) 6 to 10 p.m. Fridays and noon to midnight Saturdays, 25 cents for everyone noon to 6 p.m. Sundays. The trolley does not run at any other time. Tickets can be purchased at the Trolley Barn, East Eighth Street and South Fourth Avenue, or at East University Boulevard and North Tyndall Avenue. For ticket information, call 520/792-1802.

*Tucson Department of Transportation*

*Bike racks on Sun Tran are a relief for tired cyclists.*

## Biking in Tucson

A certified bike-friendly town, Tucson now incorporates bicycle lanes into almost all of its street projects. Lanes hug most of the major arteries and many quieter side streets (which, in any case, are usually wide). Maps are

# Tucson Street Signs

*You won't find United Way Boulevard, Mineral & Fossil Boulevard, Goal One: Graduate Boulevard, Gem Show Boulevard, or Colorado Rockies Way on any Tucson street map, but you may find them on signs along such major arteries as Speedway and Broadway. Tucson has an odd tradition of informally renaming certain streets to promote big annual events or campaigns. The temporary signs, called "metros," don't obscure the regular street names, but they can confuse visitors and residents alike. Just remember that real street-name signage is green (except sometimes in the municipality of South Tucson), whereas "metros" are usually blue, big, and strangely positioned on the pole.*

# BIKING IN TUCSON

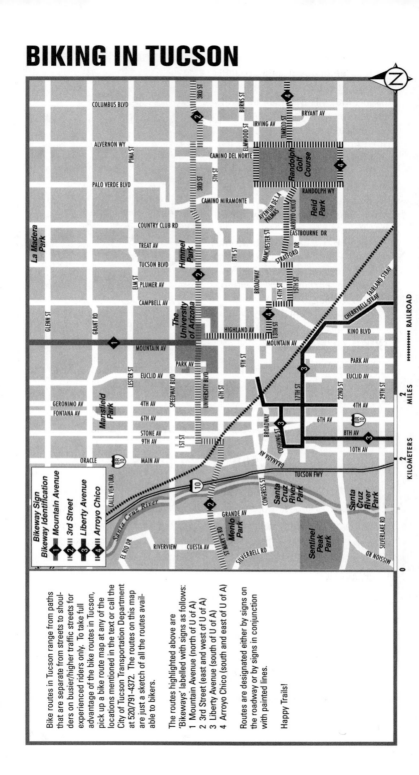

Bike routes in Tucson range from paths that are separate from streets to shoulders on busier/higher traffic streets for experienced riders only. To take full advantage of the bike routes in Tucson, pick up a bike route map at any of the locations mentioned in the text or call the City of Tucson Transportation Department at 520/791-4372. The routes on this map are just a sketch of all the routes available to bikers.

The routes highlighted above are 'Bikeways' labelled with signs as follows:

1. Mountain Avenue (north of U of A)
2. 3rd Street (east and west of U of A)
3. Liberty Avenue (south of U of A)
4. Arroyo Chico (south and east of U of A)

Routes are designated either by signs on the roadway or by signs in conjunction with painted lines.

Happy Trails!

# Top Ten Places to Photograph Tucson's Cultural Diversity

### By José Galvez
### Pulitzer Prize–winning photojournalist and owner of the José Galvez Gallery

1. **International Mariachi Conference.** Mariachi groups from across the United States gather to compete for prizes and recognition. Old friends meet at various concerts. An outdoor fiesta with music, food booths, and a children's parade also highlights the weeklong event. (April)

2. **Tucson Heritage Experience (T.H.E.).** Showcasing Tucson's various ethnic groups, from German, Cuban, and Slavic to Polynesian and many others. Dances, music, arts and crafts, and food are featured attractions. (October)

3. **Kennedy Park.** During Cinco de Mayo (May) and Mexican Independence Day (September), the park comes alive with daylong music from different Latino groups. (3700 S. Mission Road, South Side)

4. **Norteño Festival.** Latino and Native American *Norteño* music groups gather to compete for cash prizes and to see who has the best outfits and following. (Around Labor Day)

5. **Walking tour of Barrio Hollywood.** People barbecuing outside in warm weather, yard *nichos* (altars), other yard art, various murals—a cross-section of Tucson's Mexican American community. (Off Grande Avenue, west of the Santa Cruz River, West Side)

6. **Downtown Saturday Night.** First and third Saturdays of the month, along Congress Street. Young and old, grunge and leather, foothills and barrio—all come out to be entertained by each other. (See Chapter 5, Sights and Attractions)

7. **San Xavier Mission.** Rich in Tucson's Spanish, Mexican, and Tohono O'odham history; recognized the world over for its architecture and interior. (See Chapter 5, Sights and Attractions)

8. **La Fiesta de los Vaqueros.** Cowboys from across the United States gather for competition in various events. The Wild West lives on. (February, at the rodeo grounds, South Side)

9. **Barrio Historico.** With many of the original buildings from Tucson's presidio days, one can almost picture what it was like back in 1880. (See Chapter 5, Sights and Attractions)

10. **Pat's Drive-In.** People come from miles around, in suits and construction wear, to savor Pat's world-famous chili dogs. (Corner of Grande and Niagara, just south of Speedway, West Side)

available at most bike shops or from the City of Tucson Transportation Department (520/791-4372) or the Pima Association of Governments (520/792-2952). Car drivers tend to be aware of bicyclists, the city buses have bike racks, and off-road possibilities abound in the surrounding desert and mountains. The only disadvantage to city biking is that Point A can be quite distant from Point B, but tired cyclists can hitch a ride on those city buses.

Competitive cyclists should be on hand for El Tour de Tucson, a ride/ race making the circuit of the city in November, and the Tour of the Tucson Mountains, which sends cyclists around that West Side range the Sunday after Easter.

Bicycle dealers are generous with advice, even if you're not buying a bike from them. Some, like the Bike Shack (520/624-3663), Broadway Bicycles (520/296-7819), Full Cycle (520/327-3232), Sabino Cycles (520/885-3666), and University Bicycles (520/624-3663), also rent bikes. Organizers of local bike tours have come and gone over the years, but the most stable outfitter has been Arizona Off Road Adventures (520/882-6567), which offers fully supported daylong, sunset, or weeklong local excursions.

## Airports

Tucson International Airport is the area's center for commercial flights. It's an easy airport to get around; surface parking is a convenient walk from the single, two-concourse terminal (not counting a little terminal reserved for flights to and from Mexico). Taxis, shuttles, and car rental agencies are on the spot. There aren't many dining choices in the terminal, but

# Major Airlines Serving Tucson

*America West (800/235-9292)*

*American (800/433-7300)*

*Continental (800/525-0280)*

*Delta (800/221-1212)*

*Northwest (800/225-2525)*

*Reno Air (800/736-6247)*

*Sky West (800/453-9417)*

*Southwest (800/435-9792)*

*United (800/241-6522)*

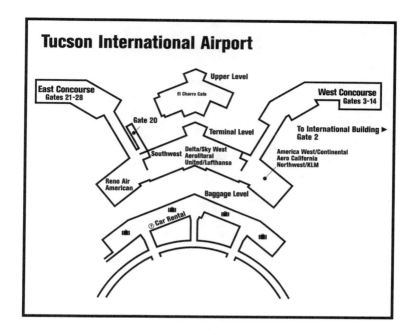

**Tucson International Airport**

Upper Level

El Charro Cafe

East Concourse
Gates 21-28

West Concourse
Gates 3-14

Gate 20

Terminal Level

To International Building ▶
Gate 2

Southwest
Delta/Sky West
Aerolitoral
United/Lufthansa

America West/Continental
Aero California
Northwest/KLM

Reno Air
American

Baggage Level

Car Rental

upstairs, El Charro operates a full-service restaurant that, while not up to the high standards of its downtown location, remains quite satisfying and authentic.

Flying in and out of Tucson can be expensive compared to the rates for Phoenix. That's because Tucson is not the hub for any major airline. To get here or get out, you usually face a layover at a major airport such as Phoenix, Dallas, or Atlanta. Some people prefer to save $50 to $200—and add two freeway hours to their trip—by flying into and out of Phoenix and taking an economical shuttle van between Tucson and Phoenix's Sky Harbor International Airport. For information, call Arizona Flying Coach (520/887-8788) or Arizona Shuttle Service (520/795-6771); reservations are necessary.

By the way, if you're heading from Tucson International Airport not to Tucson but to some nearby community, a few other shuttle options may interest you. For example, Tony's Shuttle (520/294-6788) makes hourly round trips between Tucson and Nogales. Arizona Express (520/622-2028) will cart you to Green Valley, Sun City, Casa Grande, Sierra Vista, Ft. Huachuca, Benson, Bisbee, Douglas, or Marana. In both cases you should make arrangements in advance.

Private pilots are served by the Tucson Airport Authority (administrative office, 520/573-8100), and a few smaller airfields. Most convenient is Ryan Field (520/883-2921). A couple of others exist but try to keep a low profile. If you're a pilot, you know how to look them up.

*Tucson International Airport*

## Train Service

The railroad truly opened the West, but you'd never know it by looking at today's train schedules. Nobody in southern Arizona commutes by train, although there has been talk of establishing a fast line between Tucson and Phoenix for just that purpose. The Amtrak station, at 400 E. Toole Avenue, isn't much to look at; the more interesting stations have been razed or converted into something else (sneak a peek at Carlos Murphy's restaurant, 419 West Congress Street). But it is across the street from the Ronstadt Transit Center, where the city buses gather, and near the Greyhound station (see below), one of the few places you can actually find a cab. For Amtrak reservations and schedule information, call 800/872-7245. If you need to reach the station itself, dial 520/623-4442.

## Bus Service

Greyhound is the sole bus line providing anything other than charter and tour service to Tucson. Its main station, at 2 South Fourth Avenue, throbs at the eastern end of downtown. The company and the city do a good job of maintaining the place. Taxis line up outside, and you can catch a city bus at the open-air Ronstadt Transit Center a couple of blocks to the west. Greyhound also maintains a terminal at 2424 South Sixth Avenue. Call 800/231-2222 for fare and schedule information.

Westward Look Resort

# 3

# WHERE TO STAY

*A hundred years ago, Tucson's visitors were lodged mainly in a couple of small wooden hotels near the railroad tracks—a bad location not just because of the noise, but because sparks from the engines would periodically set fire to the hostelries. Today's accommodations range from swank resorts in the foothills to spartan little motels. The bulk of the city's lodgings, of course, fall into a comfortable middle range. This chapter does not attempt to cover all the big hotel and motel chains, which are well represented and easily contacted through central reservation numbers; several have been granted listings, though, if they are located well off the usual hotel-motel strips or in zones with few other accommodations.*

*In general, midpriced and some budget motels are plentiful along Interstate 10 from Grant Road to about Park Avenue (West Side, downtown, South Side). Budget motels are concentrated along Oracle Road, from Prince Road (which provides the best access from I-10 for this purpose) down through the curve into Drachman (West Side); and near Tucson International Airport, mainly along East Benson Highway (South Side). The farther you stray from the freeways and Oracle Road, the more expensive the lodgings become— just forget about finding budget rooms on the East Side or in the Central-North area near the Catalina foothills. By the way, when the listings below give two price ratings, it usually indicates a significant difference between high-season (winter) and low-season (summer) rates.*

**Price rating symbols:**
$      $50 and under
$$     $51 to $75
$$$    $76 to $125
$$$$   $126 and up

# DOWNTOWN TUCSON

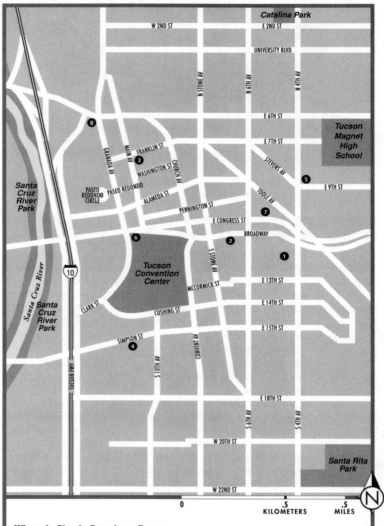

## Where to Stay in Downtown Tucson

1 Armory Park Guest House
2 Clarion Santa Rita Hotel and Suites
3 El Presidio Bed & Breakfast Inn
4 Elysian Grove Market Bed and Breakfast Inn
5 Gateway Villas
6 Holiday Inn City Center
7 Hotel Congress
8 InnSuites

One more note: Once you get past the lobby and into a room, one good hotel is sometimes hard to tell from another. Truly distinctive sleeping quarters are often found in bed-and-breakfasts, which abound in Tucson. The B&B listings here are highly selective, and many fine establishments have been ignored simply because of space restrictions. If you want something original, try one of these places.

## DOWNTOWN

### Hotels and Motels

**CLARION SANTA RITA HOTEL AND SUITES**
**88 E. Broadway Blvd.**
**Tucson, AZ 85701**
**520/622-4000 or 800/722-8848**
**$$$**
When it opened in 1904, the Santa Rita was Tucson's finest, most elegant hotel. Its fortunes have changed several times over the years, but today it is again a perfectly respectable establishment, its facelift meant to evoke the hotels of Sonora, Mexico. Its ballroom, once the city's prime passion pit, is still used on an irregular basis for concerts and dances. Across the street from the Metropolitan Tucson Convention and Visitors Bureau, the Santa Rita boasts computer connections, microwave ovens, and refrigerators in every room, among other amenities. Guests have access to a fitness center, sauna, Jacuzzi, and heated pool. Four rooms are specially equipped for wheelchair patrons. Best of all, the hotel houses Café Poca Cosa, a wonderful restaurant that brings a nouvelle cuisine touch to Mexican dishes. See Chapter 4, Where to Eat. & (Downtown)

**HOLIDAY INN CITY CENTER**
**181 W. Broadway Blvd.**
**Tucson, AZ 85701**
**520/624-8711**
**$$**
This hotel serves up only one little surprise: Small pets are allowed. That's an unexpected feature of a place that's perfectly situated for both downtown doings and freeway escapes. Just a couple of blocks from Interstate 10, right next to the Tucson Convention Center and across the street from the city and county government complex, this Holiday Inn's location could hardly be more practical. (Aesthetic placement is another matter, if you'd rather look at cactus than well-kept office buildings.) The Downtown Arts District and the surrounding historic neighborhoods are literally a few footsteps away, and guests can enjoy that rarest of Tucson perks, covered parking. The one drawback is that this hotel does plenty of convention business, so unless you have reservations, there may be no room at the inn. & (Downtown)

**HOTEL CONGRESS**
**311 E. Congress St.**
**Tucson, AZ 85701**
**520/622-8848**
**$–$$**
Cheap but chic among the urban bohemian set, this historic hotel sits at the eastern end of the Downtown Arts District, next to the Amtrak and Greyhound stations and a city bus terminal. The lobby sports an attractive Southwestern motif; the rooms themselves, each with a tub or shower, are '30s-spartan but clean. Special, extremely low rates are available to youth hostel members and students. The hotel also houses a popular little café, as well as Club Congress, the local alternative

rock mecca—so the quietest rooms are on the opposite side of the building. (Downtown)

## Bed-and-Breakfasts

### ARMORY PARK GUEST HOUSE
**219 S. Fifth Ave.**
**Tucson, AZ 85701**
**520/206-9252**
**$$–$$$**

This 1896 home with two detached guest units rests its guests in a comfortable garden setting. Doors away from the Tucson Children's Museum—originally the city's Carnegie-funded, Greek Revival–style main library—and green little Armory Park, the place is within easy walking distance of the Downtown Arts District, the Temple of Music and Art, and the Tucson Convention Center, as well as public transportation. The Armory Park neighborhood itself is full of lovely turn-of-the-century houses like this one, and deserves a stroll of its own. The Armory Park Guest House also has a Jacuzzi and access to a telephone, washer, and dryer. Breakfast is "extended continental": coffee and tea; fresh-baked pastries; dry cereals; toast; fresh fruit; yogurt; and a compote including such fruits as blueberries, boysenberries, kiwi, and strawberries. (Downtown)

### EL PRESIDIO BED & BREAKFAST INN
**297 N. Main Ave.**
**Tucson, AZ 85701**
**520/623-6151 or 800/349-6151**
**$$$**

A stately home listed on the National Register of Historic Places, El Presidio offers three suites with private entrances and phones, plus full breakfasts. Kitchenettes are also available, and antique decor and pleasant gardens enhance the quiet atmosphere. Credit cards are not accepted, though, and there's no access for wheelchairs. (Downtown)

### ELYSIAN GROVE MARKET BED AND BREAKFAST INN
**400 W. Simpson**
**Tucson, AZ 85701**
**520/628-1522**
**$$$**

Open mid-October through May, this adobe structure sports wood floors and 14-foot ceilings. It was built in the 1920s as a corner market and now sits at the edge of a historic barrio, within easy walking distance of the Tucson Convention Center, Tucson Museum of Art, and the rest of downtown's attractions. The old meat locker is now a kitchen, and the market's shelving and display cases have been traded in for fireplaces, skylights, folk art, and antiques from Mexico and the Southwest. The garden, with an abundance of desert landscaping, offers a relaxing refuge. The four bedrooms have been furnished with art, tribal rugs, and antique beds. Two of them open onto the garden through French doors, and two have been converted from the old wine cellars. Breakfast includes Mexican pastries, fresh fruit, cheese, and coffee. (Downtown)

### GATEWAY VILLAS
**228 N. Fourth Ave.**
**Tucson, AZ 85705**
**520/740-0767 or 800/484-5900**
**$$–$$$**

Describing itself as a "historic adobe apartment resort," Gateway Villas consists of five one-bedroom units built in 1897. Some units contain kitchens. All, of course, offer access to the pool and spa. This is a good choice for people desiring privacy as well as proximity to Fourth Avenue's funky shops and restaurants. The downtown core is just a few blocks away, as is the University of Arizona. (Downtown)

*Extended Stay*

**INNSUITES**
**475 N. Granada Rd.**
**Tucson, AZ 85701**
**520/622-3000 or 800/446-6589**
**$$–$$$**

# A Gangster's Demise

*In January 1934, mobster John Dillinger and his gang interrupted their violent 13-month crime spree for a relaxing break in Tucson. Dillinger wanted to duck the cops and warm up from the bitter Midwestern winter, but when he got to Tucson, he encountered more heat than he expected.*

*Members of the gang had checked into downtown's Hotel Congress. One evening they ran into some other hotel guests at a nightclub and bragged about being armed and having robbed banks, and flashed quite a bit of cash. The guests tipped off the cops, who eventually figured that the Dillinger gang was in town.*

*The day after the nightclub encounter, Hotel Congress caught fire. The gang members took their time getting out of the building, and when they finally reached the street, they bribed two firemen $12 each to go back up and rescue their heavy luggage. It was heavy, of course, because it was full of machine guns and bulletproof vests. A couple of days later, fireman William Benedict spotted pictures of the men in a magazine he was perusing—*True Detective. *The authorities now had a solid lead.*

*Within days, a ruse pulled one of Dillinger's best gunmen into Police Chief C.A. Wollard's office, and the rest of the gang was captured at a private home on Second Avenue. Dillinger surrendered to an officer who said, "Reach for the moon, or I'll cut you in half."*

*Dillinger merely remarked, "I'll be damned."*

*Dillinger would be killed in a Chicago ambush six months later. The top floor of Hotel Congress, destroyed in the fire, was never rebuilt.*

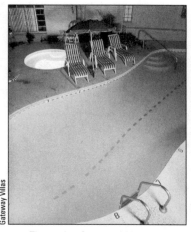

*The pool at Gateway Villas, p. 34*

The 12-acre complex has plenty of room for an Olympic-size pool and a fitness center, plus casual on-site food service at PJ's Cafe. Southwestern decor graces the whole facility, which is about four blocks removed from downtown's heaviest bustle. All rooms have coffeemakers, and some are also equipped with microwaves, refrigerators, and hair dryers. &#9855; (Downtown)

# CENTRAL-NORTH

## Resort

### WESTIN LA PALOMA
3800 E. Sunrise Dr.
Tucson, AZ 85718
520/742-6000 or 800/228-3000
$$$$
High in the Santa Catalina foothills, this resort is especially attractive to the athletically inclined. Not that golf can honestly be described as athletic, but La Paloma boasts a 27-hole Jack Niklaus Signature golf course, plus 12

tennis courts, a free-form swimming pool with a 177-foot water slide and swim-up bar, three therapeutic spas, a sand volleyball court, croquet, jogging trails, and a fully equipped health club featuring aerobics classes, a Nautilus weight room, and steam rooms. Massage, body wraps, and extensive skin care and cosmetic services are also available. If, after all this, you're too weak to drag yourself out to dinner, the resort houses five restaurants and two lounges. Before you collapse into bed, you might be lucky enough to view the city lights from a room with a balcony or terrace; if you're on the "wrong" side of the buildings for that, you can console yourself with grand desert views. As for what to do with the kids in the daytime, a variety of activities may be sampled through the Westin La Paloma Kids' Club. By the way, room rates plummet in the summer, bringing the basic no-frills cost down to the $$$ range. See also Chapter 4, Where to Eat. &#9855; (Central-North)

## Hotels and Motels

### ARIZONA INN
2200 E. Elm St.
Tucson, AZ 85719
520/325-1541 or 800/933-1093
$$$–$$$$
Right in the center of town but well off the main thoroughfares, this elegant 1930 facility surely ranks as the most beloved hotel in Tucson. The bright pink-orange stucco exterior may alarm the most sedate visitors, but everything else about the place is wholly comforting: a flower-bedecked enclosed courtyard, carefully decorated rooms (most with private patios), a gracious library complete with fireplace, and a well-regarded restaurant serving three meals a day, the lunches

and dinners favoring Continental or traditional cuisine. The Arizona Inn can be slightly tricky to find; the best route is to take Campbell Avenue to Elm, which is the first stoplight north of Speedway, then turn east and proceed just a few blocks through a quiet residential area. & (Central-North)

**DOUBLETREE HOTEL**
**AT REID PARK**
**445 S. Alvernon Way**
**Tucson, AZ 85711**
**520/881-4200 or 800/222-TREE**
**$$$–$$$$**

The DoubleTree may not be a resort, but it is right across the street from Reid Park and its public golf course, zoo, bandshell, baseball stadium, and other facilities. It's also located in a part of town not otherwise thick with hotels. If you want to get out of town fast, an airline ticket office is conveniently located downstairs. Otherwise, relax in the hotel's courtyard or pool. Rooms have the conventional amenities; an additional 11 suites each offer wet bars, turn-down service, and complimentary morning newspapers. Pets are allowed, and

# Arizona Inn

*After World War I, Tucsonan Isabella Greenway set up a furniture workshop to employ disabled veterans. Her main interest was philanthropy rather than business, and she soon found herself with a surplus of fine wicker chairs and other furnishings. In 1930 she established the Arizona Inn, claiming that she needed a place to store the stuff, and a hotel seemed like a useful place to do it.*

*The Arizona Inn's exterior walls have long been painted an arresting burnt pink, which used to shock some new Tucson residents but now is being imitated on other public buildings. Guests often suppose that the color was inspired by Tucson sunsets, or the hue of the mountains at dawn or dusk, or the color of some flower on the inn's grounds. But the truth, according to local lore, is that one day Greenway simply told her painters to reproduce the color of her nasty sunburn.*

*Greenway started spending less time in the sun when, in 1933, she became the first woman to represent Arizona in Congress.*

*Her lovely, tree-shaded complex of cottages and other buildings is still regarded as one of Tucson's finest hotels, and it continues to put all that old furniture to use.*

# GREATER TUCSON

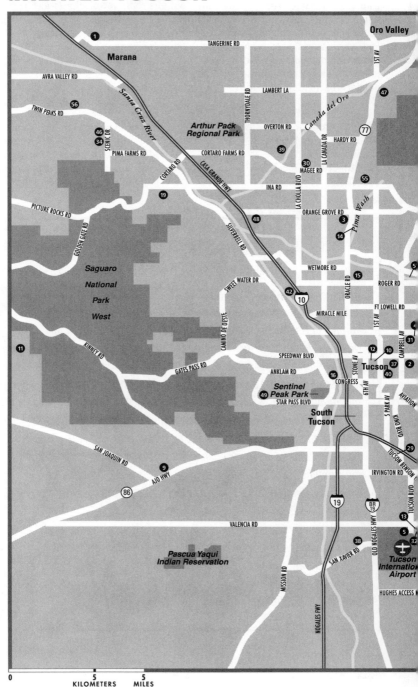

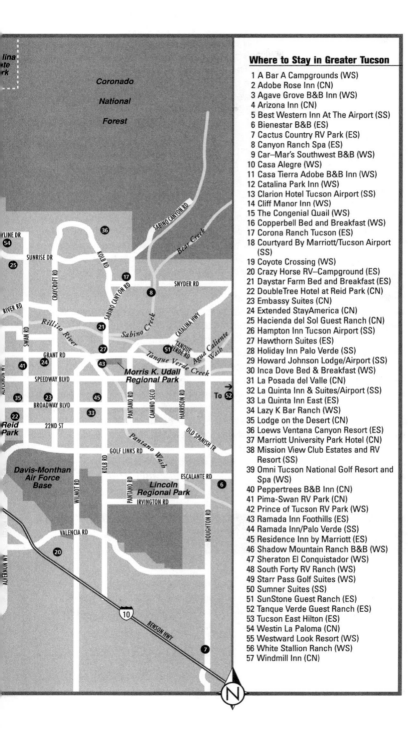

## Where to Stay in Greater Tucson

1 A Bar A Campgrounds (WS)
2 Adobe Rose Inn (CN)
3 Agave Grove B&B Inn (WS)
4 Arizona Inn (CN)
5 Best Western Inn At The Airport (SS)
6 Bienestar B&B (ES)
7 Cactus Country RV Park (ES)
8 Canyon Ranch Spa (ES)
9 Car–Mar's Southwest B&B (WS)
10 Casa Alegre (WS)
11 Casa Tierra Adobe B&B Inn (WS)
12 Catalina Park Inn (WS)
13 Clarion Hotel Tucson Airport (SS)
14 Cliff Manor Inn (WS)
15 The Congenial Quail (WS)
16 Copperbell Bed and Breakfast (WS)
17 Corona Ranch Tucson (ES)
18 Courtyard By Marriott/Tucson Airport (SS)
19 Coyote Crossing (WS)
20 Crazy Horse RV–Campground (ES)
21 Daystar Farm Bed and Breakfast (ES)
22 DoubleTree Hotel at Reid Park (CN)
23 Embassy Suites (CN)
24 Extended StayAmerica (CN)
25 Hacienda del Sol Guest Ranch (CN)
26 Hampton Inn Tucson Airport (SS)
27 Hawthorn Suites (ES)
28 Holiday Inn Palo Verde (SS)
29 Howard Johnson Lodge/Airport (SS)
30 Inca Dove Bed & Breakfast (WS)
31 La Posada del Valle (CN)
32 La Quinta Inn & Suites/Airport (SS)
33 La Quinta Inn East (ES)
34 Lazy K Bar Ranch (WS)
35 Lodge on the Desert (CN)
36 Loews Ventana Canyon Resort (ES)
37 Marriott University Park Hotel (CN)
38 Mission View Club Estates and RV Resort (SS)
39 Omni Tucson National Golf Resort and Spa (WS)
40 Peppertrees B&B Inn (CN)
41 Pima-Swan RV Park (CN)
42 Prince of Tucson RV Park (WS)
43 Ramada Inn Foothills (ES)
44 Ramada Inn/Palo Verde (SS)
45 Residence Inn by Marriott (ES)
46 Shadow Mountain Ranch B&B (WS)
47 Sheraton El Conquistador (WS)
48 South Forty RV Ranch (WS)
49 Starr Pass Golf Suites (WS)
50 Sumner Suites (SS)
51 SunStone Guest Ranch (ES)
52 Tanque Verde Guest Ranch (ES)
53 Tucson East Hilton (ES)
54 Westin La Paloma (CN)
55 Westward Look Resort (WS)
56 White Stallion Ranch (WS)
57 Windmill Inn (CN)

four rooms are especially equipped for handicapped guests. The Javelina Cantina serves drinks and food with a Mexican flair for a casual lunch or dinner inside or on the patio. The al fresco option is also available at the tonier Cactus Rose restaurant, with its Southwestern specialties. &. (Central-North)

## EMBASSY SUITES
5335 E. Broadway Blvd.
Tucson, AZ 85711
520/745-2700 or 800/362-2779
$$$
Near El Con and Park Malls, within an easy drive of the Randolph Golf Courses in Reid Park, convenient to Tucson's East-Side "restaurant row" and Davis-Monthan Air Force Base, and not too far by car from the University of Arizona, Embassy Suites offers free cooked-to-order breakfasts. They're served in part of the meeting-room complex in the middle of the hotel's shady patio area; the structure is in pleasant hacienda style, around the courtyard and pool. Data ports and modems accommodate business travelers, and coin-op laundry rooms make life easier for everyone. Pets are allowed. Evening cocktails come courtesy of the management, and complimentary health club passes are available. &. (Central-North)

## HACIENDA DEL SOL GUEST RANCH RESORT
5601 N. Hacienda del Sol Rd.
Tucson, AZ 85718
520/299-1501 or 800/728-6514
$$$–$$$$
Built in 1929 by esteemed local architect Josias Joesler as a girls' prep school, Hacienda del Sol converted to a guest ranch in the 1930s. It retains that '30s feel even today, thanks in part to the presence of many of the original (though reupholstered) furnishings. Secluded on a 34-acre site in a Catalina foothills residential district, the resort can be a little hard to find the first time; but the search is worthwhile. Amenities include a heated pool and hot tub with views of the city lights, a tennis court, massage therapy, and shuffleboard and croquet areas. The stables offer riding only in the winter. If you're wary of going out for dinner the first night, fearing (needlessly) that you won't find your way back in the dark, you can hunker down in style: The Grill at Hacienda del Sol, reopened to enthusiastic reviews in 1997 after a long inactive period, offers excellent Continental cuisine. See also Chapter 4, Where to Eat. &. (Central-North)

## LODGE ON THE DESERT
306 N. Alvernon Way

---

## T I P

The more upscale a hotel or resort is, the more likely you'll be able to save up to 50 percent by visiting in the summer instead of the winter. You're also more likely to book a room on the exact dates and at the precise hotel you prefer, without compromise.

---

Tucson, AZ 85711
520/325-3366 or 800/456-5634
$$$–$$$$
Without quite achieving the cachet or character of the Arizona Inn, which this 40-room Mexican hacienda–style facility most resembles, the Lodge on the Desert is nevertheless an entirely agreeable, long-established retreat in the central city. Near Reid Park—Tucson's answer to Central Park but with a golf course—and convenient by car to the University of Arizona, the Lodge cultivates its own spacious lawns and gardens, not forgetting to maintain a pool. Breakfast, lunch, dinner, and Sunday brunch are served in the its restaurant. Poised between Speedway and Broadway, Tucson's two major east-west arteries, the Lodge on the Desert offers a good central location for people intending to explore in every direction. Reservations are strongly advised. ♿ (Central-North)

**MARRIOTT UNIVERSITY PARK HOTEL**
880 E. Second St.
Tucson, AZ 85719
520/792-4100 or 800/228-9290
$$$–$$$$
This new four-star Diamond hotel, with an impressive high-ceilinged atrium-lobby and lounge, rises one block from the University of Arizona's main gate and Centennial Hall. It's adjacent to a brand-new block of chic college shops and pubs, and is a three-minute drive from downtown. The Mariott's 250 guest rooms are entered from eight levels of mezzanines looking down upon the lobby, with a huge skylight overhead; 69 of the rooms feature "executive work areas" with the expected modem and fax hookups. This is certainly the highest-grade hotel in the immediate vicinity of the UA. ♿ (Central-North)

**WINDMILL INN**
St. Philip's Plaza
4250 N. Campbell Ave.
Tucson, AZ 85718
520/577-0007 or 800/547-4747
$$$–$$$$
The best thing about the Windmill Inn is its location. St. Philip's Plaza lures inveterate shoppers with its large, trendy assortment of upscale clothing stores and galleries, not to mention a couple of the best restaurants in town. It's across the street from St. Philip's In The Hills Episcopal Church, a lovely 1930s building in Mission style. And the hotel overlooks the Rillito, a wide sandy wash bordered by equestrian and bicycle/running paths—you can rent a bike at the front desk. The hotel's lending library serves readers whose tastes lean toward best-sellers, which you can peruse while using the laundry or enjoying a continental breakfast, although books are probably a bad idea around the pool and whirlpool spa. As for the suites, each is stocked with multiple phones and TVs, a tiny refrigerator, and a microwave oven. ♿ (Central-North)

## Bed-and-Breakfasts

**ADOBE ROSE INN**
940 N. Olsen Ave.
Tucson, AZ 85719
520/318-4644 or 800/328-4122
$$$
A 1933 Southwestern home with foot-thick adobe walls and burnished oak floors, the Adobe Rose blooms a mere two blocks from the University of Arizona. Of the five rooms, two are in detached cottages across a bougainvillea-draped patio; one of the cottages features its own kitchen. Each room has a private bath and TV, and the entire house is furnished in classic Southwestern style. Full

breakfasts include such entrées as quiche, French toast, and pancakes; complimentary afternoon refreshments are served, too. Guests should probably leave their children at home, but senior citizens are lured with special rates. (Central-North)

## LA POSADA DEL VALLE
**1640 N. Campbell Ave.**
**Tucson, AZ 85719**
**520/795-3840**
**$$$–$$$$**

Three blocks from the university, this establishment will introduce you to an important local figure: Josias T. Joesler, the architect who designed this home and dozens of other distinctive buildings from the 1920s through the '40s. This somewhat Santa Fe–style adobe structure encloses rooms dressed with antiques from the early 1900s and Art Deco pieces from the '20s and '30s. All five rooms have private baths and entrances; some also hold a TV and kitchenette. Come hungry; gourmet breakfasts, often with an English, German, Mexican, or French theme, include a hot entrée, three kinds of muffins or breakfast breads, and real Swiss Muesli, made on the premises. Afternoon tea is also included. If you overindulge and give yourself gastric distress, University Medical Center is right across the street. Also, "Wir sprechen Deutsch," announce the owners. (Central-North)

## PEPPERTREES BED AND BREAKFAST INN
**724 E. University Blvd.**
**Tucson, AZ 85719**
**520/622-7167 or 800/348-5763**
**$$$–$$$$**

Yet another UA-area B&B, this is the oldest of all: a quaint 1905 Victorian house containing three rooms, each with a private bath, as well as a pair of two-bedroom guesthouses. Those guesthouse rooms boast kitchenettes or a washer/dryer, as well as private patios. Even if you lack access to the patios, the nicely landscaped front yard is inviting (although the pepper trees that gave the inn its name are long gone). If you'd like to reproduce the establishment's gourmet breakfast buffets at home, you can buy one of the cookbooks written by innkeeper Marjorie Martin. The meals always include fresh fruit and cereal, home-baked scones or coffeecakes, and sometimes rice pudding or fruit *tabouli*. The main course, which is generally Southwestern, could be blue pancakes, *chilaquiles*, or scrambled egg burritos. Meat is served only on the side, to accommodate vegetarians. (Central-North)

### Extended Stay

## EXTENDED STAYAMERICA
**5050 E. Grant Rd.**
**Tucson, AZ 85712**
**520/795-9510 or 800/398-7829**
**$–$$**

This establishment opened in 1997. No pool or Jacuzzi among these 120 efficiency studios; the selling points are low weekly rates and features that make an extended stay a little homier: recliners, data ports, laundry facilities, free voicemail and local calls, satellite TV. If you unfortunately are in Tucson to join a friend or loved one who is ill, this is the facility right next to Tucson Medical Center. ☧ (Central-North)

### Campground

## PIMA-SWAN RV PARK
**4615 E. Pima St.**
**Tucson, AZ 85712**

520/881-4022
$

In this centrally located little RV park near Tucson Medical Center, the 35 sites surround a laundry room and shower, with partial shade from mature trees. No recreational facilities, though—a good incentive to get out of your RV and see a bit of the city. The daily rates include full hookup (water, electricity, sewer); if you opt for the monthly rate, you pay your own electric bill. & (Central-North)

## EAST SIDE

### *Resorts*

**CANYON RANCH SPA**
**8600 E. Rockcliff Rd.**
**Tucson, AZ 85750**
**520/749-9000 or 800/726-9000**
**$$$$**
The cynics among us may mock Canyon Ranch as "Fat Farm to the Stars," but, in truth, this spa-resort has helped thousands of clients, familiar and obscure, develop more healthful lifestyles in an atmosphere as luxurious as the exercise regimens are challenging. The more routine athletic facilities include squash, racquetball, and tennis courts; indoor and outdoor pools; and gyms, plus Jacuzzis and saunas. Out-of-the-ordinary features start with the yoga dome and continue with dozens of sports and fitness classes, personalized biking and hiking regimens, weight-loss and smoking-cessation programs, and cooking classes. For every three guests, there's one staff member—a sports pro, physician, psychologist, massage therapist, fitness guru, you name it. Whether you want to slim down those thunder thighs or rest your traumatized mind, this is the place—as long as you can meet the price. & (East Side)

# Top Ten Pop Songs That Mention Tucson
### By Gene Armstrong, *Arizona Daily Star*
### popular music critic

1. "Get Back," the Beatles
2. "Under African Skies," Paul Simon with Linda Ronstadt
3. "Tucson Too Soon," Tracy Byrd
4. "Idiot Summer," the Gin Blossoms
5. "Jack Straw," the Grateful Dead
6. "Trailways Bus," Paul Simon
7. "Code of the Road," the Band of Black Ranchette
8. "You Can Sleep While I Drive," Melissa Etheridge
9. "Old Tucson," Youssou N'Dour
10. "The Lights of Tucson," Jim Campbell

*Hotel Congress, p. 33*

**LOEWS VENTANA CANYON RESORT**
**7000 N. Resort Dr.**
**Tucson, AZ 85750**
**520/299-2020 or 800/234-5117**
**$$$$**

Architecture, rather than services, distinguishes this resort from its two leading competitors, the Sheraton El Conquistador and Westin La Paloma. Of the three big resorts nestled in the Santa Catalina foothills, Ventana Canyon is the one that seems most integrated with the mountain stone—despite several expanses of water and grass across the 93 acres. As for the facility statistics: nearly 400 rooms and suites (each equipped with phone, voicemail, and computer jacks, TV, minibar, iron and board, and balcony), five restaurants and lounges, eight lighted tennis courts, two 18-hole Fazio-designed par-72 golf courses, a croquet green, 2.5 miles of fitness trails, two swimming pools, a spa, a beauty salon, and several retail outlets. Some suites also offer fireplaces and Jacuzzis. The

"Loews Loves Kids" program provides games, crafts, and recreation for guests ages 5 to 12; it's available daily, and the fee includes lunch. If you can't find enough to do on the premises, "destination services" include Jeep tours, hot-air ballooning, hiking, and something billed as "cattle drives." See also Chapter 4, Where to Eat. ⅏ (East Side)

## Hotels and Motels

**HAWTHORN SUITES**
**7007 E. Tanque Verde Rd.**
**Tucson, AZ 85715**
**520/298-2300 or 800/527-1133**
**$$-$$$**

A 90-unit brick hotel—situated in a shopping center? Actually, you can't beat the location. It's near shopping (of course) and serves up a good night's rest right in Tucson's prime dining district. The architecture is an imposing, perhaps even intimidating, mix of Medieval Romanesque and, on the interior, Southwestern. The high-ceilinged lobby, at least, is quite cozy, with an inviting fireplace for winter comfort. A pool and spa, as well as in-room coffee, provide the principal secondary entice-ments. & (East Side)

## LA QUINTA INN EAST
6404 E. Broadway Blvd.
Tucson, AZ 85710
520/747-1414 or 800/687-6667
$$–$$$

The 800 number, in case you hadn't no-ticed, spells out "new room." A good variety of amenities is provided for the money here. Each room contains the increasingly essential modem line, for example. The hotel offers a fitness center and spa, an outdoor pool, overnight delivery service, laundry and valet services, a Jacuzzi, and rooms specifically designed for handicapped patrons. Pets are allowed; children under 18 are not only tolerated but ad-mitted free, with rollaway beds and cribs available. & (East Side)

## RAMADA INN FOOTHILLS
6944 E. Tanque Verde Rd.
Tucson, AZ 85715
520/886-9595 or 800/228-2828
$$–$$$

It's not actually in the foothills, but this Ramada does sit in the heart of restaurant row, so it doesn't find it necessary to serve hot food. The complimentary breakfast is a cold buffet, and there's a free happy hour to get you in the mood to wait for a table at one of the popular restau-rants along Tanque Verde Road. This is a pleasant chain hotel with a gar-den courtyard (the grass and decidu-ous trees could make you forget you're in Tucson), heated pool, spa, and sauna. If you need more exercise than those provide, ask for a free pass to one of the nearby health clubs. Another freebie—glory be—is

unlimited free local phone calls. & (East Side)

## TUCSON EAST HILTON
7600 E. Broadway Blvd.
Tucson, AZ 85710
520/721-5600 or 800/648-7177
$$$–$$$$

The Hilton, its seven stories surround-ing a striking atrium, offers 232 guest rooms, including eight terrace suites and one presidential suite. The Sum-mit Level upgrades the amenities to include such items as complimentary continental breakfast, evening recep-tions and turn-down service. The out-door heated pool and Jacuzzi are located in a setting replete with lush vegetation and beautiful views of the mountains, even though the hotel it-self is plopped into a fully urban environment. Although the hotel is corporate- and group-oriented, the location, views, and amenities make it a popular spot for leisure travelers, particularly for those whose business or pleasure will be concentrated in Tucson's suburban far East Side, where public lodgings are scarce. & (East Side)

## *Bed-and-Breakfasts*

## BIENESTAR B&B
10490 E. Escalante Rd.
Tucson, AZ 85730
520/290-1048 or 800/293-0004
$$$

Pronounce the name in four syllables, and you have a Spanish word for "well-being." This hacienda, situated on six acres near Saguaro National Park East, is owned by a registered nurse with a holistic background. The idea here is not so much convenience to urban life—which is only ten minutes away—but a retreat in a peaceful desert environment. Gourmet breakfasts feature natural, whole foods, fresh-squeezed juices, and home-baked treats, and can accommodate any special diet. Temptations to remain on the property consist of a pool and spa, a great room with fireplace, a large library with a baby grand, plus a TV, VCR, and stereo with complimentary CDs and classic movies to borrow. Also available are complimentary horse facilities if you happen to bring along your own horse. But don't bring pets or small children, and forget about cigarettes. (East Side)

### CORONA RANCH TUCSON
7595 E. Snyder Rd.
Tucson, AZ 85750
520/529-1457
$$$
This Spanish hacienda–style facility, being near the Sabino Canyon recreational area, is well situated for hiking and horse enthusiasts. The four rooms, which the owners themselves describe as "plain but clean," are done up to echo the property's past—it began as a 1920s guest ranch. They contain a coffeemaker and refrigerator as well as antique furniture. Continental breakfast is included. Corona Ranch offers discounts for stays over three nights, or to those who rent its 4,500-square-foot banquet facility. (East Side)

### DAYSTAR FARM BED AND BREAKFAST
3312 N. Riverbend Circle E.
Tucson, AZ 85750
520/886-6461
$$$
Open September through June, this B&B is a 1940s adobe-brick ranch house on five acres, about three miles south of Sabino Canyon. There's a riding facility on the site. A brick patio wraps around the main house, and use

of brick rather than wood is a good idea here, considering the five indoor and two outdoor fireplaces. If you get too hot, you can jump into the outdoor pool. The rates include a full breakfast, plus several little extras—fancy toiletries, fresh fruit and candy supplies, terry cloth robes, and a "bottomless" cookie jar stocked with homemade goodies. No pets. (East Side)

### SUNSTONE GUEST RANCH
2545 N. Woodland Rd.
Tucson, AZ 85749
520/749-1928
$$$
A working ranch in the late nineteenth century and a dude ranch in the early 1900s, this place has more recently served as a Sikh wellness retreat. Tranquility and restfulness are still emphasized here, with a dozen separate casitas on 11 acres splashed with running-water features, grassy areas, and native mesquite bosques. Stroll around and look for the "garden angels" hidden in trees and behind flowers. The guest ranch is minutes from Saguaro National Park East, Sabino Canyon, golfing, restaurant row, and hiking in the Catalinas. If you stay put, you can take advantage of the heated pool, Jacuzzi, barbecue area, tennis and basketball courts, and horseshoes pit. The dining room is open only for breakfast. (East Side)

## Extended Stay

### RESIDENCE INN BY MARRIOTT
6477 E. Speedway Blvd.
Tucson, AZ 85710
520/721-0991 or 800/331-3131
$$$–$$$$
Copper and wrought-iron fixtures lend this inn a Southwestern character. Of the 128 rooms, 32 are penthouses with

The lobby at Westward Look Resort, p. 51

a fireplace and full-size kitchen. If you don't get your own kitchen, never fear; the Residence Inn is near the 60 restaurants and entertainment purveyors along restaurant row. There's a heated pool, Jacuzzi, free movies and VCR, free happy hour Monday through Thursday, grocery service, coin laundry, tennis and basketball courts, a barbecue area, and valet service. The rate classifications above are for by-the-night stays; ask about discounted weekly and monthly rates and further reductions for stays beyond 30 days. ⅃ (East Side)

## Campgrounds

### CACTUS COUNTRY RV PARK
**10195 S. Houghton Rd.**
**Tucson, AZ 85747**
**520/574-3000**
$

This quiet, desert-landscaped RV park is just ¼-mile north of Interstate 10 (take Exit 275). It's pretty far east of Tucson's main action, but there's a general-goods store on the premises.

Cactus Country's location advantage is proximity to the Pima Air Museum, Saguaro National Park East, Colossal Cave, and the Pima County Fairgrounds (not to mention both state and federal correctional institutions—this is a fine place to stay if you're visiting a friend in the slammer). Some of the 270 spots are shaded, and tent campers are welcome. Daily and weekly rates include full hookup; for the monthly rate, you pay your own electricity bill. ⅃ (East Side)

### CRAZY HORSE RV-CAMPGROUND
**Interstate 10 and Craycroft Rd.**
**Tucson, AZ 85706**
**520/574-0157 or 800/279-6279**
$

Children are welcome at this 154-site desert campground, and pets are, too, in certain areas. Amenities include a pool, rec hall, 24-hour Laundromat, restrooms, and showers. Tent camping is an option. Daily rates include full hookup; weekly and monthly rates require a deposit and payment of your own electricity. Six-month and yearly rates are also available. ⅃ (East Side)

## Dude Ranch

### TANQUE VERDE GUEST RANCH
**14301 E. Speedway Blvd.**
**Tucson, AZ 85748**
**520/296-6275 or 800/234-3833**
$$$$

Life for Old West cattle hands was rough, but you'd never know it at the Tanque Verde Guest Ranch, which boasts a four-star Mobil rating. The employees at this 125-year-old mountain-ringed ranch will boot you outdoors for horseback riding, swimming, fishing, tennis, and guided nature hikes and bird study programs overseen by a full-time naturalist. But temptations lie indoors as well:

Southwestern decor, a modern health spa, huge breakfast and lunch buffets, select dinner menus (with wine and liquor available), and 50 rooms and 15 suites with private baths, most with fireplaces and private patios. Further diversions include Southwest cooking demonstrations, country-western dancing, and supervised daylong children's activities. Although children are welcome, pets are not. & (East Side)

## SOUTH SIDE

### Hotels and Motels

**BEST WESTERN INN AT THE AIRPORT**
**7060 S. Tucson Blvd.**
**Tucson, AZ 85706**
**520/746-0271 or 800/528-1234**
**$$–$$$**
It's at the entrance to Tucson International Airport, but the Best Western runs a free shuttle service to the terminal, anyway—as well as to some of Tucson's malls and to the reservation casinos. If you're disinclined to venture far from the hotel, dine at its Inn Place Restaurant or loosen up at the Unwinder Lounge, complete with large-screen TV. Continental breakfast buffet and the afternoon social hour are complimentary. A swimming pool, Jacuzzi, and lighted tennis and volleyball courts are also part of the deal. Oddly, petrified chunks of 180 million-year-old trees are scattered about the courtyard; the linen is much fresher than that. & (South Side)

**CLARION HOTEL TUCSON AIRPORT**
**6801 S. Tucson Blvd.**
**Tucson, AZ 85706**
**520/746-3932 or 800/526-0550**

**$$–$$$$**
The Clarion features spiffy room accommodations, complimentary breakfast, a pool, spa, fitness center, and lush interior courtyard. Inside the building, Morgan's Food & Spirits offers diners and revelers classic American cuisine and unusual specialty drinks, amid an eclectic collection of antiques, jukeboxes, and neon. The low-season rate is less than half that of the high season. & (South Side)

**COURTYARD BY MARRIOTT/ TUCSON AIRPORT**
**2505 E. Executive Dr.**
**Tucson, AZ 85706**
**520/573-0000 or 800/321-2211**
**$$–$$$$**
A grassy, flowered interior courtyard gives each hotel in this Marriott chain its name. Twelve suites and nearly 150 rooms beckon to the airport-weary traveler—especially the business traveler, who should appreciate the computer connections, desks, irons, and ironing boards. Refrigerators are available upon request. A pool, Jacuzzi, fitness center, in-house laundry, and free HBO round out the attractions. The hotel is within walking distance of several restaurants, but its own Courtyard Cafe serves breakfast and dinner. & (South Side)

**HAMPTON INN TUCSON AIRPORT**
**6971 S. Tucson Blvd.**
**Tucson, AZ 85706**
**520/889-5789 or 800/426-7866**
**$$–$$$**
Except for the Best Western and La Quinta, this is as close as you can get to the airport without sleeping at the gate. It's OK to let poor Fluffy and other small pets out of their carrying cases at the Hampton Inn, assuming you've paid for their presence. If you splatter yourself with your own blood

while extricating Fluffy from the cage, avail yourself of the coin-op laundry rooms. The continental breakfast buffet comes free in the hotel, but room service, rather oddly, is provided by nearby Pizza Hut, Domino's, China Bay, and Denny's. Try not to spill food into the heated pool. &. (South Side)

### HOLIDAY INN PALO VERDE
**4550 S. Palo Verde Blvd.**
**Tucson, AZ 85714**
**520/746-1161**
**$$$**

Seven miles from the airport, the Holiday Inn offers 24-hour transportation there and back. It also provides easy access to Interstate 10 and has ample truck parking. The hotel is newly remodeled and features a waterfall in the lobby. Hydrophiles will also be attracted to the pool and Jacuzzi. The site includes tennis courts, laundry service, a fitness room with sauna, two restaurants, and a lounge. "Ask about discounts," advises the management. &. (South Side)

*Get a room with a view at Bienestar B&B, p. 45.*

Peggy Muller, Bienestar B&B

### HOWARD JOHNSON LODGE/AIRPORT
**1025 E. Benson Hwy.**
**Tucson, AZ 85713**
**520/623-7792 or 800/446-4656**
**$$–$$$**

There's not much to be said about a Howard Johnson's—the chain is consistent and modest—aside from pointing out its location. In this case, it's a 5- to 10-minute zip to the airport and only a few blocks away from the Veterans Administration Hospital. Just off the freeway, it's tantalizingly close to the wonderful Mexican restaurants of South Tucson (but drive, don't try to walk it). A free shuttle travels to the airport, VA Hospital, and University of Arizona. The lodge also features a pool, spa, sauna, exercise room, and free cooked-to-order breakfast. &. (South Side)

### LA QUINTA INN & SUITES/AIRPORT
**7001 S. Tucson Blvd.**
**Tucson, AZ 85706**
**520/573-3333 or 800/531-5900**
**$$–$$$**

Eight suites and 143 rooms surround the spacious two-story lobby. Geared especially to business travelers, the rooms offer voice messaging and speaker and data-port phones, as well as oversize desks and in-room entertainment systems. The only restaurants close by are in competing hotels and Tucson International Airport, but the Mexican cuisine of South Tucson is a short drive away. &. (South Side)

### RAMADA INN/PALO VERDE
**5251 S. Julian Dr.**
**Tucson, AZ 85706**
**520/294-5250 or 800/997-5470**
**$$$**

A free continental breakfast is provided; for other sustenance, try the restaurant and lounge adjacent to the inn. The guest rooms and suites have recently been redecorated, and the whole place, though of wood-frame-and-stucco construction, impersonates adobe architecture. There's an exercise room, an outdoor heated pool, four separate courtyards each with a hydrotherapy pool, valet service, and coin laundry. &. (South Side)

**SUMNER SUITES**
**6885 S. Tucson Blvd.**
**Tucson, AZ 85706**
**520/295-0405 or 800/747-8483**
**$$–$$$$**
All 122 rooms in this contemporary hotel are, as the name implies, suites—meaning that the sleeping area is separated from the parlor and kitchen areas. Close to the airport and Davis-Monthan Air Force Base, Sumner Suites caters to corporate customers, offering data ports, valet service, and a 24-hour van shuttle, as well as a heated pool, washer and dryer, and fitness center with free weights. &. (South Side)

## Campground

**MISSION VIEW CLUB ESTATES AND RV RESORT**
**31 W. Los Reales Rd.**
**Tucson, AZ 85706**
**520/741-1945**
**$**
Try not to get confused. This is three businesses in one: a mobile home park and a desert-landscaped RV park for people 55 and older, and a family mobile home park that does *not* cater to tourists. It's located on the San Xavier Indian Reservation, about two miles west of the newly restored Mission San Xavier del Bac, and, for more worldly types, half a mile east of Desert Diamond Casino. Within a

leg-stretch of your RV you'll find an indoor pool, clubhouse, shuffleboard, horseshoes, and a crafts room. Daily, weekly, and monthly rates exist, with utilities included in the first two categories. Discounts are offered for longer stays. Don't even think about asking to use a credit card here—it's close to the casino, remember? &. (South Side)

# WEST SIDE

## Resorts

**OMNI TUCSON NATIONAL GOLF RESORT AND SPA**
**2727 W. Club Dr.**
**Tucson, AZ 85742**
**520/297-2271 or 800/528-4856**
**$$$–$$$$**
In the universe of this hotel, everything orbits the golf ball. Actually, the center of the universe could be any ball zipping around the USGA 27-hole course that is often the site of the Northern Telecom Open. The faintly Mission-style facilities also include a health spa staffed by people who will do anything from clipping your nails to giving you an herbal wrap or Swedish massage. Tennis, volleyball, basketball, swimming, and aerobics are also options. Just don't expect to see much of the desert up close; the landscape is grassy fairways dotted with lakes. You may dine at the Catalina Grille but not on Sunday, not if you don't have reservations, not if you want to know exactly what to expect from the menu (it changes weekly, but the emphasis is a cross between Continental and Southwestern), and not if you're a man without a jacket—this is one of the few restaurants in town with a serious dress code. See also Chapter 4, Where to Eat. &. (West Side)

**Sleep in Tucson, support the arts. One dollar of your hotel or motel room tax is funneled into local visual and performing arts programs.**

## SHERATON EL CONQUISTADOR
10000 N. Oracle Rd.
Tucson, AZ 85737
520/544-5000 or 800/325-7832
$$$$

You want golf? You've got 45 holes beckoning, imploring you to forsake the 31 lighted tennis courts, 428 guest rooms and casitas, five themed restaurants, and two fitness centers, not to mention the possibilities of swimming, horseback riding, hiking, biking, volleyball, racquetball, Jeep tours, and hayrides. "Camp Conquistador" offers a program for children ages 5 through 12, including crafts, movies, nature-related activities, sports, and lunch. As for those rooms, each boasts two telephones with voicemail and modem hookups, and a balcony or patio with a good view (although in some cases it's a view of the pool). Of the 100 suites, half have fireplaces. Ordinary room rates plummet to around $125 or less in July and August—in other words, they're less than half-price. The Sheraton hides out on Tucson's far Northwest Side, so if you want to see a bit of the city, you need to drive your own car or take the free shuttle to Tucson Mall and hop a bus. The airport shuttle, by the way, costs more than $20 one way; it's a fairly long way. See also Chapter 4, Where to Eat. ♿ (West Side)

## WESTWARD LOOK RESORT
245 E. Ina Rd.
Tucson, AZ 85704

520/297-1151 or 800/722-2500
$$$$

Tucson's three other mainstream resorts—Loews Ventana Canyon, the Sheraton El Conquistador, and Westin La Paloma—opened in the 1980s, when bigger was better. The Westward Look dates from 1929, when people were more impressed by detail than by size. Not exactly petite, the hotel does have 244 rooms, all of them larger than the current norm and graced with private patios or balconies. But of greater interest are more subtle touches, like the exposed-beam ceilings. The place started out as a dude ranch, not a golf resort, so its lush desert landscaping holds fast to the earth. The only real reminder of the resort's equestrian past is the horseshoes court. Otherwise, distractions include tennis (subject to an hourly fee; pros are available to give you lessons), pools and whirlpools, aerobics, volleyball, basketball, softball, a jogging trail, and a fitness center. The Westward Look also prides itself as the home of one of Tucson's finest upscale restaurants, the Gold Room. See also Chapter 4, Where to Eat. ♿ (West Side)

## Hotels and Motels

### CLIFF MANOR INN
5900 N. Oracle Rd.
Tucson, AZ 85704
520/887-4800 or 800/736-6767

**$–$$**

This inn does, indeed, hug the edge of a cliff overlooking a par-3 golf course; the rooms boast fine views of the Santa Catalina Mountains by day and the city lights by night. Twelve are casitas with kitchenettes; eight "hospitality" rooms provide cooking facilities. All have cable TV. One Jacuzzi burbles on the premises, in the company of a heated swimming pool, and there's a tennis club within walking distance. Tucson Mall is a mile and a half away. The hotel has recently installed a nightclub, the faux-Florida-atmosphered The Keys, offering a more energetic alternative to its quiet restaurant with splendid views. & (West Side)

**STARR PASS GOLF SUITES**
**3645 W. Starr Pass Blvd.**
**Tucson, AZ 85745**
**520/670-0500 or 800/503-2898**
**$$$–$$$$**
Starr Pass would dearly love to sell you a home near its 18-hole championship desert golf course, but it is

also willing to rent its one- and two-bedroom Southwestern-style casitas with open-beam ceilings, Mexican *saltillo* tile floors, fireplaces, and balconies or patios. Other facilities include LaEstrella Restaurant, a heated pool, Jacuzzi, tennis courts, and a fitness center. If you're planning to travel in a pack, Starr Pass can accommodate groups up to 50. & (West Side)

### Bed-and-Breakfasts

**AGAVE GROVE BED AND**
**BREAKFAST INN**
**800 W. Panorama Rd.**
**Tucson, AZ 85704**
**520/797-3400**
**$$$**
"Casual elegance" is emphasized here. Each of the five sleeping rooms is differently themed (there's a Sonoran Desert Suite, Caribbean Room, and so on). All rooms include cable TV. The guesthouses have private entrances; more public are the breakfast room and a family room with a billiard table. Just down the road from the desert lushness of Tohono Chul Park, Agave Grove depends largely but not entirely on desert landscaping; the area includes fruit trees, large yuccas, plenty of agaves, a putting green, a pool with a waterfall, an in-ground spa, a barbecue area, and three covered patios. Breakfast generally consists of an egg dish, specialty items such as blintzes or stuffed French toast, plus the expected muffins, coffees, and teas. & (West Side)

**CAR-MAR'S SOUTHWEST**
**BED & BREAKFAST**
**6766 W. Oklahoma Rd.**
**Tucson, AZ 85746**
**520/578-1730 or 888/578-1730**
**$$–$$$**

*The Congenial Quail, p. 54*

The Congenial Quail

"Car-Mar" is owner Carole Martinez, who designed and helped build the home in 1980 and turned it into a B&B in '93. Four rooms and a guesthouse share 2.5 desert-landscaped acres. Three rooms have a private patio or garden, and each is decorated in a different style—Santa Fe, Victorian, and so on. Martinez herself built some of the furniture. A pool, Jacuzzi, free-standing fireplaces, and on-site massage therapist complete the facility. It's close to Old Tucson, the Desert Museum, and San Xavier Mission, and offers easy access to Kitt Peak and both freeways. Breakfast typically involves a fresh fruit cup, a main course such as French toast (several versions, including a pineapple-upside-down variety), hash browns or cottage fries, sausage or bacon for omnivores, and scrambled eggs on the side. The rate categories above are for the rooms; inquire about the weekly guesthouse rate. (West Side)

## CASA ALEGRE
316 E. Speedway Blvd.
Tucson, AZ 85705
520/628-1800 or 800/628-5654
$$$

Not only is Casa Alegre moderately priced by B&B standards, but it manages to be both charming and conveniently located—right on Speedway, a major east-west thoroughfare, extremely close to downtown as well as to the University of Arizona, and within a few paces of The Garland, a very nice vegetarian-friendly restaurant. The World War I–era house is a good example of local bungalow style, which dominates the surrounding neighborhoods—high ceilings but a squat, cozy overall feel. The decor and furnishings, too, emphasize historical continuity rather than current trends. Each of the four rooms has a

private bath, but the phone and TV are situated only in a common room, with a pool and patio out back. Full breakfasts benefit from the inclusion of home-baked breads. (West Side)

## CASA TIERRA ADOBE B&B INN
11155 W. Calle Pima
Tucson, AZ 85743
520/578-3058
$$$

In a secluded desert area minutes from the Desert Museum, Saguaro National Park, and Old Tucson, this rustic adobe home was built in Mexican hacienda style, with an interior garden courtyard, brick and tile floors, viga ceilings, and Mexican furnishings. The place also promises a hot tub and excellent hiking and birding opportunities. Each of the three rooms has a private bath, private patio and entrance, microwave, and refrigerator. Above all, Casa Tierra's special distinction is its full vegetarian breakfast. No credit cards accepted. (West Side)

## CATALINA PARK INN
309 E. First St.
Tucson, AZ 85705
520/792-4541 or 800/792-4885
$$–$$$

This stately 1927 residence stands well within the city, not far from downtown and the University of Arizona. According to the owners' own description, "Richly hued walls set off an energetic collection of antiques, tag-sale treasures and handsome fabrics," which should interest all but the most ascetic traveler. Each of the four rooms has a private bath, phone, and TV, but there the similarities end. Two, for example, enjoy furnished balconies; another opens onto a private garden. Continental breakfast is served either in your quarters or in the convivial breakfast room. (West Side)

## THE CONGENIAL QUAIL
4267 N. Fourth Ave.
Tucson, AZ 85705
520/887-9487 or 800/895-2047
$$–$$$
Pioneer history, wildlife, and literary sensibilities converge in this B&B owned by two English teachers. It's located on three acres of former Mormon farmland now bordering a city park. Wild quail and desert squirrels abound. All four rooms are themed, with eclectic art and plenty of books. *Saltillo* tile covers the floor, impervious to feet wet from the hot tub. Local foods are featured in the gourmet Southwestern breakfasts. ♿ (West Side)

## COPPERBELL BED AND BREAKFAST
25 N. Westmoreland Ave.
Tucson, AZ 85745
520/629-9229
$$$
Six rooms lie at the foot of Sentinel Peak, which most locals insist on calling "A" Mountain. The two rooms in the 1908 lava-rock main house share a bath; the guesthouses have private baths. This is one of the most remarkable looking B&Bs in town, beginning with that locally quarried lava rock and continuing with the wooden floors, stained glass, large porch, and handmade quilts. Copperbell is very close by car to downtown and the Tucson Convention Center but a bit of a trudge on foot. The German owners speak their native language and French as well as English, and they serve a full German breakfast. No pets, no credit cards, and no children under 10. (West Side)

## COYOTE CROSSING
6985 N. Camino Verde
Tucson, AZ 85743
520/744-3285
$$$
Secluded but still convenient to the freeway, Coyote Crossing consists of four rooms, each with a desert theme as well as private bath, cable TV, and refrigerator. All access the pool and patio. The house is situated on four acres of desert in the ragged foothills of the Tucson Mountains, with Old Tucson Studios and the Arizona–Sonora Desert Museum nearby. The proprietors serve what they call a "continental-plus, high-energy" breakfast: coffee and tea, fruits, breads and muffins, yogurt, cereals, and juices. No credit cards accepted. ♿ (West Side)

## INCA DOVE BED & BREAKFAST
1341 W. Liddell Pl.
Tucson, AZ 85704
520/797-7004 or 800/299-1747
$$–$$$
Take your choice: Stay in the main house, a Territorial ranch home, or in the guesthouse with a private patio and shared kitchen. All four rooms have private baths. *Saltillo* tile and antique furniture grace the house, which is near Tohono Chul Park, golf courses, two shopping malls, several restaurants, horseback riding, hiking, and a fitness center. Room rates include a breakfast of fruit and muffins, an egg dish, sometimes potatoes, and meat. The rule of the house is, "You don't leave hungry." The proprietor says children are welcome, "but not the little, sticky ones." Neither are credit cards. ♿ (West Side)

## SHADOW MOUNTAIN RANCH B&B INN
8825 N. Scenic Dr.

*Armory Park Guest House, p. 34*

Tucson, AZ 85743
520/744-7551 or 888/9-SHADOW
$$$–$$$$
Yet another hacienda tucked into the desert vegetation of the Tucson Mountains, Shadow Mountain Ranch's accommodations include a poolside two-bedroom, two-bath villa with full kitchen, a luxury king suite, and queen rooms and daybed/trundle facilities, meaning that this B&B can handle small groups and families as well as individuals. There's also a pool and spa. Breakfast is continental, and there's a 10 percent discount for weekly stays. (West Side)

## Campgrounds

### A BAR A CAMPGROUNDS
9015 W. Tangerine Rd.
Marana, AZ 85653
520/682-4332
$
This 85-spot RV park and campground rests in a desert setting about 25 miles from downtown Tucson. Tenters can stake out a grassy area. There are new restrooms and showers, and the place is upgrading to include a recreation building and laundry facilities. It's located near Breakers Water Park, with easy access to I-10. Pets are allowed at the manager's discretion. The daily and weekly rates include full hookup; monthly rates are also available. (West Side)

### PRINCE OF TUCSON RV PARK
3501 N. Freeway Rd.
Tucson, AZ 85705
520/887-3501
$
Reasonably close to Tucson Mall and right along Interstate 10, the 210-spot Prince features a pool, Jacuzzi, shuffleboard, two lounges, and a convenience store on the property. The rules 'n' regs allow a maximum of two pets. Nightly, weekly, and monthly rates are available. &. (West Side)

### SOUTH FORTY RV RANCH
3600 W. Orange Grove Rd.
Tucson, AZ 85741
520/297-2503

**$**

One of Tucson's most established RV parks, the South Forty has been herding recreational vehicles into its 229-space corral since 1973. It occupies a desert setting not far from Tohono Chul Park, a bit farther from Saguaro National Park West. Access to I-10, restaurants, and shopping is easy. Facilities include a pool, rec hall, spa, library, card room, exercise room, and billiards room. Neither dogs nor credit cards are accepted. Daily, weekly, and monthly rates. (West Side)

## Dude Ranches

### LAZY K BAR RANCH
8401 N. Scenic Dr.
Tucson, AZ 85743
520/744-3050 or 800/321-7018
$$$$

Open mid-September through mid-June. If you want a telephone and television in your room, seek lodging elsewhere. This place is all about horseback riding, with the ranch's wranglers ready to assist riders of any (or no) skill. The Lazy K also features team penning, a horse and cattle game which takes place in an arena; riders of various skill levels may participate. Other features include scenic mountain and desert trails, weekly picnic rides into Saguaro National Park, and sunrise and moonlight rides. Once you're ready to put a little temporary distance between yourself and the horses, you can check out the heated pool, spa, tennis courts, hayrides drawn by a Percheron team, country-western dance lessons with live music, or the trapshooting, hiking, and birdwatching options. It's a smallish ranch, with 23 rooms concentrated in eight cottages. Free airport transfers, too. (West Side)

### WHITE STALLION RANCH
9251 W. Twin Peaks Rd.
Tucson, AZ 85743
520/297-0252 or 888/977-2624
$$$$

Open from September to May, this 3,000-acre working cattle ranch west of town sets aside 29 rooms for greenhorns and tenderfoot tourists. Organized horseback rides range from sedate jaunts to rigorous outings, and the hands put on a weekly rodeo for the entertainment of the guests. Non-equestrian activities range from hiking and swimming to tennis, basketball, pool, and shuffleboard. Furnishings in the ranch buildings have retained their 1940s look, complete with rough oak chairs and cholla lamp stands. Some rooms have whirlpool tubs—always an attractive option after a day in the saddle. (West Side)

Westward Look Resort

# 4

## WHERE TO EAT

Until the 1970s, Tucson diners were restricted mainly to steakhouses, standard meat-and-potato American fare, and Mexican and Chinese restaurants. Such establishments remain plentiful, but they have been joined by everything from wonderful little Ethiopian and Guatemalan joints to trend-setting purveyors of nouvelle Southwestern cuisine.

Mexican food, of course, remains the cuisine most closely associated with Tucson. But the term "Mexican" covers a variety of styles. The local version ignores chili, to the distress (or smug satisfaction?) of Tex-Mex fans. It has never adopted the flat enchiladas (enchiladas montadas) common in New Mexico. Rolled tacos, which you'll find as close by as Yuma, are an anomaly in Tucson. Fajitas are regarded as a trendy import. Tucson's style of Mexican food is based on northern Sonoran fare, as adapted over the decades by border chefs. Shredded beef plays a significant role. Flour tortillas wrap around a variety of fillings, from beef and chicken to refried beans. During the Christmas season the household tamale makers go into high gear, and you're likely then to find individuals standing outside every supermarket selling them by the dozen.

This chapter begins with a list of restaurants organized by the type of food each offers. Each restaurant name is followed by a geographic zone abbreviation and the page on which you can find a description of the restaurant. The descriptions are organized alphabetically within each zone. Dollar-sign symbols indicate how much you can expect to spend per person for a meal (appetizer, entrée, and dessert).

### Price rating symbols:
$   **$10 and under**
$$   **$11 to $20**
$$$   **$21 and up**

## American/Grills

Catalina Grille (WS), p. 81
City Grill (ES), p. 74
El Corral (CN), p. 67
The Grill at Hacienda del Sol (CN),
p. 70
La Cocina (DT), p. 62
Last Territory Steakhouse and Music
Hall (WS), p. 82
Li'l Abner's Steakhouse (WS), p. 82
Little Anthony's Diner (ES), p. 76
The Metropolitan Grill (WS), p. 82
Ovens Restaurant (CN), p. 72
Pinnacle Peak (ES), p. 76
Presidio Grill (CN), p. 73
Ranchers Club of Arizona (CN), p. 73
Tohono Chul Tea Room (WS), p. 83
The White Dove (WS), p. 83

## Asian/Pacific Rim

AZ Stixx (CN), p. 63
China-Thai Cuisine (ES), p. 74
India Oven (CN), p. 70
New Delhi Palace (ES), p. 76
Old Peking (CN), p. 72
Oriental Garden (CN), p. 72
Sakura Teppan Steak and Sushi (ES),
p. 77

## Cafés and Bistros

B&B Café (DT), p. 59
The Blue Willow (CN), p. 63
Café Magritte (DT), p. 59
Café Terra Cotta (CN), p. 66
Dakota Café and Catering Co. (ES),
p. 74
The Dish (CN), p .67

## Continental

Anthony's in the Catalinas (CN), p. 63
Café Sweetwater (DT), p. 61
Gold Room (WS), p. 81
The Ventana Room (ES), p. 77

## Delicatessen

Sausage Deli (CN), p. 74

## French

Le Mélange (ES), p. 76
Le Rendez-Vous (CN), p. 71
Penelope's Restaurant Français (CN),
p. 72

## German/Czech

Mountain View Restaurant (CN), p. 71

## Greek

Athens on 4th Avenue (DT), p. 59
Olive Tree Restaurant (ES), p. 76

## Italian

Capriccio Ristorante (CN), p. 66
Ciao Italia (WS), p. 81
Daniel's (CN), p. 66
DaVinci's (CN), p. 66
Magpie's Gourmet Pizzas (DT), p. 62
Michelangelo (WS), p. 82

## Mexican/Latin American/
## Native American

Birrieria Guadalajara (SS), p. 78
Café Poca Cosa (DT), p. 59
Casa Molina (WS), p. 80
Cora's Cafe (SS), p. 78
Crossroads (SS), p. 78
El Adobe Café (DT), p. 61
El Charro (DT), p. 61
El Minuto (DT), p. 62
El Saguarito Mexican Food (WS), p.81
El Torero (SS), p. 79
Guillermo's Double L (SS), p. 79
La Costa Brava (SS), p. 79
La Indita (DT), p. 62
Mariscas Chihuahua (SS), p. 79
Maya Quetzal (DT), p. 63
Micha's (SS), p. 79
Mi Nidito (SS), p. 80
Sanchez Burrito Company (WS),
p. 83
Su Casa (SS), p. 80
Taqueria Pico de Gallo (SS), p. 80
Yoeme Café (WS), p. 84

## Middle Eastern

Le Mediterranean (ES), p. 75

## Seafood
Keaton's (ES, WS), p. 75
KingFisher (CN), p. 71
The Maine Course (WS), p. 82

## Southwestern
The Cottonwood Café (CN), p. 66
¡Fuego! (ES), p. 75
Janos (CN), p. 71
Jonathan's Tucson Cork (ES), p. 75
The Tack Room (ES), p. 77

## Vegetarian-friendly
El Saguarito Mexican Food (WS),
  p. 81
Govinda's (CN), p. 70

# DOWNTOWN

## ATHENS ON 4TH AVENUE
**500 N. Fourth Ave.**
**520/624-6886**
**$$**
This charming Hellenic bistro exudes bright cleanliness; its menu is similarly dependable, with the expected *spanakopita*, moussaka, gyros, lamb dishes, and other Greek favorites, served in rather large portions (it's quite easy to make a satisfying meal of appetizers and soup). The side vegetables are braised especially well, and the quality of the main dishes, if not Olympian, is thoroughly satisfactory. Athens can be easy to miss from the street; it's in an old house set back slightly from the northeast corner of Fourth Avenue and Sixth Street. Lunch, dinner. Reservations are suggested on Saturday nights. ♿ (Downtown)

## B&B CAFÉ
**330 S. Scott Ave.**
**520/792-2623**
**$$**
Located in the lovely Temple of Music

and Art, the B&B offers a short but interesting menu of dishes evolved from the establishment's origin as a deli. Fresh salads, light entrées, comforting soups, a surprising number of vegetable options, and delectable desserts constitute the fare. At lunchtime, take advantage of the mix 'n' match plate, whereby you assemble a meal from about a dozen menu selections and pay according to the number of items selected. Service can be disorganized but not rude. If the high-ceilinged, exposed-brick interior doesn't suit you, sit outside in the Temple's relaxing, fountain-splashed courtyard. Because the B&B is the logical spot for dinner before an Arizona Theatre Company performance, it can be difficult to be seated between 6 and 8 p.m. without reservations. Lunch, dinner. ♿ (Downtown)

## CAFÉ MAGRITTE
**254 E. Congress St.**
**520/884-8004**
**$$**
Named for the surrealist painter, Café Magritte was actually opened by a fine Tucson artist who has decorated the place with an appropriately surreal whimsy, as well as with images by Magritte himself. Even the restrooms here are a hoot. As for the food, it's offbeat and eclectic, yet never bizarre. Dishes range from unremarkable red beans and rice to wonderful cheese tortellini with pine nuts and cilantro pesto. Hummus and odd cheeses find their way into a number of enticing dishes. The dessert tray may be small, but its contents are select. Lunch, dinner. ♿ (Downtown)

## CAFÉ POCA COSA
**Santa Rita Hotel**
**88 E. Broadway Blvd.**
**520/622-6400**

# DOWNTOWN TUCSON

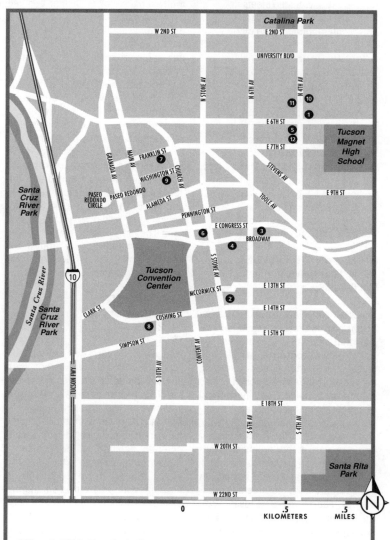

**Where to Eat in Downtown Tucson**

1 Athens on 4th Avenue
2 B&B Café
3 Café Magritte
4 Café Poca Cosa
5 Café Sweetwater
6 El Adobe Café
7 El Charro
8 El Minuto
9 La Cocina
10 La Indita
11 Magpie's Gourmet Pizzas
12 Maya Quetzal

## $$

Sonoran Mexican food meets nouvelle cuisine sensibilities in this remarkable local favorite. Don't let the word "nouvelle" lead you to anticipate small portions—plates are loaded down, with at least half given over to a generous salad of trendy greens (no iceberg lettuce within two blocks). Beans, rice, and warm corn tortillas are always served on the side. As for the flavorful but not necessarily spicy main dishes, they pull chicken, beef, seafood, pork, and vegetables into recipes of Mexican origin with a special panache. The chicken *mole*—chicken in a chocolate sauce (no, it's not really sweet)—is one of the more conventional choices on a menu that changes often enough that it's kept on a blackboard rather than on paper. Be daring and go for the chef's choice, which serves up three of the day's entrées on one plate—but you won't know *which* entrées until they arrive. A hole-in-the-wall Poca Cosa lies just down the street, at 20 S. Scott Avenue. Lunch, dinner. & (Downtown)

## CAFÉ SWEETWATER
### 340 E. Sixth St.
### 520/622-6464
### $–$$

Seafood and pasta are the primary choices, and they're usually given a neat Southwestern twist—the blackened mussels are tossed in a honey jalapeño dressing, for example. The kitchen help seems to be tossed, too, from time to time, judging from Sweetwater's occasional flirtation with drabness. Still, the place is good enough often enough to be worth a chance. If nothing else, sidle up to the bar and sample a nice variety of wines by the glass and Latin jazz or blues on the weekend. Lunch, dinner. & (Downtown)

## EL ADOBE CAFÉ
### 52 W. Congress St.
### 520/624-6133
### $

Mexican food often wobbles with fat, but El Adobe prides itself on a menu balanced with "heart-healthy" options as tasty as the regular fare. Vegans and vegetarians can even partake of certain interesting varieties of burrito, without having to rely on the usual refried-bean variety. El Adobe bills itself as the home of the "Perfect Margarita," a controversial claim held with some justification. There's no argument about the perfect patio area, fine for dining during much of the year. Lunch, dinner. & (Downtown)

## EL CHARRO
### 311 N. Court Ave.
### 520/622-1922
### $$

That phone number is significant—El Charro has been operated by the same family since 1922. It hasn't been located in this same house since then; urban renewal once sent it packing. But El Charro has always been resilient and now constitutes a local restaurant empire. The branches at the airport and on the East Side at Broadway and Wilmot, however, often fail to meet the standards of the downtown original. Meat lovers owe this place a pilgrimage; it prides itself on its air-dried *carne asada* (spiced shredded beef). If you arrive early enough in the day, go out to the patio and look for the baskets of beef hoisted up near the roof. The *carne seca* earns high marks, and some more heart-healthy dishes have found their way into this domain, too. During the likely for your table, check out the restaurant's cozy cantina, ¡Toma! Lunch, dinner. (Downtown)

Tucson claims to be the birthplace of the *chimichanga*, the deep-fried version of the burro/burrito. Unfortunately, it's an unverifiable claim, and one the city may be less willing to press now that fried foods are anathema to our increasingly health-conscious culture.

**EL MINUTO**
**354 S. Main Ave.**
**520/882-4145**
**$**
Ordinary, no-frills Sonoran-style Mexican food is hardly done better than at El Minuto, right between the Tucson Convention Center and the old barrio. You can't go wrong with the *carne seca* or chiles rellenos, and the usual range of burritos, *chimichangas*, tacos, and tamales gets sympathetic treatment in this kitchen. The place is open late on Fridays and Saturdays, and mariachi musicians stroll through on an irregular schedule. While you're here, mosey over to the next lot south on Main and inspect the wishing shrine El Tiradito (see Chapter 5, Sights and Attractions). Lunch, dinner. & (Downtown)

**LA COCINA**
**201 N. Court Ave.**
**520/622-0351**
**$**
Even more than the food, La Cocina's setting holds special appeal; it occupies one corner and the courtyard of Old Town Artisans, a block of adobe buildings in which fine Southwestern and Mexican arts, crafts, and jewelry are purveyed. While you relax and dine in the courtyard, you can imagine what life was like for well-heeled Tucsonans a century ago. The menu itself makes no particular claim to historical authenticity; it centers on

mesquite-grilled beef, chicken, and seafood, with a nice variety of sandwiches, quiches, soups, and salads offered as alternatives. Lunch, dinner; often open late. & (Downtown)

**LA INDITA**
**622 N. Fourth Ave.**
**520/792-0523**
**$**
La Indita doesn't merely pay lip service to Tucson's "Indian" heritage, it serves the palate as well, with a Tohono O'odham take on food styles from the Mexican state of Michoacán, rather than the more usual Sonoran fare. A concoction that might be self-consciously trendy elsewhere, like mushroom enchiladas, seems entirely natural in this unpretentious restaurant. The various chicken dishes, particularly the daily specials, are favorites among the regulars, but vegetarians do very well here, too. Food is cooked only in vegetable oil, never lard, and fat content in general is kept low. If there's anything at all negative to report about this endearing restaurant, it's that the southern room facing Fourth Avenue can get hot on a summer evening. Lunch (except on Saturdays), dinner, and Sunday breakfast. (Downtown)

**MAGPIE'S GOURMET PIZZAS**
**605 N. Fourth Ave.**
**520/628-1661**
**$–$$**

Great pizza doesn't come cheap at Magpie's, but it comes often. Try the rich pesto pizza, the savory Greek pizza, the chicken picante, or the several lowish-fat versions, or—well, just about anything on the menu. Decor is bare-bones in this storefront pizzeria, and you order at the counter even if you'll ultimately eat in rather than carry out. So what? Where else can you order eggplant or asparagus on your pizza, outside of a tony trendoid restaurant? Magpie's has established several satellite locations, mainly for takeout; check the phone book for the nearest locations. No reservations. Lunch, dinner. ₺ (Downtown)

## MAYA QUETZAL
**429 N. Fourth Ave.**
**520/622-8207**
**$**

This is a Guatemalan, not Mexican, restaurant, and a delightful one it is. The cuisine is similar to Mexico's, with tostadas, chiles rellenos, tamales, and such, but the seasoning tends to be milder, even a little sweet. Chicken is often served in a spicy cream sauce; pastry dough encases such odd combinations as spinach and walnuts. Black beans and rice are readily available. Don't neglect the beverage menu; try the rice-based *horchata* or the hibiscus-flavored tea called *jamaica*. No reservations. Lunch, dinner. (Downtown)

# CENTRAL-NORTH

## ANTHONY'S IN THE CATALINAS
**6440 N. Campbell Ave.**
**520/299-1771**
**$$$**

Tucked up near the top of Campbell Avenue, Anthony's offers a spectacu-

lar view of the valley—and a wine list to match, with a 1,600-item inventory ranging from perfectly good table wine to the sort of vintage you (and your banker) can only fantasize about. The cuisine is no less impressive: the tender, flaky lamb Wellington is a standout, followed not far behind by a variety of veal, fish, and beef dishes. Anthony's lavishes equal attention on its appetizers—anyone for duck liver pâté?—and desserts, including airy soufflés, light pastries, and assorted extravagances. The dining rooms themselves reflect the elegance of the food and service. Reservations recommended. Lunch, dinner (open Sunday only for dinner). ₺ (Central-North)

## AZ STIXX
**3048 E. Broadway Blvd.**
**520/323-3701**
**$$**

The cutesy name constitutes the only drawback at this newish midtown restaurant. Contemporary pan-Asian cuisine emerges from the kitchen, ranging from traditional Chinese favorites (*moo shu duck*, for instance) to such postmodern concoctions as shrimp and cilantro potstickers. Quick service, a good wine and microbrew list, and half a hundred varieties of single-malt Scotch contribute to the lively, casual atmosphere. It's also one of the few places in town open late. Lunch, dinner. ₺ (Central-North)

## THE BLUE WILLOW
**2616 N. Campbell Ave.**
**520/795-8736**
**$–$$**

Maintaining its original Sensitive Seventies atmosphere without a trace of kitsch or insincerity, this café serves wholesome, hearty food, with an emphasis on breakfast fare. The menu

# GREATER TUCSON

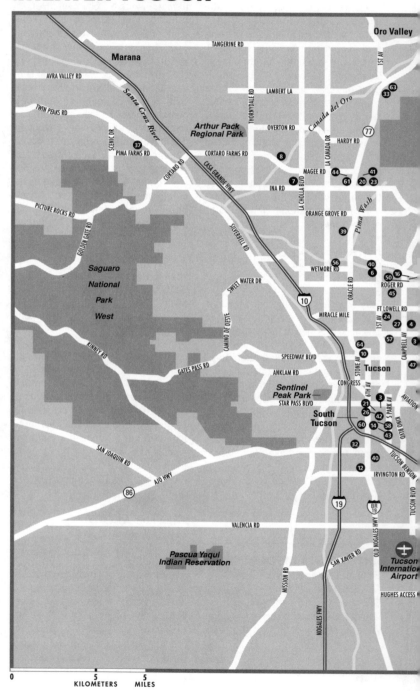

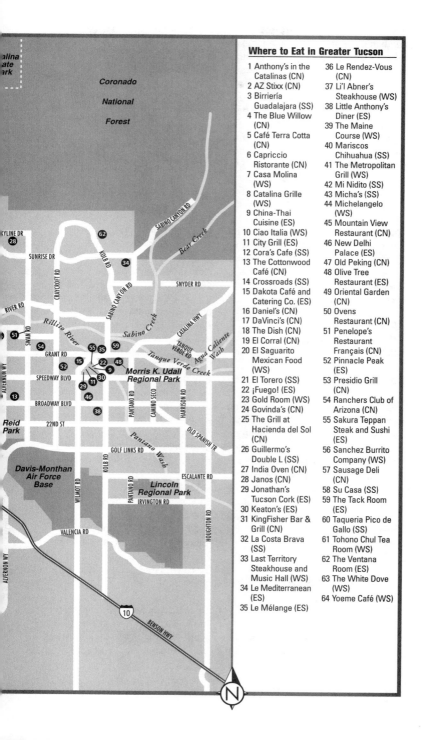

## Where to Eat in Greater Tucson

1 Anthony's in the Catalinas (CN)
2 AZ Stixx (CN)
3 Birriería Guadalajara (SS)
4 The Blue Willow (CN)
5 Café Terra Cotta (CN)
6 Capriccio Ristorante (CN)
7 Casa Molina (WS)
8 Catalina Grille (WS)
9 China-Thai Cuisine (ES)
10 Ciao Italia (WS)
11 City Grill (ES)
12 Cora's Cafe (SS)
13 The Cottonwood Café (CN)
14 Crossroads (SS)
15 Dakota Café and Catering Co. (ES)
16 Daniel's (CN)
17 DaVinci's (CN)
18 The Dish (CN)
19 El Corral (CN)
20 El Saguarito Mexican Food (WS)
21 El Torero (SS)
22 ¡Fuego! (ES)
23 Gold Room (WS)
24 Govinda's (CN)
25 The Grill at Hacienda del Sol (CN)
26 Guillermo's Double L (SS)
27 India Oven (CN)
28 Janos (CN)
29 Jonathan's Tucson Cork (ES)
30 Keaton's (ES)
31 KingFisher Bar & Grill (CN)
32 La Costa Brava (SS)
33 Last Territory Steakhouse and Music Hall (WS)
34 Le Mediterranean (ES)
35 Le Mélange (ES)
36 Le Rendez-Vous (CN)
37 Li'l Abner's Steakhouse (WS)
38 Little Anthony's Diner (ES)
39 The Maine Course (WS)
40 Mariscos Chihuahua (SS)
41 The Metropolitan Grill (WS)
42 Mi Nidito (SS)
43 Micha's (SS)
44 Michelangelo (WS)
45 Mountain View Restaurant (CN)
46 New Delhi Palace (ES)
47 Old Peking (CN)
48 Olive Tree Restaurant (ES)
49 Oriental Garden (CN)
50 Ovens Restaurant (CN)
51 Penelope's Restaurant Français (CN)
52 Pinnacle Peak (ES)
53 Presidio Grill (CN)
54 Ranchers Club of Arizona (CN)
55 Sakura Teppan Steak and Sushi (ES)
56 Sanchez Burrito Company (WS)
57 Sausage Deli (CN)
58 Su Casa (SS)
59 The Tack Room (ES)
60 Taqueria Pico de Gallo (SS)
61 Tohono Chul Tea Room (WS)
62 The Ventana Room (ES)
63 The White Dove (WS)
64 Yoeme Café (WS)

lists more varieties of omelet than you have fingers and toes; they're big and come accompanied by your choice of toasted breads, as well as fruit and potatoes. Much of the breakfast menu is served throughout the day, which may distract you from the quiches, soups, veggie-and-rice dishes, and other substantial offerings. Save room for one of the desserts, which are baked on the premises and generally intended to prove that chocolate is an independent food group. Try dining on the pleasant, enclosed patio. By the way, the entrance of the Blue Willow sports a funky gift shop; this would be a perfect place to purchase cards or a silly but good-quality souvenir. Reservations accepted; the place is often packed for breakfast and lunch, less so for dinner. ♿ (Central-North)

### CAFÉ TERRA COTTA
**4310 N. Campbell Ave.**
**520/577-8100**
**$$**
New Southwestern cuisine rules in trendy St. Philip's Plaza, particularly from Terra Cotta's kitchen. The dining rooms behind the verdigris front door can be noisy, so consider a table on the refreshingly peaceful side patio. The clever dishes include *poblano* chiles stuffed with chicken and shrimp, prawns stuffed with herbed goat cheese, some highly regarded seafood offerings, and a few economical (yet distinctive) pizzas from a wood-burning oven. Reservations recommended. Lunch, dinner. ♿ (Central-North)

### CAPRICCIO RISTORANTE
**4825 N. First Ave.**
**520/887-2333**
**$$–$$$**
When you begin to yearn for something Italian but *not* spaghetti and

meatballs, try the sophisticated fare at Capriccio. It's the sort of restaurant the brothers in the movie *Big Night* would operate if they were in Tucson today: pasta as a separate, early course rather than main dish (although you are welcome to make it the centerpiece of your meal), creamy risotto, roast duck with a sauce of Grand Marnier and green peppercorn, veal porterhouse sautéed in a white-wine sauce. Reservations essential on weekends, recommended weeknights. Dinner. ♿ (Central-North)

### THE COTTONWOOD CAFÉ
**60 N. Alvernon Way**
**520/326-6000**
**$–$$**
Now, how many places serve raspberry *chipotle* sauce with mesquite-grilled meat, or mix Indian corn and black beans into a seafood paella? Perhaps more and more restaurants will, once word of the Cottonwood's cuisine gets around. Sprawling noisily through a rambling midtown home with a fine patio and a comforting, quiet lounge, the Cottonwood Café has rapidly become a local favorite. Around back, the Cottonwood Club offers dancing and an odd variety of live music late into the evening. Lunch, dinner, Sunday brunch. ♿(Central-North)

### DANIEL'S
**4340 N. Campbell Ave.**
**520/742-3200**
**$–$$ (lunch); $$$ (dinner)**
Yet another of the fine restaurants in St. Philip's Plaza, Daniel's sets itself apart with its Northern Italian rather than contemporary Southwestern cuisine, as well as its intriguing Art Deco decor. Even the simplest things here—an appetizer of roasted eggplant and mushrooms, perhaps—can be exquisite, to say nothing of

*The dining area and bar in Café Terra Cotta*

the more complex flavors brought to the likes of duck or ribeye steak. Perhaps the most arresting specialty of the house is a dessert called *torta di tartufo liquefatto*, a sort of brownie soufflé. Closed Mondays. Lunch served October through May only. Reservations recommended. &#x267F; (Central-North)

### DAVINCI'S
**3535 E. Ft. Lowell Rd.**
**520/881-0947**
**$$**

If you are determined to overstuff your stomach and clog your arteries, you'll have a fine time doing it at DaVinci's. From the pasta-and-red-sauce standards to veal, chicken, and specialty dishes, all the food comes in enormous portions. Closed Sundays. Dinner, with lunch on Saturdays. &#x267F; (Central-North)

### THE DISH
**3200 E. Speedway Blvd.**
**520/326-1714**
**$$**

During Prohibition, you might have found liquor flowing in speakeasies hidden behind a respectable restaurant. Well, The Dish is a fine bistro hidden behind one of Tucson's leading wine shops, The Rumrunner. Here you'll find far more wines (30 by the glass) than tables (about a dozen), and a concise menu of winning appetizers and entrées, from saffron mussels to *penne Piacenza* and anise-crusted pork tenderloin. Given the tight surroundings, reservations are a must. Dinner. &#x267F; (Central-North)

### EL CORRAL
**2201 E. River Rd.**
**520/299-6092**
**$$**

This incredibly popular steakhouse doesn't fool around; the offerings consist of various cuts of beef, most notably prime rib, with a few token chicken entrées for variety. Period. You can have potato or tamale pie on the side, and dessert is basically a good chocolate mud pie, but red meat grilled without frills is what this place

# Mexican Food Glossary

**Albóndigas**: *meatballs; a popular soup ingredient*
**Arroz**: *rice*
**Barbacoa**: *barbecued meat*
**Burro/burrito**: *a large flour tortilla wrapped around a filling, usually beans, spicy beef, or some combination*
**Caldo**: *soup*
**Camarón**: *shrimp*
**Carne**: *beef, or meat in general*
**Carne seca**: *beef jerky, spiced and shredded*
**Cerveza**: *beer; Corona and Dos Equis are the ubiquitous Mexican brands*
**Ceviche**: *salad of fish marinated in lime juice*
**Chilaquiles**: *a casserole of corn tortilla pieces covered with enchilada sauce and cheese*
**Chile relleno**: *large chile stuffed with cheese, dipped in egg and deep-fried*
**Chimichanga** *(literally "thingamajig")*: *deep-fried* burro
**Chorizo**: *extremely spicy pork and beef sausage, often served with eggs or in a* burro
**Cilantro**: *coriander; a distinctive small-leaf ingredient in salsas*
**Empanada**: *turnover; a favorite pastry snack*
**Enchilada**: *corn tortilla dipped in red chile sauce, rolled around cheese, chicken, beef, sour cream, or whatever's handy, and topped with more sauce and cheese*
**Ensalada**: *salad*
**Flan**: *baked, caramel-coated custard; the most popular Mexican dessert*
**Flauta** *(literally "flute")*: *corn tortilla tightly rolled around a filling, then deep fried; the* flauta *is to the* enchilada *as the* chimichanga *is to the* burro
**Frijoles**: *beans, usually pinto;* frijoles refritos *are beans cooked a first time, then fried and mashed*

**Guacamole**: *mashed avocado dip or topping*
**Huevo**: *egg*
**Mariscos**: *shellfish*
**Masa**: *usually a dough of ground hominy, employed mainly in tamales*
**Menudo**: *tripe soup; a traditional cure for hangovers, served primarily for breakfast on the weekend*
**Mole** *(pronounced MOE-lay)*: *unsweetened chocolate and chile sauce, often served on chicken*
**Nopales**: *cactus pads cooked like okra*
**Pescado**: *fish*
**Picante**: *hot to the taste buds*
**Poblano**: *a variety of chile; the central ingredient in a chile relleno*
**Pollo**: *chicken*
**Postre**: *dessert*
**Quesadilla**: *flour tortilla folded over cheese and grilled; a Mexican grilled-cheese sandwich*
**Queso**: *cheese*
**Salsa**: *sauce; restaurant salsa is usually spicy and red, designed as a condiment for food or scooping up with tortilla chips; there's sometimes a green option*
**Sopa**: *soup*
**Taco**: *corn tortilla folded over a filling, usually shredded chicken or beef, with lettuce and cheese*
**Tamal** *(plural is* tamales*)*: *usually* masa *encasing a bit of chile or beef, all wrapped in a cornhusk*
**Tequila**: *distilled liquor made from agave, or century plant; the alcoholic ingredient in a margarita*
**Topopo**: *usually, a large salad contained in a deep-fried tortilla shell*
**Tortilla**: *thin, flat bread made from wheat flour or corn masa; a Mexican food staple*
**Tostada** *(literally "toasted")*: *fried or toasted corn tortilla onto which are piled beans, lettuce, and cheese*

is about. Huge portions and the adobe-ranch house atmosphere make up for the inevitably long wait for a table. No reservations. Dinner. & (Central-North)

## GOVINDA'S
**711 E. Blacklidge Dr.**
**520/792-0630**
**$**

With all those Krishna devotees selling incense in airports, you wonder why someone doesn't retaliate by selling airline tickets outside this quirky but alluring cafeteria-style restaurant run by the Hare Krishnas, complete with an incense and clothing shop right inside the front door. Tucked into a compound on a side street off First Avenue, Govinda's offers a different variety of vegetarian and vegan dishes from night to night; sometimes it's Indian-oriented but often not. Yes, some of the recipes employ tofu, and they taste just fine, thank you; someone in the kitchen knows how to handle herbs and spices. You may eat in a conventional dining room, sit on cushions on the floor at low tables (remove your shoes before entering this room), or amble outside to the quiet patio with its juice bar. On Thanksgiving, the turkey from Govinda's small aviary is allowed to roam with confidence

among the patrons. Lunch, dinner. & (Central-North)

## THE GRILL AT HACIENDA DEL SOL
**5601 N. Hacienda del Sol Rd.**
**520/529/3500**
**$–$$$**

It's not quite clear what the owners mean when they say that The Grill serves "Hacienda-style" cuisine, but it must have something to do with inventive uses of mesquite-grilled steak, veal, lamb, and seafood. Recently resurrected after a long period of inactivity, this restaurant in one of Tucson's most charming old former dude ranches has quickly earned high marks from local connoisseurs. Dine on the patio and enjoy a view of the mountains; dine inside and enjoy a view of the chefs at work. Dinner. & (Central-North)

## INDIA OVEN
**2727 N. Campbell Ave.**
**520/326-8635**
**$–$$**

Tucson boasts an ever-increasing number of Indian restaurants; all of them are, at the very least, good. India Oven is generally agreed to be one of the best, even though it's fairly new (and is the least self-conscious about Indian decor). Sizzling meats

For a great, cheap lunch on your way to or from Old Tucson or the Desert Museum, take Speedway west of I-10 and turn south on Grande (at the Arizona Schools for the Deaf and Blind). Within a couple of blocks you'll find two wonderful little joints. Grande Tortilla Factory, a family business since 1947, prepares all sorts of Mexican standards to go (or to carry out to the tables adjoining the parking lot); you could buy a dozen tortillas and nibble on them through the day. Or try Pat's Drive-In, the home of the best spicy chili dogs in the known world.

from the tandoor oven compete for attention with creamy vegetable dishes, all based on recipes brought over from the owners' native Punjab. The lunch buffet, as usual at Indian restaurants, is a real bargain. Lunch, dinner. & (Central-North)

## JANOS
**3770 E. Sunrise Dr.**
**520/615-6100**
**$$–$$$**

This magnificent restaurant—one of the two or three best high-end establishments in Tucson—was recently evicted from its longtime home in a historic adobe building downtown to allow expansion of the Tucson Museum of Art. Chef Janos Wilder is worth following anywhere; he virtually invented, and certainly perfected, nouvelle Southwestern cuisine, employing mostly locally grown ingredients in a menu that changes seasonally. Even something as ordinary as grilled beef tenderloin can be dressed up remarkably, layered with roasted chiles and served with an eggplant taco. Portions are small for the price, but the summer samplers are good deals. And if you partake sufficiently from Janos' superb wine list, you'll care less about the quantity and more completely savor its excellent quality. Reservations recommended. Closed Sundays year-round and on Mondays in the warm months. Dinner. & (Central-North)

## KINGFISHER BAR & GRILL
**2564 E. Grant Rd.**
**520/323-7739**
**$$$**

Fresh seafood is what hooks most diners at this trendy locale, but various American regional dishes share the menu, especially during the summer, when the restaurant offers "road trip"-themed specials. Depending on the time of year, you might indulge in a salmon tostada, pasta with grilled vegetables, or even buffalo prime rib. The oyster bar claims a great many adherents, and the regular bar offers charms of its own, including an astonishingly large selection of wines by the glass. KingFisher has been known to remain open as long as people come in and order food, which means service after 11 p.m. if there are enough late diners around to keep the chef busy. Reservations are recommended. Lunch, dinner. & (Central-North)

## LE RENDEZ-VOUS
**3844 E. Ft. Lowell Rd.**
**520/323-7373**
**$$$**

Settle into one of the intimate dining rooms, preferably with one intimate companion, and prepare your taste buds for a sensual evening. Le Rendez-Vous serves one outstanding classic French dish after another, from the pâtés and vichyssoise to the succulent rack of lamb through to a finale of flaky pastries or Grand Marnier soufflé. Other house specialties include mussels, duck, veal, and beef Wellington. Are reservations needed? *Mais oui*. Lunch Tuesdays through Fridays and dinner. Closed Mondays. & (Central-North)

## MOUNTAIN VIEW RESTAURANT
**1220 E. Prince Rd.**
**520/293-0375**
**$$**

Local opinion remains sharply divided on this German/Czech establishment. There just aren't many sources in Tucson for Wiener schnitzel, chicken schnitzel, and sauerbraten, and Mountain View ably fills that culinary gap. Beef, especially, is done to melting tenderness, and the various noodles are full-bodied but not gummy. Still, some diners find the flavors plain by Central European standards, and the service can sometimes be indifferent. For food wimps, there's also a selection of steaks, ribs, and other American standards. Lunch, dinner. & (Central-North)

## OLD PEKING
**2522 E. Speedway Blvd.**
**520/795-9811**
**$$**
Although Chinese-Americans have been firmly established in Tucson for more than a century, the city lacks truly outstanding Chinese restaurants. Several *very* good ones, however, have remained in business through the years, and Old Peking has long been a local favorite for its extensive Mandarin and Szechuan menu. Crispy, greaseless Peking duck is usually available without advance reservation, and the more common fare—eggplant in garlic sauce, spicy General Tso's chicken, and the like—adheres to respectable standards. Vegetarians can salivate over an array of fleshless dishes that'sbroad even by Chinese standards—noodles, bean curd, vegetables, even vegetarian spring rolls. Lunch, dinner. & (Central-North)

## ORIENTAL GARDEN
**15 N. Alvernon Way**
**520/326-4700**
**$$**
This restaurant offers a nice variety of non-Chinese, nonnouvelle Asian cuisine, with the emphasis on Japanese delights and Korean barbecue. Sushi addicts consider Oriental Garden's wraps to be better than average. Unlike many Asian restaurants, this one offers a fully stocked bar and cocktail lounge, not to mention the dreaded karaoke facilities. Takeout is also available. Lunch, dinner. & (Central-North)

## OVENS RESTAURANT
**4280 N. Campbell Ave. #37**
**520/577-9001**
**$$**
Yet another first-rate restaurant lodged in St. Philip's Plaza, this one proudly takes its name from its wood-burning ovens, which produce unusual pizzas, grilled meats and seafood, and such delicious oddities as Thai chicken pasta and *moo shu* calzone. Quantity is as generous as quality. Despite the tony nature of the cuisine, Ovens' atmosphere is entirely casual and a bit noisy; a lovely patio offers refuge. Reservations recommended. Lunch, dinner, Sunday brunch. & (Central-North)

## PENELOPE'S RESTAURANT FRANÇAIS
**3071 N. Swan Rd.**
**520/325-5080**
**$$$**

*KingFisher Bar & Grill, p. 71*

KingFisher Bar & Grill

Tucked away just a bit off the main road in a quiet, fine old house, Penelope's presents French cuisine of both classic and countryside varieties, beginning with the *escargots à la bourguignonne* and ending with chocolate mousse. As for the outstanding wine cellar, relax and let the sommelier steer your choice and you won't go wrong. The locals complain that Penelope's is overpriced by Tucson standards—but fine French restaurants tend to be overpriced, even in France. This doesn't frighten away people in search of an exquisite dining experience. Lunch, dinner. ♿ (Central-North)

## PRESIDIO GRILL
**3352 E. Speedway Blvd.**
**520/327-4667**
**$$–$$$**

Chic, postmodern, noisy, and irresistible, this yuppie hangout replicates the upscale neighborhood grills of lower Manhattan. The changing menu blends urban American and Southwestern trends, ranging from the basics (roasted garlic and brie) to such concoctions as duck and ancho chile quesadillas and pasta with *andouille* sausage and shrimp. Open late Friday and Saturday, and for breakfast Sunday. Reservations recommended. Lunch, dinner. ♿ (Central-North)

## RANCHERS CLUB OF ARIZONA
**5151 E. Grant Rd.**
**520/321-7621**
**$$$**

You have, after all, come to cattle country, and the steers aren't out there on the range just to keep the grass from getting too tall. They wind up on the grill, and one of the best grills is here at the Ranchers Club, in the Sheraton Tucson Hotel and Suites. It's quite a struggle to decide on one of several meat options—aged prime beef, lamb, pork, poultry, some seafood—but the most interesting choices begin with which sort of aromatic wood will the food be grilled over. You could select the current favorite, mesquite, or go back to the old standard of hickory, or opt for something unusual like sassafras or wild cherry. Then there's the question of which sauce for your entrée: Béarnaise? Curried apple chutney? Or one of two dozen others? Oh, and which two grilled vegetables would you prefer? (Vegetarians in your company are welcome to a platter of grilled vegetables, along with the standard accompaniments of soup or salad.) This is no steakhouse; it's an elegant restaurant (despite the trophy heads staring from the walls), and you'll want to spiff up a bit before you arrive. Reservations recommended.

**TIP**

If you absolutely must grab some fast food, at least patronize a Tucson-based chain. That would be eegee's, which makes up for what it lacks in capital letters with reasonably wholesome deli sandwiches (including a vegetarian option). The prime attraction is the "eegee's" itself; it resembles a Sno-cone, but instead of a dollop of syrup over crushed ice, an "eegee's" is made with ice and shaved frozen fruit, bits of which you're sure to find in your cup.

Closed Sundays. Dinner; lunch on weekdays. ⅍ (Central-North)

**SAUSAGE DELI**
**2334 N. First Ave.**
**520/623-8182**
**$**

Billing itself as "Tucson's alternative to fine dining" with "festival-style parking," this madcap joint happily serves up satisfying cholesterol-laden deli sandwiches, first-rate sides like artichoke salad, tasty lemonade, and a cool jukebox. You don't go to a place like this for atmosphere; you go to stuff your face, and you're not likely to find better stuffing than the Sausage Deli's. No reservations. Lunch, dinner. (Central-North)

## EAST SIDE

**CHINA-THAI CUISINE**
**6502 E. Tanque Verde Rd.**
**520/885-6860**
**$**

The name lays it out plainly. If you want to play it safe with familiar Chinese dishes like *moo goo gai pan* and shrimp egg foo yung, you'll do well here. But if your palate calls out for

something more adventuresome, something fiery like Thai curry or *pad Thai*, you'll find satisfaction here. The prices are economical, takeout and limited delivery are available, and the only remarkable thing about the casual dining room's atmosphere is its totally smokeless nature. Lunch, dinner. ⅍ (East Side)

**CITY GRILL**
**6350 E. Tanque Verde Rd.**
**520/733-1111**
**$–$$**

It's gaining a reputation as a clattery hangout for upscale young singles, perhaps in part because of the attentive service from hip waiters. But City Grill welcomes anyone with an appetite for gourmet wood-fired pizzas, inventive sandwiches, nouvelle pastas, grilled seafood, and rotisserie chicken. Entertainment, other than people-watching, is provided by the exhibition kitchen and full bar. Open late. Lunch, dinner. ⅍ (East Side)

**DAKOTA CAFÉ AND CATERING CO.**
**6541 E. Tanque Verde Rd.**
**520/298-7188**
**$$**

Tucked away into the Western kitsch of Trail Dust Town is this restaurant that doesn't pretend to be anything other than an excellent contemporary American establishment offering pasta entrées, fresh seafood, and grilled meat, often doused with inventive sauces (prickly pear/port on lamb loin, for instance). Equally attractive is the choice of dining areas: the high-ceilinged, postmodern interior or the sunny enclosed patio. The prices are good considering the sophistication of much of Dakota's fare. Closed Sundays. Lunch, dinner. ♿ (East Side)

## ¡FUEGO!
### 6858 E. Tanque Verde Rd.
### 520/886-1745
### $$–$$$

Chef Alan Zeman's latest endeavor sits firmly in the New Southwestern category, although all that means these days is an eclectic menu of exotic combinations, most of them involving some regional ingredient or other. Consider a single appetizer: scampi, *chorizo*, pepper, and roasted garlic flambé. The rest of any meal will proceed apace, through a variety of meats and pastas. Noisy and bright, ¡Fuego! stays open late. Reservations recommended. Lunch, dinner, Sunday brunch. ♿ (East Side)

## JONATHAN'S TUCSON CORK
### 6320 E. Tanque Verde Rd.
### 520/296-1631
### $$–$$$

When chef Jonathan Landeen took over this purveyor of such standard Southwestern fare as prime rib and steak, and added items like ostrich and buffalo, some traditionalists complained that the menu was straining to be outlandish. Well, half the menus in town strain to be outlandish, and many of them come through with worthy, exciting dishes.

Jonathan's Tucson Cork is no exception, and if you're curious about ostrich steak (ranched right here in Arizona), this is as fine a preparation as you'll find. The wine list, too, is unconventional but attractive. Reservations recommended. Lunch, dinner. ♿ (East Side)

## KEATON'S
### 6464 E. Tanque Verde Rd.
### 520/721-1299
### $$

Seafood is the specialty but not the fixation at this family American grill. Sharing the menu with salmon, swordfish, crab cakes, and oysters are free-range veal, New York sirloin, and bodacious burgers. Don't pass up the basket of zucchini bread, and carefully study the potato and rice choices that accompany the entrées—you might find something arrestingly Southwestern and new. Reservations recommended. Lunch, dinner. Another location in Foothills Mall, 7401 N. La Cholla Blvd. (520/297-1999). ♿ (East Side)

## LE MEDITERRANEAN
### 4955 N. Sabino Canyon Rd.
### 520/529-1330
### $$

Despite its French name, this restaurant borrows its cuisine not from the Riviera but from the eastern end of the Mediterranean basin. Outstanding Lebanese, Turkish, and Greek dishes, from simple hummus through traditional moussaka to a stew of lamb and green beans, provide savory alternatives to the American- and Continental-centered fare that dominates Tucson's East Side. Just stepping through the door and sniffing the air tells you you've entered the realm of cumin, lemon, and feta cheese. Not to mention the sight of the belly dancer performing on Fridays and Saturdays. Reservations recommended. Dinner. &. (East Side)

## LE MÉLANGE
**6761 E. Tanque Verde Rd.**
**520/298-2233**
**$$$**
What used to be a solid spot for hearty breakfasts and lunches has become a fine French restaurant with Swiss inflections. The real catch on the menu is seafood, and we're not talking fish sticks: swordfish with pesto and oyster mushrooms, ragout of monkfish with artichoke hearts, salmon poached in saffron sauce, sole that supposedly swam within view of Dover's white cliffs. Classic French treatments of beef and lamb also grace the menu. Concentrate on the entrées here; the starters and desserts haven't been up to quite the same standard. Breakfast, lunch daily; dinner Tue–Sat. &. (East Side)

## LITTLE ANTHONY'S DINER
**7010 E. Broadway Blvd.**
**520/886/9428**
**$**
A great place to take the kids and a cool outing for baby boomers who wax nostalgic for the 1950s, Little Anthony's reeks *Happy Days* atmosphere with its diner decor, its background score of early rock 'n' roll classics, and, of course, its food. Burgers and pizza are the prime attractions, with supporting roles given to such diner standards as chicken-fried steak, meatloaf, and soda fountain specials. Lunch, dinner; breakfast on the weekend. &. (East Side)

## NEW DELHI PALACE
**6751 E. Broadway Blvd.**
**520/296-8585**
**$$**

One of the first Indian restaurants to arrive in Tucson, New Delhi Palace remains a favorite for its spicy tandoori specialties and wide range of vegetarian dishes. Like most other Indian restaurants in town, this has gone through a few stale periods, but it keeps reviving its fare and retaining its regulars. The lunch buffet is a tasty bargain. Another special attraction: 35 brands of imported beer. Lunch, dinner. &. (East Side)

## OLIVE TREE RESTAURANT
**7000 E. Tanque Verde Rd.**
**520/298-1845**
**$$**
Greek food gets a classy treatment in this East Side establishment that also serves Continental specialties. Roast lamb, cinnamon chicken, and finely executed fish dishes share menu space with the usual moussaka, dolmathes, and shish kebab. The interior decor is soothing and the atmosphere is quiet, but when the weather's fine the beautiful treelined patio is the place to be. Lunch (except Sundays), dinner. Reservations recommended. &. (East Side)

## PINNACLE PEAK
**6541 E. Tanque Verde Rd.**
**520/296-0911**
**$**
This tourist-oriented steakhouse in Trail Dust Town draws plenty of locals, especially families, with its kitschy Old West atmosphere. The place proclaims its specialty to be "mesquite-broiled cowboy steaks," implying that it's the ranch hand who's been carved up. A few dissenters claim you couldn't tell the difference between cowboy and cow in this kitchen, but it's silly to expect a haute cuisine experience in such a barnlike, Wild West environment. The

> For a special Sunday brunch, consider the Cottonwood Café, La Fuente, Ovens, the White Dove, or ¡Fuego!

cooking satisfies enough people that there's usually a wait for a table, even though Pinnacle Peak seats 550. By the way, if you're dying to get rid of that lurid necktie Aunt Thelma gave you last Christmas, wear it here. The staff scissors off every tie brought through the door. No reservations. Lunch, dinner. & (East Side)

### SAKURA TEPPAN STEAK AND SUSHI
**6534 E. Tanque Verde Rd.**
**520/298-7777**
**$$–$$$**

Sushi, tempura, and other Japanese dishes receive the imperial treatment here, but if you order a *teppan-yaki* meal, you get a floor show, too: a flamboyant chef will grill your chicken, shrimp, or steak entrée at your table, whipping his knives through the air, juggling ingredients and utensils, and generally making it impossible to concentrate on anything besides the food preparation. The resulting portions can be small, but tasty. The sports bar serves food until 1 a.m. Lunch weekdays, dinner. & (East Side)

### THE TACK ROOM
**2800 N. Sabino Canyon Rd.**
**520/722-2800**
**$$$**

Since 1973, the Tack Room has gotten a lot of mileage out of its AAA five-Diamond rating. This restaurant has long maintained a stable of stalwart regulars, but some naysayers contend that the food has slipped from its high standard and that it's getting by on arrogance rather than expertise. Still, things haven't declined to such a state that the curious gourmand shouldn't investigate what all the fuss has been about. Housed in an elegant, quiet adobe hacienda, the restaurant features such fare as rack of lamb Sonora and slow-roasted duckling on a menu that changes daily. Reservations recommended. Dinner. & (East Side)

### THE VENTANA ROOM
**Loews Ventana Canyon Resort**
**7000 N. Resort Dr.**
**520/299-2020, ext. 5194**
**$$$**

Situated high in the Catalina foothills, the Ventana Room is as close to heaven as you'll get in a Tucson restaurant. Sumptuous American regional cuisine, superb presentation, excellent service, wonderful views of the city (*ventana* does mean "window," after all), and elegant appointments characterize this establishment. Grilled seafood, meat, and game—sometimes including venison or caribou—form the centerpieces of most meals, with exacting attention lavished on even the simpler appetizers and desserts. The wine list stands as one of the city's most extensive, and for the indecisive, a prix fixe chef's tasting menu comes to the rescue. Reservations recommended. Dinner. & (East Side)

*Jonathan's Tucson Cork, p. 75*

## SOUTH SIDE

### BIRRIERÍA GUADALAJARA
**304 E. 22nd St.**
**520/624-8020**
**$**

Nothing but counter service and picnic tables here, but you'll be too stirred up to linger anyway once you've consumed some of the wonderfully fiery, or at least unusual, food inspired by the cuisine of the Mexican state of Jalisco. In the "unusual" category are the *tacos de cabrito* (made with goat meat) and tongue burros. More conventional is the moist, lightly seasoned *carne asada*. *Birriería*, more commonly spelled *birria* in these parts, is a spicy, lime-dusted stew of shredded goat meat; beef is substituted here. The *birria* meat also finds its way into tacos and burritos. Neither credit cards nor reservations are accepted. Breakfast, lunch, dinner. &#9855; (South Side)

### CORA'S CAFE
**24 W. Irvington Rd.**
**520/294-2146**
**$**

A neighborhood working-class favorite, Cora's can't be beat for its extensive variety of Mexican soups, which tend to be light but spicy. They're all here, all the time: *arroz con pollo* (chicken and rice), *caldo de queso* (vegetables and cheese in a broth rather than cream base), *pozole* (hominy, pork, and beans), *albóndigas* (spicy meatballs and vegetables), and many more. *Menudo*, or tripe soup, traditionally a weekend dish, is available only Friday through Sunday. If you prefer something you can sink your teeth into, Cora's also offers the Sonoran standards—enchiladas, chiles rellenos, tacos, and so forth. Lunch. Closed Mondays. (South Side)

### CROSSROADS
**2602 S. Fourth Ave.**
**520/624-0395**

**$**

This started out as a drive-in, as you can tell from the architecture and the survival of cheeseburgers on the menu. But Crossroads is now a sit-down Mexican establishment adorned with bullfight paintings and an interesting mural. The place is notorious for its tear-inducing red chile; other house specialties include *carne asada*, *chimichangas*, and chiles rellenos. Lunch, dinner. ᕼ (South Side)

## EL TORERO
**231 E. 26th St.**
**520/622-9534**
**$**

Alongside the green corn tamales and *albóndigas*, El Torero offers such novelties as turkey *flautas* and crab *topopo* salad. The restaurant, which announces its presence with a sign depicting a bullfighter, lies just off Fourth Avenue. Lunch, dinner. Closed Tuesdays. ᕼ (South Side)

## GUILLERMO'S DOUBLE L
**1830 S. Fourth Ave.**
**520/792-1585**
**$**

Few restaurants can please asbestos-tongued locals and dove-tonsiled tourists with equal flair, but Guillermo's somehow manages. Perhaps that's because the place neither dumbs down its recipes nor courts the macho-mouthed diner who's impervious to subtleties. Take the green chile enchiladas: tender beef, onions, and chiles wrapped in corn tortillas and topped with red sauce, cheese, and sour cream—traditional, simple, flavorful. The huge *topopo* salads contain a veritable garden of vegetables as well as shrimp or chicken. Fajitas and chile con carne also hold their own against the competition. Lunch, dinner. Closed Sundays. ᕼ (South Side)

## LA COSTA BRAVA
**3541 S. 12th Ave.**
**520/623-1931**
**$$**

Adjacent to the L.H. Rodriguez Fish Market, and owned by Levi Rodriguez himself, La Costa Brava specializes in Mexican seafood dishes. Under maritime decor, the restaurant serves surprisingly fresh fish, given Tucson's distance from anything resembling running water. The menu changes seasonally; in the winter, try the *cabrilla*. Lunch, dinner (early closing on Sundays). ᕼ (South Side)

## MARISCOS CHIHUAHUA
**3901 S. Sixth Ave.**
**520/741-0361**
**$–$$**

*Mariscos* means "shellfish." Shellfish do not thrive in the landlocked desert Mexican state of Chihuahua. The etymology of this restaurant's name is complicated, but suffice it to say that the shellfish half is the more important. You'll find it and its soft-scaled relatives in nearly every dish: seafood cocktails, fish soup, spicy shrimp *endiablados* style, fish Culichi style (in a green chile and cheese sauce), octopus entrées, and ceviche. Some day they'll probably figure out some sort of fishy dessert, too—chocolate-covered prawns? Lunch, dinner. ᕼ (South Side)

## MICHA'S
**2908 S. Fourth Ave.**
**520/623-5307**
**$**

Most Tucsonans would be loathe to name the one best Mexican restaurant in town, but half of the few who dared an opinion would probably single out Micha's (the other half would vote for Mi Nidito, below). There are no tricks or trends to identify here, just reliable Sonoran fare prepared with care and served in generous portions. Aside from the usual Mexican menu items, you'll find a choice of about five soups, plus seafood and vegetarian plates. Breakfast, lunch, and dinner (no dinner on Mondays). 🏷 (South Side)

## MI NIDITO
**1813 S. Fourth Ave.**
**520/622-5081**
**$$**

Your chances of being seated immediately upon arriving are about equal to those of winning the lottery. Mi Nidito ("My Little Nest") is one tremendously popular place, and people are willing to wait for a table for up to 20 or 30 minutes (or two hours on a weekend) rather than duck into some other nearby Mexican joint. One reason: the chiles rellenos, fresh, light, puffy, with just a little spicy bite to them. Another: the Burro Deluxe, a large flour tortilla wrapped around beans, green chile, avocado, cheese, and more. Another: the quirky desserts, including the choco-taco and the mango *chimichanga*. No reservations. Closed Monday and Tuesday. Lunch, dinner.🏷 (South Side)

## SU CASA
**2205 S. Fourth Ave.**
**520/628-1931**
**$**

"Your House," indeed; everything is done by hand, as if in a modest household kitchen. Daily lunch specials at this Sonoran-style restaurant are incredibly cheap and include beans, rice, and dessert. *Menudo* is available every day, not just for weekend hangovers. Closed Sundays; open late Fridays and Saturdays. Breakfast, lunch, and dinner. 🏷 (South Side)

## TAQUERIA PICO DE GALLO
**2618 S. Sixth Ave.**
**520/623-8775**
**$**

*Pico de gallo* is a spicy Mexican fruit cup, and this restaurant originated as a little *pico de gallo* cart. Now it's housed in a modest building and serves regular food—if "regular" encompasses such items as manta ray *burros* and tongue tacos. Many more conventional dishes are offered here, including *carne asada*, seafood, and bean *burros*. Wash it all down with a glass of *horchata* or limeade or a tasty fruit drink made in the kitchen, not bought from some wholesaler. Table space is scarce, so consider ordering at the counter and eating on the run. No credit cards accepted. Lunch, dinner. 🏷 (South Side)

# WEST SIDE

## CASA MOLINA
**Foothills Mall**
**7401 N. La Cholla Blvd.**
**520/297-5000**
**$–$$**

Lard has been discarded in favor of canola oil, but otherwise this remains an old-guard classic Sonoran restaurant. Casa Molina stands as one of the city's real veterans, having been founded in 1947. The *chimichangas* are a little skinnier than elsewhere, but they make up for that by jutting crisply over each side of the plate. Everything else on the menu is either long, plump, or at least generously proportioned. Meat eaters must try the smoky *carne seca*, and anyone should enjoy a dessert of light sopapillas with honey. Also at 4240 E. Grant Road (520/326-6663), and the home office at 6225 E. Speedway (520/886-5468). Most locations offer

*Chef Jonilonis of the Gold Room*

live entertainment toward the weekend. Lunch, dinner. ⅋ (West Side)

## CATALINA GRILLE
**Omni Tucson National Golf Resort**
**2727 W. Club Dr.**
**520/297-2271**
**$$$**

The Catalina Grille got off to a slow start, but it's shaping up to be another interesting mainly Southwestern kitchen. Now, "Southwestern" implies little more than a special touch with seasoning and accouterments; but this restaurant's main ingredients are especially far-flung, including Sonoma lamb, cranberry-spiced Iowa pork loin, and Seattle salmon. Unlike other restaurants of its type, the Catalina Grille is actually quiet enough for you to converse without shouting. For now, lunchtime probably offers the best balance of quality and price. Reservations recommended. ⅋ (West Side)

## CIAO ITALIA
**1535 N. Stone Ave.**
**520/884-0000**

**$$**

When you begin to yearn for something Italian, *especially* pasta, Ciao Italia is the local favorite. Unpretentious, casual decor sets the scene for some of the finest fettucine and tortellini around, as well as entrées revolving around beef, chicken, seafood, and veal. Closed for several months after a fire, the restaurant reopened in 1997 with a slightly pricier and fancier menu than before; the old customers have been clamoring for an exact duplication of the beloved old Ciao Italia, and some fine-tuning is underway. Lunch weekdays, dinner nightly. ⅋ (West side)

## EL SAGUARITO MEXICAN FOOD
**7216 N. Oracle Rd.**
**520/297-1264**
**$**

Unpretentious yet attractive to tourists for the crafts and curios it sells in the entryway, El Saguarito strives to serve nothing but low-fat food that will give you a taste of Mexico without clogging your arteries. Even up on Oracle Road, where the Mexican food gets rather bland, this restaurant can sometimes fool you into thinking you're eating in South Tucson. The Sonoran standards are all here, often with vegetarian alternatives in which the only shredded ingredients are the lettuce and cheese. Lunch, dinner. ⅋ (West Side)

## GOLD ROOM
**Westward Look Resort**
**245 E. Ina Rd.**
**520/297-1151**
**$$$**

One of the few restaurants in Tucson that offers a view of both the city and the mountains beyond, the Gold Room specializes in extras. Begin with a glance at the elegant Southwestern decor and then consider the presentation of the food; for starters, the complimentary chicken liver pâté appetizer is served on a plate on which the resort's logo is painted in mustard. Main courses include lamb, seafood, beef, and now even buffalo and ostrich. Side vegetables are never afterthoughts. If dinner here is off your budget, consider showing up for one of the most elegant Sunday brunches around. Reservations recommended. Breakfast, lunch, and dinner. & (West Side)

**LAST TERRITORY STEAKHOUSE
AND MUSIC HALL
Sheraton El Conquistador Resort
10000 N. Oracle Rd.
520/544-1738
$$$**
If you're staying in town, there's honestly no need to drive all the way out to the Sheraton El Conquistador for this experience, but if you're lodged at the resort, it's a fine way to get your Western kitsch fix. Set up as part of a mock–Wild West town, the steakhouse offers good mesquite-grilled steaks, ribs, chicken, and seafood, accompanied by nightly Western music performances. Reservations recommended. Lunch, dinner. & (West Side)

**LI'L ABNER'S STEAKHOUSE
8501 N. Silverbell Rd.
520/744-2800
$–$$**
Why, oh why, do so many steakhouses tart themselves up in cutesy decor? Li'l Abner's, at least, shows a modicum of restraint, concentrating mainly on its limited menu of meat, ranch beans, and potatoes. The meat is chicken, ribs, and, of course, steak, served in two varieties: large (16 ounces) and huge (32 ounces). It's all cooked over the outdoor mesquite

grill. Try to arrive before sunset, so you can enjoy what's left of the natural desert landscape along Silverbell during the longish drive. Dinner. & (West Side)

**THE MAINE COURSE
5851 N. Oracle Rd.
520/887-5518
$$$**
It's sometimes criticized as inconsistent and overpriced, but what do you expect of a lobster restaurant in the middle of the desert? Maine lobster is the featured attraction at this cozy New England–style restaurant, and it is the most reliably well-prepared item from the kitchen, whether served whole, as a bisque, or in some other incarnation. Scallops, mussels, crab, shrimp, and clams also vie for attention, with a few token chicken and beef dishes offered to diners who prefer not to get their culinary feet wet. Reservations recommended. Dinner. & (West Side)

**THE METROPOLITAN GRILL
7892 N. Oracle Rd.
520/531-1212
$$**
Fairly new but quickly proven a reliable purveyor of contemporary American fare, the Metropolitan Grill dispenses rotisserie chicken, chops, pizza, and prime rib alike from its exhibition kitchen. Pasta, seafood, and entrée salads also feature prominently on the menu. The look is upscale, and the wine selection is respectable, but the pricing is comparatively economical. Lunch, dinner. & (West Side)

**MICHELANGELO
420 W. Magee Rd.
520/297-5775
$$**

Weight-watchers must look the other way for the homemade pasta and hand-stretched pizza make no concession to calorie counters. Seafood, veal, and chicken also get the Italian treatment here, making this about the most dependable Italian restaurant on Tucson's expanding Northwest Side. Lunch, dinner. ᕪ (West Side)

## SANCHEZ BURRITO COMPANY
**1350 W. Wetmore Rd.**
**520/887-0955**
**$**

This indispensable local chain has also popped up at 2530 N. First Avenue (520/622-2092), 2526 E. Broadway Boulevard (520/795-3306), and 1060 N. Craycroft Road (520/747-0901). As the name implies, the specialty of the house is the burrito: not one but two flour tortillas wrapped around the filling of your choice, usually beans, meat, or some combination thereof. You can have them topped with enchilada sauce, sour cream, cheese, even rice, for a little extra. Quesadillas, enchiladas, chiles rellenos, and a few other Sonoran standards are also available at most locations. The food is simple, delicious, and cheap. It's served faster than you can say "barbacoa," and designed mainly for takeout, although some seating is available. Note that some of the locations are sprucing up their decor and assuming more hoity-toity names, although each retains the "Sanchez." No reservations. Lunch, dinner. ᕪ (West Side)

## TOHONO CHUL TEA ROOM
**Tohono Chul Park**
**7366 Paseo del Norte**
**520/797-1711**
**$–$$**

Although it's undergone management changes in recent years, the

*Cafe Poca Cosa, p. 59*

Tohono Chul Tea Room is usually run by some leading restaurateur as an elegant little sideline, an outlet for gourmet sandwiches, inventive entrées, and sumptuous desserts. One thing that always holds true is its location in a rustic brick house within Tohono Chul Park, a beautiful, lush oasis of desert plants. Breakfast, lunch, afternoon tea; twilight dinner served occasionally. ᕪ (West Side)

## THE WHITE DOVE
**Sheraton El Conquistador Resort**
**10000 N. Oracle Rd.**
**520/544-1788**
**$$$**

Snubbed for a time as overpriced and mediocre, the White Dove has rebounded under the guidance of chef Guy Hulin. The eclectic menu fuses American and European inclinations. Seafood, pastas, specialty pizzas, and grilled items dominate. The place is still noisy, which some people find appealing and others find, well, loud. Lunch, dinner, Sunday brunch. ᕪ (West Side)

## YOEME CAFÉ
**1545 N. Stone Ave.**
**520/623-2046**
**$**

Operated by members of the Pascua Yaqui tribe, Yoeme Café (the name means "the people") serves Mexican food with a refreshing Native American twist. The flat enchiladas—something you're much more likely to find in New Mexico or south of the border than in Arizona—mound finely minced white onions and green olives with a sweet and fiery chile sauce onto a round of *masa* cake. This tiny place is one of Tucson's undiscovered treasures, mainly because it can't afford to advertise, the neighborhood is not aesthetically appealing, and the dining room is too small to accommodate hordes of people even if they did show up. Make a pilgrimage, laugh with the friendly ladies behind the counter, and join the small coterie of Yoeme devotees. Closed Sundays and Mondays. No credit cards. Lunch, early dinner (closes around 6 p.m.). & (West Side)

© Metro Tucson CVB/Gill Kenny—San Xavier del Bac

# 5

# SIGHTS AND ATTRACTIONS

*As a typical Western city, Tucson capitalizes on its wide open spaces. That means it's a poor walking town (but it's a great hiking town—just out of town). Downtown is the one district where you can take a stroll and see plenty of sights: the city's historic center boasts a concentration of old buildings and landmarks. Just remember that around here, "old" means only a century or so. For the rest of the city, you're best off in a car or on a tour. To see the finest neighborhoods, take a spin through the area roughly between the University of Arizona and Reid Park. Or head north, into the hoity-toity Catalina foothills.*

*Reid Park itself has a very nice midsize zoo that takes animal comfort as well as human fun into account. As for the University of Arizona, it's speckled with public art, museums, and, for star-gazers, Flandrau Planetarium. Real telescope fanatics will want to make a half-day excursion to Kitt Peak to inspect one of the world's leading observatories. (Don't bother showing up at night; only scientists—with appointments—may look through the 'scopes.)*

*Remember that Tucson's greatest attraction is its scenic beauty, which lies at the city's extreme eastern and western ends (in the two units of Saguaro National Park) and to the north, in Coronado National Forest (see Chapter 10, Sports and Recreation). If tramping around in the wild doesn't interest you, then catch some scenery despite yourself on your way to Old Tucson and the Arizona–Sonora Desert Museum in the west, Colossal Cave in the east, and Biosphere 2 in the north.*

## CITY TOURS

**CELESTIAL SAFARI**
**5100 N. Sabino Foothills Dr.**

**520/760-2100**
Because its skies remain clear and dry most of the year, Tucson has attracted enough observatories and

telescopes to bill itself as the Astronomy Capital of the World. You might say, then, that the Milky Way is in the neighborhood, and worth a tour while you're in town. That's what Celestial Safari is about—telescopic viewing of stars, planets, comets, far-flung galaxies, and clouds of gas (no, the 'scopes do not point toward City Hall). Reservations are required.

## CENTER FOR DESERT ARCHAEOLOGY
### 3975 N. Tucson Blvd.
### 520/881-2244

While you're out wandering through the desert, you'll probably stumble by plenty of little bumps and hollows that mean nothing to you but say "pit house" or "ball court" to an archaeologist. Tucson has been continuously inhabited for more than two millennia, and the only sure way to tour the really *old* neighborhoods is with a specialist. This nonprofit center offers half-day and full-day tours to nearby petroglyph (900-year-old graffiti) sites and similar areas of interest.

## DESERT VIEW TOURS
### 520/887-6933

If your time in Tucson is limited or you lack private transportation, Desert View will get you to the main attractions of your choice: Old Tucson Studios, the Arizona–Sonora Desert Museum, Mission San Xavier del Bac, Biosphere 2, Sabino Canyon, or intriguing nearby towns like Tombstone and Bisbee.

## GETAWAY ADVENTURE DRIVING TOURS
### 800/288-3861

Singing movie cowboy Rex Allen, no less, is your guide to southern Arizona in a series of cassette tapes designed for playback as you drive yourself along the local highways and byways. Allen provides patter about Arizona history, tidbits about the sights you pass, and cues for turning the tape off and on again so it remains in synch with your travels. The narration, neither shallow nor obscure, lets you get the lowdown at your own pace and avoid having to stick your nose in a guidebook every few minutes. Driving tour tapes for Bisbee, Tombstone, Sonoita, and Sierra Vista are available at local bookstores or by calling the number above.

## LET'S GO TOURS
### 4725 E. Sunrise Dr., Suite 351
### 520/299-6647

These folks will whisk you from your hotel directly to the usual destinations (Old Tucson, San Xavier, and all the rest), or get you started on a shopping trip in Nogales, Mexico, or custom-design a tour to your specification. Reservations required.

## OLD PUEBLO TOURS
### 520/795-7448

Six-and-a-half-hour tours depart around 9:30 a.m. Monday through Saturday for stops at DeGrazia's Gallery in the Sun, the Arizona Historical Society Museum, downtown, Old Town Artisans, Sentinel Peak, and Mission San Xavier del Bac, besides passing through the University of Arizona and Barrio Historico. Half-day tours are also available. Reservations required.

## TRAIL DUST JEEP TOURS
### 520/747-0323

Take the word "dust" seriously, but forget the idea that getting out into the Arizona wilds means anything arduous. These guides will take you on leisurely rides like the Sunset Champagne Tour or on more informative

# Top Ten Views of Tucson

**By Walter A. Clark Jr., retired FAA tower chief,
Tucson International Airport**

Clark used to commute from his Willcox home every day by
private plane; he's an expert on bird's-eye views of the city.

1. **Valencia Road** just west of the Tohono O'odham reservation
   provides a picture-perfect view, especially at sunset.

2. **"A" Mountain** (Sentinel Peak), just west of downtown, reveals
   a panoramic view of the entire Tucson Valley.

3. **The Catalina Highway**, just north of Tucson in the majestic
   Santa Catalina Mountains, affords city views as well as a
   look toward Mexico.

4. **Redington Pass**, just northeast of Tucson, offers a different
   view, especially during sunrise. Follow Tanque Verde Road
   east until it becomes Redington Road. The way over the pass
   is gravel but does not require four-wheel drive; just travel
   slowly.

5. **Gates Pass** on Speedway, west of town in the Tucson
   Mountains, is lined with almost every variety of cactus,
   flower, and native bush in the Tucson Valley. The road is
   excellent, but recreational vehicles are prohibited because of
   the hairpin turns.

6. **Mission Road** provides a beautiful scenic drive from just
   south of Sentinel Peak down to Mission San Xavier del Bac.

7. **Daniel's**, 4340 N. Campbell Ave., offers fine cuisine and a
   fantastic view of the city from the north. Most restaurants in
   the foothills have patios from which you can view the city.

8. **Oracle Road**, north of River Road, is the home of many good,
   moderately priced restaurants, and the drive back south into
   town after dark heads into a panorama of city lights.

9. **Saguaro Corners**, 3750 S. Old Spanish Trail, is a beautiful
   restaurant with a fabulous view of desert wildlife and the
   Tucson Valley.

10. **Tucson International Airport** has short charter flights for the
    most spectacular view of Tucson, and numerous fixed-base
    operators fly over the city day or night.

outings revolving around desert ecology, gold panning, and such. Overnight tours are available, too. Reservations are required.

## TUCSON TOURS
### 520/297-2911
Another provider of guided transportation to the area's most popular tourist sites, Tucson Tours will also take you as far as the Grand Canyon. Perhaps its most valuable offering is a 90-minute fact-filled tour of the city itself; the van rarely stops, but the guide keeps up a constant, informative patter strong on local history. Reservations a day or so in advance are suggested.

# DOWNTOWN

## ARMORY PARK NEIGHBORHOOD
### Between Stone and Second Aves. and 12th and 19th Sts.
Around the turn of the century, this was the mod place to live. The thick-walled adobe and Spanish Mission styles were left behind west of Stone Avenue; as Tucsonans moved east physically, if only a few blocks, their architecture also moved east, toward the Atlantic and "progressive" tendencies. Two-story wood construction with front yards, porches, and sloping roofs became the standard; gables and even turrets put in occasional appearances. This Victorian style was gradually given up as Tucsonans moved even farther east, toward the university, so the Armory Park area stands as a charming, unique neighborhood. The well-maintained but decidedly lived-in houses, lining remarkably wide yet quiet streets, provide pleasant surroundings for a stroll or bike ride. ♿ (Downtown)

## BANK ONE BUILDING
### 2 E. Congress St.
Completed in 1929, this bank building rose 11 stories to become Tucson's first skyscraper, towering over the one- and two-level structures that gave the city its original "Old Pueblo" character. Nothing indigenous went into this building; its arrangement, using different materials to set off the base and top from the sober red-brick seven-story body, imitated early skyscrapers elsewhere. Old-timers still refer to this as the Valley National Bank building, its identity from 1935 into the 1990s. Besides the name change, another recent development is the pleasant tree-shaded brick patio on the south side, offering a place to rest, even if it is on a noisy corner. The lobby is open to the public during business hours. ♿ (Downtown)

## BARRIO LIBRE (BARRIO VIEJO, BARRIO HISTORICO)
### Between Interstate 10 and Stone Ave. and Cushing and 17th Sts.
In the late nineteenth century, this was the Mexican American side of town; the Anglos clustered north of what is now the Tucson Convention Center. Called "Barrio Libre" because the Anglos left the residents fairly free to follow their own laws within their neighborhood, this district boasts several blocks of intriguing thick-walled adobe (sun-dried mud-brick) homes built more than a century ago. The houses appear squat because their roofs are flat; these were originally packed dirt—great insulation—held aloft by wood beams overlaid with ocotillo or saguaro ribs. The variety of paint colors from house to house, by the way, is no modern eccentricity; pink, blue, yellow, and green are right in

# DOWNTOWN TUCSON

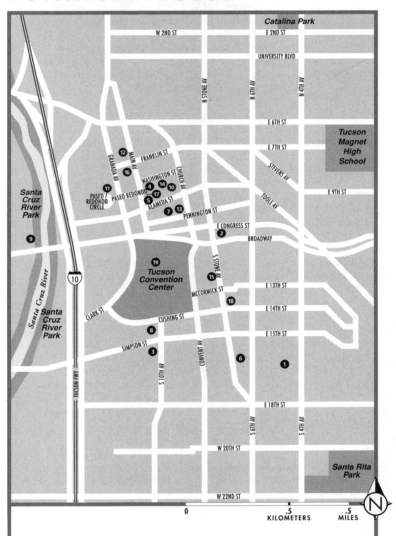

**Sights in Downtown Tucson**

1 Armory Park Neighborhood
2 Bank One Building
3 Barrio Libre
4 Corbett House
5 Edward Nye Fish House
6 El Fronterizo
7 El Presidio Park
8 El Tiradito
9 Garden of Gethsemane
10 La Casa Cordova

11 Manning House
12 Owls' Club Mansion
13 Pima County Courthouse
14 Romero House
15 Saint Augustine Cathedral
16 Steinfeld Mansion
17 Stevens House
18 Temple of Music and Art
19 Tucson Convention Center/La Placita Plaza

line with nineteenth-century aesthetics. Most of the houses sit flush with the sidewalk; private outdoor space was afforded by interior courtyards. Today some of these structures are collapsing and melting back into the earth, but most have been nicely restored. The little house at 363 South Meyer is probably one of Tucson's oldest buildings, dating to the 1850s or earlier. In contrast, 388 and 392 South Convent are modern infill construction, hewing to traditional designs. Most of these buildings remain private homes or have been turned into offices, so you'll have to admire them from the outside. & (Downtown)

## CORBETT HOUSE
### 257 N. Main Ave.
Another part of the Tucson Museum of Art Historic Block, this relatively new house—built in 1906 to a design by D. H. Holmes—is named for J. Knox Corbett, a Southern-born entrepreneur who moved to Tucson in 1880 and eventually rose to the position of mayor. The 4,400-square-foot house is an oddity by the standards of its neighborhood; it eschews the simple Sonoran adobe style in favor of Mission Revival, with red brick instead of adobe walls and a tile roof. It's now filled with early-twentieth-century arts, crafts, furniture, and such lovely examples of the local participation in the Arts and Crafts movement as Tiffany lamps, Roycroft candle sconces and ashtrays, and a rocker by L. & J.G. Stickley. In other words, an antique-lover's delight. Open Sun noon–4, Mon–Sat 10–4. Admission included with that to the Tucson Museum of Art: $2 adults, $1 seniors and students, free for children under 12; free for everyone Tue. & (Downtown)

## DOWNTOWN SATURDAY NIGHT
### In the blocks surrounding Congress St. from Church Ave. to Fourth Ave.
On the first and third Saturdays of each month, the usually sleepy Downtown Arts District springs to life with free street performances and extended gallery and shop hours (to about 9 p.m. in most cases). At various spots, little stages feature musicians of all sorts, dancers, and the occasional unclassifiable act. If you're from a city with an annual First Night celebration on New Year's Eve, you'll know generally what to expect, but on a smaller scale and with an artsy rather than strictly family orientation. A few vendors set up shop near the Ronstadt Transit Center (a big city bus stop) to sell beads, bumper stickers, and whatnot. All the downtown and Fourth Avenue galleries keep their doors open and are often jammed with people. In good weather, this is a highly popular event, crowded but not in any way threatening. You'll have to park a few blocks away, because Congress is unnavigable on these evenings, but it's worth putting on your walking shoes and seeing downtown at its best. & (Downtown)

## EDWARD NYE FISH HOUSE
### 120 N. Main Ave.
Built in 1868 on the site of old barracks, the Fish House (named for its original owner, a prominent businessman) is a fine example of mid-nineteenth-century Tucson architecture. The adobe walls, 2 feet thick, rise 15 feet to meet ceilings of *vigas* (beams) laced with saguaro ribs. Don't expect period furnishings, though; the old Fish residence now houses the Tucson Museum of Art's collection of Western art. Open Sun noon–4, Mon–Sat 10–4.

*The trolley operators on the Old Pueblo Trolley, p. 95*

Admission included with that to the Tucson Museum of Art: $2 adults, $1 seniors and students, free for children under 12; free for everyone Tue. ♿ (Downtown)

## EL FRONTERIZO
### 471 S. Stone Ave.

During its reconstruction in the 1970s, this building offered clues to its original use. Workers found, under the floorboards, some old hand-set type (that's why the dirt under and around downtown structures is always carefully sifted during renovation—you never know what relics will turn up). This was the printing office of a Spanish-language newspaper founded in 1878 by Carlos Y. Velasco. One adobe wall of this building, which is a National Register site, is a remarkable five feet thick. ♿ (Downtown)

## EL PRESIDIO PARK
### West of the Pima County Courthouse

Eleven months before East Coast colonists signed the Declaration of Independence to begin ousting their English overlords, the Spanish government took a significant step to strengthen its power in what is now Arizona. On August 20, 1775, j9the Spanish army under Lt. Col. Hugo O'Conor (an Irish mercenary) staked out the site of a fortress, or presidio, that would soon become the center of Tucson. The presidio's structures are long gone, but its presence is noted by plaques in this paved plaza, surrounded on three sides by government buildings.

El Presidio Park constitutes the southern half of the fortress, an area known in the nineteenth century as the Plaza de las Armas. A hundred years ago this was a prime fiesta site, and today the park hosts October's Tucson Heritage Experience festival, among other celebrations. Otherwise, you won't find much history here, aside from the 1927 courthouse. All this is the product of early 1970s urban renewal, with tallish government office buildings lining the park's southern and western boundaries, within which lie a few fountains (one of them large and geometric, in '70s style), some welcome if nonindigenous trees, and several pieces of contemporary statuary. It's a good place to rest or enjoy a light picnic lunch, although homeless people often stake out the shadiest spots. ઙ (Downtown)

## EL TIRADITO
### 354 S. Main Ave.
At the back of a simple dirt lot is a little grotto waxy and oily from decades of burning candles. It's one of America's more interesting folk shrines, because it's a wishing shrine dedicated to sinners. Details of its origins vary and even conflict, but the official version holds that a herder named Juan Oliveras, the unlucky member of a lovers' triangle, was killed on this spot. Because he was buried in unconsecrated ground, his pious neighbors came here to light candles and pray for his soul. (Even today, you will see roadside white crosses and garlands of flowers marking the scenes of fatal traffic accidents.) Over the years, the locals gave up on old Juan and started looking out for their own interests; folklore has it that if you make a wish here and light a candle, and if your candle burns all through the night, your wish will come true. So it's best to visit El Tiradito ("The Castaway") in the evening, although in the dark you may overlook, west of the shrine, El Ojito, an artesian spring that has supplied water to the community since Spanish Colonial days. ઙ (Downtown)

## GARDEN OF GETHSEMANE
### Western bank of the Santa Cruz River, north side of Congress St.
Here's a small enclosed garden patio maintained as part of the Santa Cruz River Park by the city of Tucson and other organizations. It cradles religious statuary by local sculptor Felix Lucero, who, when injured during World War I, vowed to God that he would create just such a place if he survived. Lucero created these works from only concrete, sand, and debris he found in the Santa Cruz. The garden includes larger-than-life sculptures of the Last Supper, Joseph and Mary, Jesus on the cross and in a tomb, and a small diorama depicting Pontius Pilate. Catholic visitors often leave flowers and votive candles as offerings. Open daily during daylight hours. ઙ (Downtown)

## LA CASA CORDOVA
### 175 N. Meyer Ave.
Continuously inhabited by Mexican American families from 1848 until it became part of the Tucson Museum of Art Historic Block in the 1970s, this house is named for its last resident, Maria Navarette Cordova. Now a Mexican heritage museum, its five rooms have been restored to their original style. If you're curious about what the original Spanish garrison looked like, a small replica is displayed here. The best time to visit La Casa Cordova is between late November and early March; that's when Maria Luisa Teña's elaborate folk-art *nacimientos*, or nativity scenes, are shown. Open Mon–Sat 10–4, Sun noon–4. Admission included with that to the Tucson Museum of Art: $2 adults, $1 seniors and students, free for children under 12; free for everyone Tue. ઙ (Downtown)

## MANNING HOUSE
### 450 W. Paseo Redondo
Built in 1907 as a 12,000-square-foot home for then-mayor Levi Howell Manning, this Henry Trost–designed mansion eventually passed into the hands of the Elks Club, which was largely responsible for its expansion

to 36,000 square feet of banquet, dining, and kitchen facilities. After the usual vicissitudes that befall old downtown buildings, the Manning House received a $4 million renovation in 1997 and has reopened to the public. Palm trees and bougainvillea grace the grounds of this combination Spanish Colonial and Santa Fe Territorial building. Most of the building and the tile outside are original. The mansion's front section, with its unusual round, two-story turret, is now a restaurant and tap room called Hugo O'Conor's, after an Irish soldier in the Spanish Colonial army who played a key role in Tucson's early development. Luscious carved redwood graces the interior throughout the building. It's worth a drink at Hugo O'Conor's just for the rare pleasure of gaining entry to one of Tucson's old Snob Hollow homes—and one of the few that wasn't built in an alien mock-Tudor style. ♿ (Downtown)

*Owls' Club Mansion*

## OWLS' CLUB MANSION
**378 N. Main Ave.**
Henry Trost designed this pink two-story building in 1902. It's an eclectic affair, picking up Chicago architect Louis Sullivan's Modern style of arches and geometrical frieze decoration, while adding Sonoran *canales*—drainpipes—to jut out from just below the roofline, and a façade decoration that invokes Mission San Xavier del Bac. The building now houses private offices, but its history as a home for the Fraternal Order of Owls is inextricable from its design: a sculpted owl surveys the street from its ornate, circular perch at the third-story level. (Downtown)

## PIMA COUNTY COURTHOUSE
**115 N. Church St.**
Newer than it looks, the courthouse

was built in 1927 in Spanish Colonial style. Although a business trip to the courthouse can be anything but restful, depending on your errand, just strolling around the grounds and viewing the structure from front and back can be quite pleasurable. Columns and arches create an arcade around a grassy front courtyard and large fountain. The main part of the courthouse is topped with a lovely tiled dome. The whole package, with its vaguely Moorish and neo-Baroque elements, nicely evokes Tucson's early Spanish heritage, which left no physical traces other than Mission San Xavier del Bac. Well, that's not quite true; a portion of the original presidio wall is displayed on the courthouse's first floor. ♿ (Downtown)

## ROMERO HOUSE
**101 W. Washington St.**
Changing tastes in architectural style are evident in this single home. Leonardo Romero, a carpenter who helped build Saint Augustine Cathedral, may well have had a hand in

*Tucson Convention Center Arena, p. 96*

erecting this house in 1868. Romero was, after all, its first resident. Over the next few decades, the home's owners gradually tried to disguise its adobe origins. Brick has replaced some of the adobe walls, and the flat mud roof now supports a gabled structure. What's happened to the interior will remain a mystery to you, unless you're in town long enough to take a class here—it's now the Tucson Museum of Art School. ⑤ (Downtown)

### SAINT AUGUSTINE CATHEDRAL
### 192 S. Stone Ave.
This cathedral has stood since 1896, but it looks nothing like the original plans. A 1920 renovation transformed it from a half-heartedly Gothic Victorian brick church into an older Mission-style house of worship, inspired by Mexico's Cathedral of Queretaro. The renovation brought with it domed towers, a white plaster exterior, and an impressive, ornate sandstone façade. Inside you can more properly view the stained-glass windows, as well as a 1900 painting

of Our Lady of Guadalupe and a grand dome of wooden slats. A mariachi mass is celebrated every Sunday, generally at 8 a.m., and visitors are welcome. Photographers, note: Saint Augustine's exterior is strikingly illuminated at night. ⑤ (Downtown)

### STEINFELD MANSION
### 300 N. Main Ave.
One of the noblest and most alluring mansions in the formerly upper-class quarter known as Snob Hollow, this brick and stucco house was built in 1900 and bought four years later by department store head Albert Steinfeld. It had been designed in 1898 as the original Owls' Club (see entry above); like its larger successor, this building shows architect Henry Trost's fascination with Mission Revival forms (check out the tiled roof and arched portico) as well as more modern decorative trends. Today this fine old home is subdivided into offices. Go around to the back to inspect the shaded, intimate, sometimes mustysmelling courtyard with its curved double staircase. (Downtown)

## STEVENS HOUSE
### 150 N. Main Ave.

This, along with the Edward Nye Fish House next door, was the center of Tucson's upper-crust social life in the late nineteenth century. Built in 1865, the adobe house served as the seat of the empire of cattle baron Hiram Sanford Stevens; the home was overseen by his wife, the much younger Petra Santa Cruz. The oleander in the back patio, which may be approached from the Tucson Museum of Art courtyard, was planted by Stevens himself. The cattle business literally dried up for Stevens in 1893; depressed, he shot Petra and killed himself. Petra survived, though—the bullet ricocheted off a large comb in her hair. The house found happier occupants from the 1970s well into the '90s, as the site of the exquisite Janos restaurant (see Chapter 4, Where to Eat). Janos has recently been evicted, however, so the Tucson Museum of Art may expand into the space. ⅍ (Downtown)

## TEMPLE OF MUSIC AND ART
### 330 S. Scott Ave.
### 520/884-8210

Built in 1927 at the instigation of local matrons (who also helped raise much of the construction funding) demanding a proper hall in which to present fine concerts, the Temple of Music and Art carries a grandiose name and largely lives up to it. Near the end of a quiet, treelined street, the Temple rises two stories in solid yet graceful Southwestern style. A modest but appealing fountain bubbles on the cobbled patio. The main building houses a 600-seat balconied theater occupied about 85 percent of the time by Arizona Theatre Company, an excellent regional theater. On the second floor is a little art gallery. The south wing contains, on the ground floor, the appealing B&B Café; directly above it is a 90-seat cabaret theater. The north wing holds the ATC box office and gift shop, where you can find theatrical souvenirs, printed plays, and fine note cards. The whole place was splendidly renovated around 1990. Free backstage tours of the facility are given most Saturdays at 11:30 a.m., October through April. ⅍ (Downtown)

## THURSDAY ARTWALK
### Along Congress St.
### 520/624-9977

Downtown Tucson's 40 or 50 art galleries stay open until 7:30 every Thursday as part of the ArtWalk, a free, docent-led, two-hour tour of maybe a half-dozen galleries, the roster changing weekly. There's usually a mix of folk art, commercial art, and art for art's sake. Gung-ho art lovers may prefer a self-guided ArtWalk using the brochure supplied by each participating gallery. Note that many of the ArtWalk participants are actually "Phantom Galleries"—murals, or displays in windows of empty shops. The walk also takes in a few restaurants and cafés, and several artists' personal studios. The ArtWalk spreads from Congress Street to Barrio Historico, Armory Park, El Presidio, and Fourth Avenue. The free tours meet at 5:30 p.m. in the lobby of the Park Inn International Santa Rita, 88 E. Broadway ⅍ (Downtown)

## TROLLEY TOURS
### Fourth Ave./University Blvd.
### 520/792-1802

All that remains of Tucson's original mass transit system is a single line, resurrected only a few years ago, that runs from the Trolley Barn at East

Eighth Street and South Fourth Avenue, up Fourth to University Boulevard, then east to the main gate of the University of Arizona. It's a charming little ride from the ex-hippie Fourth Avenue shopping district through a few shady residential blocks to the trendier two shopping blocks in front of the UA, and a good way to get from the free parking around Fourth Avenue to campus and back. It's not a guided ride, so just sit back and gawk or talk, resting your feet. It costs $1 each way (50 cents for seniors and kids under 12) 6 to 10 p.m. Fridays and noon to midnight Saturdays, 25 cents for everyone noon to 6 Sundays. The trolley does not run at any other times. Buy tickets at the Trolley Barn

at Eighth and Fourth, or at East University Boulevard and North Tyndall Avenue. (Downtown)

**TUCSON CONVENTION CENTER/LA PLACITA PLAZA**
**260 S. Church Ave.**
Several blocks of old adobe homes were plowed under to make way for this urban renewal project in the late '60s and early '70s. The Tucson Convention Center (originally called Tucson *Community* Center; you can tell how the priorities have shifted) is the city's principal performing arts complex, made of blocks supposed to evoke, without quite succeeding, the local volcanic rock with which many early Anglo houses were built. The

# Tucson's Public Art

*Public art has become a booming industry in Tucson, where a small percentage of government project construction costs is set aside for sculpture and other artistic enhancements. Much of it is scattered across the University of Arizona campus. More may be found on a number of buildings and water-pumping station walls around town, mainly in the area concentrated around downtown.*

*Other major pieces of public art worth a look include the Father Kino equestrian statue, by Julian Martínez, overlooking Kino Parkway, on the west side of the street between 22nd and Broadway (Central-North); and the Holocaust Memorial, by Ami Shamir, at the Jewish Community Center, Dodge Boulevard and River Road (Central-North). See also David Hoyt Johnson's Top Ten Works of Public Art, listed in Chapter 7, Museums and Galleries.*

*You may be able to obtain a full list of the more than 100 public art works in Tucson by calling the Tucson/Pima Arts Council at 520/624-0595.*

Music Hall, with its mainly glass façade and lobby chandeliers fronting a large fountain (which does spew water over authentic local volcanic rocks), tries too hard to imitate New York's Lincoln Center or Los Angeles' Dorothy Chandler Pavilion, on a much smaller budget. On its own terms it is a satisfactory, if hardly acoustically resplendent, 2,200-seat home for the Tucson Symphony Orchestra and Arizona Opera. Nearby, the Leo Rich Theatre is a smaller space best for straight plays but used mainly as a venue for the Arizona Friends of Chamber Music. The Arena fills with the usual array of sporting events and popular-music concerts, and two groups of exhibition halls handle the convention trade. The architectural interest is mild, but odd sculptures—abstract and amusingly representational—are popping up all over the grounds, along with a few interesting fountains. La Placita, adjoining the TCC on the north, was intended to be a fancy shopping plaza. Retailers never got a good foothold here, so now it's mainly an office complex. But it is an attractive series of two-story buildings in ambling Southwestern style, with some shady places to sit, a couple of modest eateries, and a footbridge across Congress and Broadway north to the government office buildings and El Presidio Park. ⓑ (Downtown)

# CENTRAL-NORTH

## BENEDICTINE MONASTERY
### 800 N. Country Club Rd.
Only the sanctuary is open to the public for worship, but you can enjoy the flavor of this Spanish Colonial Revival complex by spending a

moment in the side parking lot. Designed in 1940 by Roy Place (who would soon abandon this look for the Modern style), the monastery features a tile-domed tower, an arcaded front, and a sloping Mexican-tile roof that together provide a pleasing distraction that may slow the passing traffic, especially since the look is so different from anything nearby. ⓑ (Central-North)

## COLONIA SOLANA NEIGHBORHOOD
### South of Broadway Blvd. between Country Club Rd. and Reid Park
Development of this area of posh, graceful homes, and of the similar El Encanto neighborhood on the other side of Broadway, began in the 1920s. The houses have a heavier, more permanent look than the overpriced stucco specials in the foothills; many of them are valued at more than $500,000. This is the nesting place of doctors, attorneys, and financiers who have some sense of historical continuity. You'll know you're approaching the area when you spot its major landmark, the big stucco-faced, tile-roofed water tower with a cast-iron miner-and-burro weathervane just southwest of the intersection of East Broadway and South Randolph Way. ⓑ (Central-North)

## EL ENCANTO NEIGHBORHOOD
### Between E. Fifth St. and Broadway Blvd., immediately west and north of El Con Mall
Developed in the late 1920s, El Encanto is a neighborhood of elegant, mostly Spanish- or Moorish-style houses laid out along streets that form circles around a central plaza. As you drive through, keep an eye out for the anomalous 65 N. Camino Español. That's the home of Lisa

# GREATER TUCSON

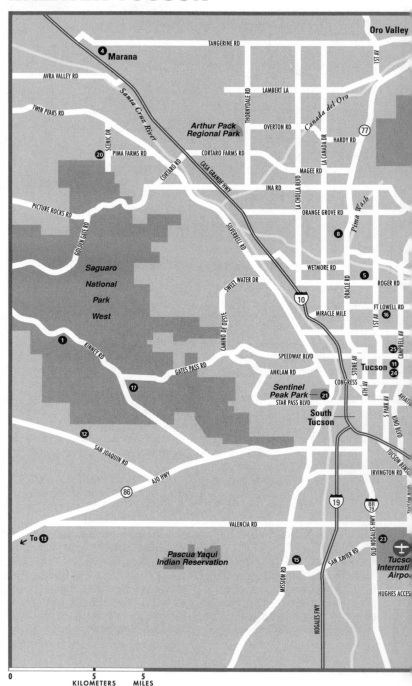

Oro Valley

TANGERINE RD

❹ Marana

AVRA VALLEY RD

TWIN PEAKS RD

Santa Cruz River

SCENIC DR

❷⓪ PIMA FARMS RD

PICTURE ROCKS RD

GOLDEN GATE RD

Saguaro
National
Park
West

❶

KINNEY RD

GATES PASS RD

❶⓻

❶❷

SAN JOAQUIN RD

AJO HWY

⑧⑥

← To ❶❸

VALENCIA RD

Pascua Yaqui
Indian Reservation

❶❺

MISSION RD

NOGALES FWY

LAMBERT LA

THORNYDALE RD

OVERTON RD

Arthur Pack
Regional Park

CORTARO FARMS RD

CORTARO RD

CASA GRANDE FWY

INA RD

SILVERBELL RD

SWEET WATER DR

CAMINO DE OESTE

SPEEDWAY BLVD

ANKLAM RD

Sentinel
Peak Park — ❷❶
STAR PASS BLVD

South
Tucson

Cañada del Oro

1ST AV

❼❼

HARDY RD

LA CAÑADA DR

MAGEE RD

LA CHOLLA BLVD

ORANGE GROVE RD

Pima Wash

❽

WETMORE RD

ORACLE RD

❺

ROGER RD

❶⓪

MIRACLE MILE

FT LOWELL RD

1ST AV

❶❻

CAMPBELL AV

❷❺

STONE AV

Tucson ❶❶
❷❹

CONGRESS

6TH AV

S PARK AV

KING BLVD

AVIATION

TUCSON BENSON

IRVINGTON RD

OLD NOGALES HWY

❶❾

BR
❶❾

❷❸

Tucson
Internati
Airpo

SAN XAVIER RD

HUGHES ACCES

0        5        5
    KILOMETERS    MILES

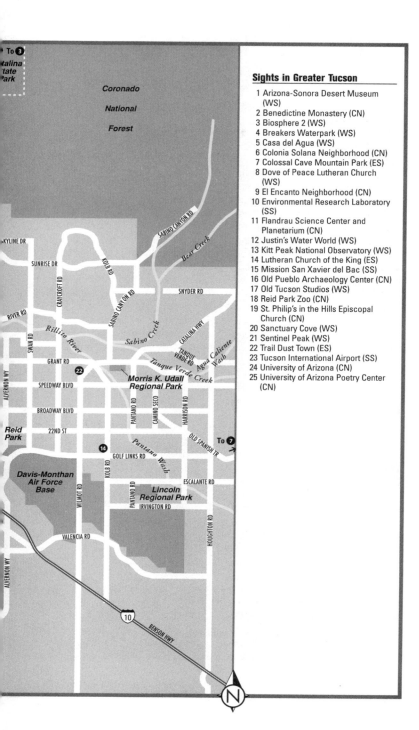

To ③
Catalina
State
Park

Coronado

National

Forest

Bear Creek

SABINO CANYON RD.

KYLINE DR

SUNRISE DR

KOLB RD

CRAYCROFT RD

SABINO CANYON RD

SNYDER RD

RIVER RD

Rillito River

CATALINA HWY

SWAN RD

Sabino Creek

TANQUE VERDE RD

Agua Caliente Wash

GRANT RD

22

Tanque Verde Creek

ALVERNON WY

SPEEDWAY BLVD

**Morris K. Udall Regional Park**

BROADWAY BLVD

PANTANO RD

CAMINO SECO

HARRISON RD

OLD SPANISH TR

**Reid Park**

22ND ST

Pantano Wash

To ⑦

14

GOLF LINKS RD

**Davis-Monthan Air Force Base**

KOLB RD

WILMOT RD

PANTANO RD

ESCALANTE RD

**Lincoln Regional Park**

IRVINGTON RD

HOUGHTON RD

VALENCIA RD

ALVERNON WY

10

BENSON HWY

N

## Sights in Greater Tucson

1 Arizona-Sonora Desert Museum (WS)
2 Benedictine Monastery (CN)
3 Biosphere 2 (WS)
4 Breakers Waterpark (WS)
5 Casa del Agua (WS)
6 Colonia Solana Neighborhood (CN)
7 Colossal Cave Mountain Park (ES)
8 Dove of Peace Lutheran Church (WS)
9 El Encanto Neighborhood (CN)
10 Environmental Research Laboratory (SS)
11 Flandrau Science Center and Planetarium (CN)
12 Justin's Water World (WS)
13 Kitt Peak National Observatory (WS)
14 Lutheran Church of the King (ES)
15 Mission San Xavier del Bac (SS)
16 Old Pueblo Archaeology Center (CN)
17 Old Tucson Studios (WS)
18 Reid Park Zoo (CN)
19 St. Philip's in the Hills Episcopal Church (CN)
20 Sanctuary Cove (WS)
21 Sentinel Peak (WS)
22 Trail Dust Town (ES)
23 Tucson International Airport (SS)
24 University of Arizona (CN)
25 University of Arizona Poetry Center (CN)

Frank, she of the colorful sticker and notebook series hoarded by prepubescent girls. You can tell—it's the house with the purple, blue, and hot-pink highlights. & (Central-North)

## FLANDRAU SCIENCE CENTER AND PLANETARIUM
### University of Arizona
### Cherry Ave. and University Blvd.
### 520/621-STAR

Shows in this domed science center include sometimes stunning astronomy-oriented presentations and family laser extravaganzas, with light beams dancing to music ranging from Bach to Pearl Jam. In the exhibition facilities, you can stroke a meteoroid, see a holographic image blow you a kiss, challenge yourself with spatial reasoning puzzles, learn about minerals and optics, and, weather permitting, peer through Flandrau's telescope (but only Tuesday through Saturday after 8:30 p.m.). The gift shop sells science-related toys and books. Open Mon–Fri 9–5, Sat–Sun 1–5, plus evening hours of Wed–Thu 7–9, Fri–Sat 7–midnight. Admission: $3–$5. & (Central-North)

## OLD PUEBLO ARCHAEOLOGY CENTER
### 1000 E. Fort Lowell Rd.
### 520/798-1201

This center offers opportunities—especially for kids—to dig for "planted" artifacts on its own replica of a Hohokam pit house site. You can find at the end of your trowel metates and manos (concave stones and smaller stones used for grinding), ax heads, seashell jewelry, and broken pottery, much of which can be reassembled (but not taken home with you). The program is designed primarily for groups and schools, but individuals might be able to piggyback onto a

group's dig. The center also organizes archaeologist-guided tours of the Sabino Canyon Ruin, where Hohokam Indians built apartmentlike structures, pit houses, and irrigation canals 650 to 1,000 years ago. Reservations are always necessary. & (Central-North)

## REID PARK ZOO
### Reid Park, off E. 22nd St.
### between S. Country Club Rd. and
### S. Randolph Way
### 520/791-4022

Over the years, Tucson's traditional zoo (not to be confused with the more specialized Arizona–Sonora Desert Museum) has torn out its bar-and-concrete enclosures and replaced almost all of them with more natural habitats, comfy homes for more than 400 types of mammals, reptiles, and birds from around the world. Reid Park Zoo has developed a successful captive breeding program for endangered species; its program for the giant anteater is especially remarkable, and the long-snouted beast has been incorporated into the zoo's logo.

*Anteaters at the Reid Park Zoo*

**TIP**

If you've visited the University of Arizona and haven't tired yourself out, take a stroll through one of the nearby neighborhoods. To the east lies the reasonably tony Sam Hughes neighborhood (bounded by Campbell Avenue, Sixth Street, Tucson Boulevard, and Speedway). To the west stretches the firmly middle-class and logically named West University district, featuring quaint dwellings from the first third of the twentieth century, and bounded by Stone Avenue, Sixth Street, Euclid Avenue, and Speedway.

The animal enclosures are arranged in habitat areas that more or less keep one continent's critters separate from another's. The fine new South America Habitat Loop does this especially well, with overgrown vegetation providing atmosphere for llamas, the flightless bird called Darwin's rhea, tapirs, sloths, the crocodilelike dwarf caiman, and the carnivorous piranha, as well as many bird species in a lush new aviary. Open daily 9–4; closed Christmas. Admission: $3.50 adults, $2.50 senior citizens, 75 cents children 5–14, free for kids 4 and under. & (Central-North)

### ST. PHILIP'S IN THE HILLS EPISCOPAL CHURCH
**4440 N. Campbell Ave.**

This church was designed in 1936 by the beloved and busy local architect Josias Joesler to mimic a Mexican town plaza: A little park is edged with buildings, some of which are in turn built around a small, pretty courtyard immediately east of the sanctuary. Rustic materials, clean proportions in the Spanish Colonial Revival style, and enthusiasm for tasteful ornament make the complex seem much older than it really is. Inside is one of the city's three finest organs, a neo-Baroque instrument whose console is set back under the choir loft rather than near the altar. A magnificent arched altar window looks out to the desert and mountains. The church is open for services. (Central-North) &

### UNIVERSITY OF ARIZONA
**Cherry Ave. and University Blvd.**
**520/621-5130**

Despite annual budget cuts, the UA maintains an aggressively research-oriented program that makes it especially strong in the hard sciences, with perfectly good arts and humanities programs receiving less administrative attention (and funding). The campus sprouted timidly from the desert in 1891 with Old Main, a veranda-ringed two-story building a block east of the UA's main gate, at University Boulevard and Park Avenue. Since then, the UA has spread for blocks, sometimes consuming neighborhoods in its path, generating more variations on red-brick construction than you'd think possible. Since the 1960s, and especially in the 1990s, the UA has placed a special emphasis on public art. Sculpture is tucked into all sorts of places but congregates near the fine arts complex at Park and Speedway and along the Mall, the wide grassy median that would be University Boulevard/Third Avenue if it were still open to traffic. The main library was regularly ranked as one of the nation's top 20 research libraries in the 1980s, but budget cuts haven't allowed it to keep up its rapid acquisitions rate. Parking on campus can be a trick, and it isn't cheap. Most lots are restricted to permit-holders; the best bets are the garages near Euclid and University (a bit of a walk), Park and Speedway, on Second Avenue east of Mountain, and just south of the Visitors Center at Cherry and University. Guided tours of campus are provided every Thursday and Saturday at 9:30 a.m., September through May, from the Visitors Center at Cherry Avenue and the Mall. A wheelchair-accessible shuttle bus tour is also offered on the first Saturday of the month. & (Central-North)

## UNIVERSITY OF ARIZONA POETRY CENTER
**1216 N. Cherry Ave.**
**520/321-7760**
To be absolutely certain your day doesn't descend to the prosaic, visit the UA Poetry Center, an archive of 30,000 books, periodicals, and video- and audiotapes all devoted to the well-turned word. It's an essential resource for poetry scholars and a comfortable refuge for anyone who wants simply to read some verse. The center also sponsors a free reading series in the UA Modern Languages Auditorium, featuring the school's students and faculty as well as distinguished visiting poets. Open Mon–Thu 9–8, Fri 9–5, Sun 1–4. & (Central-North)

# EAST SIDE

## COLOSSAL CAVE MOUNTAIN PARK
**Old Spanish Trail, 11 miles past Saguaro National Park East, or Interstate 10 to the Vail-Wentworth exit, then 5 miles north.**

**520/647-7275**
This cool cave is a smart family destination, especially as a brief refuge from the summer heat; the temperature is 70 degrees year-round. A hideout for bandits in the late nineteenth century, the cave is rumored still to hold stolen gold in one of its unexplored caverns. Although it's dry now, water seepage through this limestone cave formed room after room of stalactites and stalagmites in formations that have lent themselves to such fanciful names as "The Frozen Waterfall" and "Kingdom of the Elves." Kids will be either reassured or terribly disappointed to learn that all visits are in guided groups—no solo exploring allowed. The tour route is a half-mile long and takes about 45 minutes, along nicely accessible and well-lighted walkways. Guides describe the cave's history, legends, and geology, and may even turn out the lights for a moment (with warning) for a truly spooky experience. The surrounding park offers wooded picnic areas, guided trail rides, birding, and hiking. Open Mon–Sat 9–5, Sun and holidays 8–7. Mid-March through mid-September: Open Mon–Sat 8–6, Sun 8–7. Admission: 17 and older $6.50, ages 11–16 $5, ages 6–10 $3.50. & (East Side)

## LUTHERAN CHURCH OF THE KING
**2450 S. Kolb Rd.**
Designed by Ned Nelson in 1958, this building makes the most of extremely unremarkable materials—particularly boring brown cinder block, which is hidden on the east and south by an intricately patterned brick screen that also offers protection from the sun. A sawtooth roof allows the interior to stretch free of structural columns, while clerestory windows bring natural if indirect light into the sanctuary. The church is open only for services,

but you can get the gist of it from outside. ᯤ (East Side)

## TRAIL DUST TOWN
### 6541 E. Tanque Verde Rd.
### 520/296-4551

If you lack the time, budget, or inclination to soak up the Old West kitsch at Old Tucson, you can get a quick taste of it at Trail Dust Town. Wander around the frontier-façade street free of charge, perhaps stopping for lunch or dinner at Pinnacle Peak Steakhouse at one end or the Dakota Café at the other (see Chapter 4, Where to Eat). A few shops are open for business, including a gallery of Western art, a photo studio where you can get photographed in Western garb, an arcade, an old-style sweet-shop, and a couple of curio and apparel dealers. Nightly, on the hour, there's a stunt show/gunfight for an extra charge. You also pay individually to ride the old-fashioned carousel or take a little train trip through a mine tunnel and around the premises. ᯤ (East Side)

*4-meter Mayall Telescope at Kitt Peak National Observatory, p. 106*

© Metro Tucson CVB/Gill Kenny

# SOUTH SIDE

## ENVIRONMENTAL RESEARCH LABORATORY
### 2601 E. Airport Dr.
### 520/741-1990

Because of the one-way traffic restrictions, you have to drive by the Tucson International Airport terminal and begin heading back out in order to reach this facility. The center consists of environmental agriculture research labs, where specialists develop methods of intensive food production, seawater crop irrigation, and heating and cooling the world's hot spots. Visit a talapia fish farm, find out how a cooling tower works, or just relax in the lab's shady, desert-landscaped picnic area. Tours are conducted at 1:30 p.m. on the first Tuesday of each month. ᯤ (South Side)

## MISSION SAN XAVIER DEL BAC
### 1950 W. San Xavier Rd.
### 520/294-2624

Zip down Interstate 19 about 10 miles south of downtown Tucson and follow the signs. You can easily spot the mission from the freeway—a bright, white, frontier-Baroque structure rising from the desert scrub. The mission was completed in 1797—except for one of its two towers, which remains domeless to this day. A working Catholic parish, San Xavier serves the people of the Tohono O'odham Reservation—and the thousands of tourists who visit every week. Outside, the building's graceful arches and domes provide fascinating contrast to its squared-off towers. Nearly every inch of the interior was painted with intricate designs and murals during the nineteenth century, and the entire mission was beautifully restored just in time for its bicentennial. The main altar is a highly regarded example of

# Top Ten Tucson Architectural Landmarks

(Results of a 1997 *Arizona Daily Star* readers' poll, choosing from among buildings nominated by local architects)

1. Mission San Xavier del Bac
2. Pima County Courthouse
3. Benedictine Monastery
4. Arizona Inn
5. St. Philip's in the Hills Episcopal Church
6. Old Main (University of Arizona)
7. Loews Ventana Canyon Resort
8. Owls' Club Mansion
9. Arizona State Museum (University of Arizona)
10. Steinfeld Mansion

a Spanish retable, perhaps the best one north of Mexico. The reclining statue to the left, behind dozens of votive candles, represents St. Francis Xavier. Don't forget to inspect the other little chapels and shrines on the grounds. You can purchase Tohono O'odham crafts and food at a small marketplace across the dirt parking lot from the mission. & (South Side)

## TUCSON INTERNATIONAL AIRPORT
**7250 S. Tucson Blvd.**
**520/573-8100**
Find out what's behind those little doors where the luggage comes out onto the conveyer belts. Get a jolt from the airport's own power station. Inspect the weapons and other potentially lethal objects that security people have confiscated from passengers. Take a behind-the-scenes look at airport operations on tours of-

fered every Wednesday at 9 a.m. and every second and fourth Saturday at 9:30 a.m. They're recommended for ages 16 and up. Reservations are required for Saturday tours. If you can get a group of people together, call to set up a separate guided tour of the Airport Fire Department (open to any age), Sky Chefs flight kitchen (age 6 or over), a commercial airliner (any age), or the Air Traffic Control Tower (at least age 13; this locale may be designated off-limits before long). Free. & (South Side)

## WEST SIDE

## ARIZONA–SONORA DESERT MUSEUM
**2021 N. Kinney Rd.**
**520/883-2702**
If you have time for only one time-consuming destination while you're in

town, this should be it—unless you have absolutely no interest in spying on desert critters and learning about this area's ecology and geology. Not really a museum at all, this is more of a zoo featuring animals and plants of the Sonoran Desert, most of them living in areas that painstakingly re-create their natural habitats. The reptiles aren't quite so lucky, but you probably wouldn't want to get this close to a rattlesnake or a sidewinder without the nice sheet of glass between you. The prairie dog "town" is always a popular stop; you'll also encounter everything from bighorn sheep to otters (yes, desert *wetlands* otters). Step into the hummingbird aviary and come face to beak with some of its 300 residents. There's also an interesting Earth Sciences Center, consisting mainly of a convincing simulated cave, and informative plant exhibits. If you get hungry, pick up some Mexican, vegetarian, or generically American sustenance at the museum's Ironwood Terrace. The best time to visit the Desert Museum, especially in the summer, is in the early morning hours, when the animals are

most active. Open daily, including all holidays, October through February 8:30–5; March through September 7:30–6 (sometimes extended to 10 on Saturdays). Admission: $8.95 for adults, $1.75 for kids 6–12, free for children 5 and under. ♿ (West Side)

## BIOSPHERE 2
### Oracle Road (Arizona 77) north
### 520/896-6200

Biosphere 1, in case you were wondering, is planet Earth. Biosphere 2 was developed in 1991 as a self-contained mini-Earth, with a number of different microecologies that would support eight sealed-in humans for a couple of years. The initial experiment failed from the self-sufficiency angle, and the place has been retooled by Columbia University as a more general laboratory for earth sciences. Guided tours begin with a film about the center's history and mission, and continue with visits to the greenhouses—not actually part of the Biosphere enclosure itself, but nurseries for plants from tropical to desert areas. You will walk away with some idea of what it's

*Biosphere 2*

like inside Biosphere 2. There's also a laboratory exhibit; a peek through Biosphere 2's glass walls at its little rain forest, savanna, ocean, and farm; a visit to the mission crew's living quarters; and, for the kids, Biofair, a hands-on science park with a tornado simulator and other attractions that allow your precious babes to play God. A café and restaurant are on the grounds, so you won't have to grow your own lunch. You should, however, show up with good walking shoes and a hat. Tours leave about every hour. Reservations are no longer required, but you should call for directions, hours, and ticket prices, the last of which change frequently. Open daily except Christmas. & (West Side)

### BREAKERS WATERPARK
**8555 W. Tangerine Rd.**
**520/682-2530**
Off Interstate 10 about a dozen miles north of Tucson, Breakers boasts one of the world's largest wave pools, making waves every 15 minutes. One of its five hydrotube slides is called "The Black Hole," which allows you to zip through in the dark. Away from the water, shade trees are a plus. Open daily 10–7, Memorial Day weekend through Labor Day. Admission: $9.95 adults, $7.95 kids 4–12. & (West Side)

### CASA DEL AGUA
**4366 N. Stanley Pl.**
**520/887-1185**
This water conservation demonstration and education house focuses on historical and current water usage in Tucson and promotes water-saving features. It's a private home remodeled by the University of Arizona Office of Arid Lands Studies, Tucson Water, and other organizations to showcase water-conservation techniques.

Low-flow toilets, recycling "used" water for irrigation, and similar measures cut water use for this house in half—and it's a real, honest-to-goodness family home, not some 9-to-5 research lab. Tours, conducted by the family, are available Sunday noon–4. (West Side)

### DOVE OF PEACE
### LUTHERAN CHURCH
**665 W. Roller Coaster Rd.**
Designed in 1969 by W. Kirby Lockard, this award-winning church managed to come through well designed despite a low budget. The exterior may now seem too blocky and white, but true elegance remains in the sanctuary, with its central altar lighted by a multisided skylight. From the outside, it's an abstract four-pointed crown, cradling the steeple. Open for services. & (West Side)

### JUSTIN'S WATER WORLD
**3551 S. San Joaquin Rd.**
**520/883-8340**
Water conservation is not the issue here. Water slides are—curving slides, straightaway slides, side-by-side racing slides, gentle kiddie slides, all for your hydroplaning pleasure. Justin's features several pools, one of which is for adults only. Mature trees provide lots of shade, and picnic tables await your use. Perhaps you could give this place some credit for water conservation, since it's only open Friday through Sunday and holidays 10–5, from late May through Labor Day. Admission: $8.50 (free for children 5 and under, and seniors 60 and over). & (West Side)

### KITT PEAK NATIONAL
### OBSERVATORY
**56 miles southwest of Tucson, off**

*The Mission Show at Old Tucson Studios*

### Ajo Way/Arizona 86 on the Tohono O'odham Reservation
### 520/318-8600

A pleasant drive out of town and up a 6,882-foot mountain brings you to the largest collection of ground-based optical telescopes in the world. Twenty-two universities around the nation have a hand in the research here, which is conducted with 4-meter and 2.1-meter telescopes that are open to the public, as well as with the world's three largest solar telescopes. A good many other 'scopes that are monopolized by working astronomers are inaccessible to the public. The 4-meter Mayall optical telescope occupies a white, 18-story domed building; it spends evenings peering at distant galaxies and quasars. Climb up to the observation deck for a grand 100-mile view of southern Arizona and even a bit of northern Mexico. In the visitors center and museum you'll find astronomy exhibits and films. Pick up a brochure and wander at your leisure, or join a guided tour at 9:30, 11:30, 1, or 2:30 daily (the first tour sometimes runs only on weekends). The surroundings offer snow cover in the winter, cool air in the summer, and picnic tables if you've brought your own lunch. Open daily 9–3:45; closed Thanksgiving, Christmas Eve, Christmas Day, and New Year's Day. & (West Side)

### OLD TUCSON STUDIOS
### 201 S. Kinney Rd.
### 520/883-0100

Half-destroyed by fire in 1995, Old Tucson rose from the ashes a year later with even more attractions than before. Built as a set for the movie *Arizona* in 1939, it had a spotty history until it was aggressively developed in the 1960s as a combination film location and Wild West theme park. Few movies are shot here anymore, the production companies having moved to more remote ghost towns and other facilities, but as a theme park the place is booming. Literally. Staged gunfights break out along the faux–frontier town streets at intervals throughout the day, with stunt men getting into fist fights and blasting each other off the roofs. More sedate visitors may prefer a variety of rides, including one through the legendary (and haunted) Iron Door Mine. Or venture into the Arizona Ruins, with its Native American–themed Storyteller's Theater; Mexican Plaza, with the rebuilt Mission Santa Maria; or the Young Riders' Park, a kid-friendly play area. Other attractions include Western wear and curio stores, an old-fashioned ice cream parlor, and a theater showing a history of the Hollywood Western. If you mosey through in October, check out "Nightfall," Old Tucson's nighttime Halloween bloodfest. Open daily 10–6, 9–7:30 in the summer. Admission: adults $14.95, children 4–11 $9.45. ♿ (West Side)

## SANCTUARY COVE
### 8001 N. Scenic Dr.
### 520/744-2375
Not at all a tourist destination and not even qualifying as a park, Sanctuary Cove is a simple, serene outdoor retreat intended by the All Creeds Brotherhood as a meditation spot in a beautifully vegetated desert setting. Getting there is a scenic drive itself:

Take Silverbell Road north to Pima Farms Road, then take Pima Farms west to Scenic Drive, at which you turn south and continue about a quarter mile. Open dawn to dusk daily. ♿ (West Side)

## SENTINEL PEAK
### Sentinel Peak Road
Locals persist in calling this fine rise immediately west of town "A" Mountain, because every autumn since 1915, University of Arizona freshmen whitewash over the stone "A" for Arizona that defaces the eastern slope. This visually jarring result of a Homecoming ritual (all too common, in Western communities) distracts us from Sentinel Peak's historical importance. An excellent lookout point commanding a view of the entire Tucson basin, the little peak has cast its shadow across human dwellings for more than 2,000 years. Today you can drive up for a romantic view of the city lights at night or to get your directional bearings during the day. A few grills line the road near the top. The road is closed from 10:30 p.m. to about dawn. ♿ (West Side)

# 6

## KIDS' STUFF

*With great weather and plenty of open space, Tucson can be an exciting place for kids. Even science and history can come alive for younger ones—from the timeless drama of desert life at the Arizona–Sonora Desert Museum to the modern drama of Cold War strangeness at the Titan Missile Silo Museum.*

## ANIMALS AND THE GREAT OUTDOORS

### ARIZONA–SONORA DESERT MUSEUM
**2021 N. Kinney Rd.**
**520/883-2702**
Don't let the word "museum" scare you (not that it should); this is really a splendid zoo featuring animals and plants of the Sonoran Desert, most of them living in areas that painstakingly re-create their natural habitats. Press your nose against the glass and flick your tongue at a rattlesnake, visit the prairie dog "town," get a good look at coyotes and bighorn sheep, and find out how stinky javelina really are. There's also an aviary that's home to 300 hummingbirds, and an interesting

Earth Sciences Center consisting mainly of a convincing simulated cave. The best time to visit the Desert Museum, especially in the summer, is in the early morning hours, when the animals are most active. Open daily, including all holidays, October–February 8:30–5; March–September 7:30–6 (sometimes extended to 10 on Saturdays). Admission: $8.95 for adults, $1.75 for kids 6–12, free for children 5 and under. ♿ (West Side)

### BIOSPHERE 2
**Oracle Road (Arizona 77) north**
**520/896-6200**
Biosphere 2 was developed in 1991 as a sort of planet Earth in a bottle, with a number of different microecologies, that would support eight sealed-in

## TIP

The classic place to entertain kids is at a public park. Reid Park, the city's largest (see Chapter 8, Parks, Gardens, and Recreation Areas), boasts great grassy expanses for running, jumping, and hollering, as well as swings, a big duck pond, and a bandshell. Himmel Park, about a block south of Speedway, immediately east of Tucson Boulevard, contains the usual playground equipment as well as a locomotive engine. Other city parks are listed in the phone book.

humans for a couple of years. Today the place is a more general laboratory for earth sciences. Guided tours begin with a film about the center's history and mission, and continue with visits to the greenhouses—not actually part of the Biosphere enclosure itself, but nurseries for plants from tropical to desert areas; this will give you some idea of what it's like inside Biosphere 2. There's also a laboratory exhibit; a peek through Biosphere 2's glass walls at its little rain forest, savanna, ocean, and farm; a visit to the mission crew's living quarters; and, especially for kids, Biofair, a hands-on science park with a tornado simulator and other attractions. Tours leave about every hour; reservations are no longer required, but you should call for directions, hours, and ticket prices, the last of which change frequently. Open daily except Christmas. (West Side) &

### CENTER FOR DESERT ARCHAEOLOGY TOUR PROGRAM
3975 N. Tucson Blvd.
520/885-6283
This organization offers group tours of several archaeology sites around Tucson, including a petroglyph site, food-processing and Hohokam village site in Catalina State Park, and a petroglyph tour in the Tucson Mountains.

It also offers guided tours of downtown sites—including the Presidio Wall Excavation, the location of an eighteenth-century Spanish presidio, tenth-century Hohokam village, and even older settlements. Tours last four to five hours and are led by a professional archaeologist. (Central-North)

### COLOSSAL CAVE MOUNTAIN PARK
Old Spanish Trail 11 miles past Saguaro National Park East, or Interstate 10 to the Vail–Wentworth exit, then 5 miles north
520/647-7275
The cool cave, 70 degrees year-round, was a hideout for bandits in the late nineteenth century; stolen gold may still lie in one of the unexplored caverns. Although the cave is dry now, water seepage created room after room of stalactites and stalagmites in formations that have lent themselves to such fanciful names as "The Frozen Waterfall" and "Kingdom of the Elves." Kids will be either reassured or terribly disappointed to learn that all visits are in guided groups—no solo exploring allowed. The tour route is a half-mile long and takes about 45 minutes, along well-lighted walkways. Guides describe the cave's history, legends,

and geology, and may even turn out the lights for a moment (with warning) for a truly spooky experience. The surrounding park offers wooded picnic areas, guided trail rides, birding, and hiking. Open Mon–Sat 9–5, Sun and holidays 8–7. Mid-March through mid-September: Mon–Sat 8–6, Sun 8–7. Admission: 17 and older $6.50, ages 11–16 $5, ages 6–10 $3.50. ⑤ (East Side)

### INTERNATIONAL WILDLIFE MUSEUM
**4800 W. Gates Pass Rd.**
**520/629-0100**

People either love or hate this center, a mock-castle that exhibits the stuffed hides of more than 290 species of mammal and bird from various parts of the globe. Some find it pretty creepy—maybe it's all those glass eyes staring out from the heads of what used to be living lions, rhinos, penguins, and whatnot—but they must admit that it's a memorable place. Open daily (except Christmas and Thanksgiving) 9–5; the ticket window closes promptly at 4:15. (West Side)

### OLD PUEBLO ARCHAEOLOGY CENTER
**1000 E. Fort Lowell Rd.**
**520/798-1201**

Just because you're not at the beach doesn't mean you can't dig in the sand. Old Pueblo Archaeology has planted artifacts on its own replica of a Hohokam pit house site. Kids 7 and older get to play Indiana Jones and dig them up (harrowing chases and Nazi thugs not included). You'll probably find grinding stones, ax heads, seashell jewelry, and broken pottery, much of which can be reassembled (but not taken home). Reservations are always necessary. One Saturday a month November through March, the

organization offers a public tour of the authentic Sabino Canyon Ruin, site of an ancient Hohokam Indian dwelling. The group tour is led by a professional archaeologist. Children 8 and older also may experience supervised, hands-on archaeological field training at the Sabino site and dig for actual Hohokam artifacts. This five-hour "Dig for a Day" program costs $69 per person, with discounts for groups or multiple days. ⑤ (Central-North)

### REID PARK ZOO
**Reid Park, off East 22nd St.,**
**between S. Country Club Rd. and**
**S. Randolph Way**
**520/791-4022**

This traditional zoo has taken its animals out of jail—old-style cages—and put them all in comfy natural habitats. It can be a little frustrating to spot certain animals that aren't feeling sociable, because they're free to duck behind a boulder or crawl into a hole. But if you miss one bashful beast, you can try your luck with more than 400 other types of

*"Dig for a Day" at Old Pueblo Archaeology Center*

Old Pueblo Archaeology Center

mammals, reptiles, and birds from around the world. The animal enclosures are arranged in habitat areas that more or less keep one continent's critters separate from another's. The South America Habitat Loop does this especially well, with overgrown vegetation providing atmosphere for llamas, a flightless bird called Darwin's rhea, tapirs, sloths, the crocodilelike dwarf caiman, and the carnivorous piranha, as well as many bird species in a lush new aviary. Open daily 9–4 except Christmas. Admission: $3.50 adults, $2.50 senior citizens, 75 cents children 5–14, free for kids 4 and under &(Central-North)

### TUCSON BOTANICAL GARDENS
**2150 N. Alvernon Way**
**520/326-9686**
Five and a half acres of plants might not thrill your kids, but a children's multicultural garden does plop a play ramada into an international garden; it's designed to foster an appreciation of cultural diversity as well as environmental conservation. Open daily 8:30–4:30. Admission: $4 adults, $3 seniors (over 62), free for children under 12. & (Central-North)

## MUSEUMS AND LIBRARIES

### ARIZONA HISTORICAL
### SOCIETY MUSEUM
**949 E. Second St.**
**520/628-5774**
The big draw for kids here is "Exploring 1870s Tucson," a hands-on exhibit that re-creates three frontier settings: a ranch house, a Native American dwelling, and a town shop. Each allows children to get physically involved. Similarly, the mining exhibit offers an underground tunnel

and an assay office. Other features are rooms decorated in Territorial style and a small collection of old weapons, plus changing exhibits. Open Mon–Sat 10–4, Sun noon–4. Admission is free, but donations are encouraged. & (Central-North)

### FLANDRAU SCIENCE CENTER
### AND PLANETARIUM
**University of Arizona**
**Cherry Ave. and University Blvd.**
**520/621-STAR**
One minute you're sitting in a domed theater; then the lights go down, a big projector looking like a robot insect comes up, and the stars appear overhead. It's cool enough to cause shivers, guaranteed. Shows vary from little dramas that are really astronomy presentations to family laser extravaganzas with light beams dancing to music ranging from Bach to Pearl Jam. In the exhibition facilities, you can stroke a meteoroid, see a holographic image blow you a kiss, challenge yourself with spatial reasoning puzzles, learn about minerals and optics, and, weather permitting, peer through Flandrau's telescope (but only Tue–Sat after 8:30 p.m.). The gift shop sells science-related toys and books. Open Mon–Fri 9–5, Sat–Sun 1–5, plus evening hours of Wed–Thu 7–9, Fri–Sat 7–midnight. Admission: $3–$5. (Central-North) &

### TITAN MISSILE SILO MUSEUM
**1580 W. Duval Mine Rd.**
**Sahuarita/Green Valley**
**520/625-7736**
Kids may have studied the Cold War in school, but a one-hour tour of this facility (located about 25 miles south of Tucson) will bring it into stark reality. Visit the control center, experience a simulated launch sequence, and peer down through the silo closure

# A Trip to the Past

From the texture of clothing worn by a ranch family to the scent of candy sold at a general store, a long-term, tactile exhibit at the Arizona Historical Society gives kids the feel and smell of life in 1870s Tucson. The three-pronged exhibit shows family life at a Mexican American ranch house, a Jewish mercantile, and a Tohono O'odham village.

In the Tohono O'odham area, kids can crawl into a grass hut, practice carrying pots on their heads, handle sticks for a women's field hockey game called toka, check out traditional farm implements, and sift through the tepary beans, wheat, and corn that those tools helped cultivate. They can also see and hear the musical instruments that would have been used by tribal elders.

The exhibit's ranch area includes a kitchen, a living room displaying the period's typical fine embroidery, and a bedroom complete with period clothes that kids may try on. Outside, children can move bread in and out of a clay oven, clamber into the Sinaloan saddle of a full-size fiberglass horse, or inspect the most popular element of the exhibit, the outhouse.

The mercantile store includes examples of drugs, fabrics, and canned foods popular in the 1870s, sacks of flour and coffee that children may weigh on scales, and soap and candies to smell. Attached living quarters contain upholstered Victorian furniture and other items that were difficult to obtain before Tucson became a railroad town.

The three cultures under study got along remarkably well because they were loosely united against a common enemy, the Apaches. O'odham pots turn up in the ranch house and store, and cloth displayed at the store reappears as a dress at the ranch. Still, the Native American farmers sleep in a grass hut, but the townspeople live in adobe buildings with glass windowpanes and wooden floors. Ranch children play with cloth dolls, but the doll at the merc has a fragile china head. Weekdays tours are given from noon to 4 p.m.

door to see the actual, deactivated Titan II—which carried the largest single warhead of any U.S. Inter-continental Ballistic Missile. Open daily November–April, Wed–Sun May–October. Guided tours leave every half-hour, starting at 9 a.m. (last tour of the day leaves at 4 p.m.). Reservations are recommended. Take Exit 69 off Interstate 19, go west on Duval Mine Road. Handicapped accessible if you tell them at time of reservation. (West Side)

### TUCSON CHILDREN'S MUSEUM
### 200 S. Sixth Ave.
### 520/884-7511
Housed in the old Carnegie Library downtown, the Tucson Children's Museum offers hands-on exhibits and displays that teach kids about the world around us. Kids can try on fire-fighters' helmets and turnout gear in the firehouse, learn about energy dis-tribution in the electricity exhibit, and make their own projects in crafts or science-activity classes. Open Tue–Fri 9:30–5, Sat 10–5, Sun noon–5. The last admission is sold half an hour before closing, and kids must be accompanied by an adult. On the third Sunday of every month, you can tour the museum for free. (Downtown)

### TUCSON INTERNATIONAL
### AIRPORT TOUR
### 7250 S. Tucson Blvd.

### 520/573-4868
Not exactly a museum trek, the 90-minute guided tour of Tucson's international airport is nonetheless educational and kid-friendly (mainly for kids nearing and in their teens). It covers aviation history, airport safe-ty, TIA's expansion plans—and offers plenty of opportunities to ogle airlin-ers and feel the inner workings of a busy airport. The free tour is offered every Wednesday at 9 a.m., as well as on the second and fourth Saturdays of every month. Call for reservations and wear comfortable shoes. (South Side)

## THEATER

### ARIZONA YOUTH THEATRE
### 5671 E. Speedway Blvd.
### 520/546-9805
This troupe produces live stage shows, from *Cinderella* to *A Mid-summer Nights Dream*, written and performed by kids. It also offers occasional performance workshops. Shows are given year-round, Fri at 8 p.m., and Sat at 11, 2, and 4. Reser-vations required. (Central-North)

## STORES KIDS LOVE

### BIG KIDS (TOO) COMICS
### 8791 E. Broadway Blvd.

Childsplay is a first-rate theater company that happens to specialize in plays for children. Employing adult actors and producing sophisticated scripts written for kid audiences by noted playwrights, Childsplay offers top-grade entertainment. Unfortunately, the Phoenix-based company performs in Tucson on an irregular basis; check the newspaper for announcements.

**520/290-5080**

Big Kids Too specializes, as you would anticipate, in comic books—Marvel, DC, Image, and smaller press publications—new and collectible. If two dimensions won't suffice, you can opt for the action figures (*Spawn*, original and new *Star Wars* items), and Beanie Babies. Open Mon–Tue 12–6, Wed 12–7, Thu–Fri 11–6, Sat 10–6, Sun 12–4. Also at 3930 W. Ina Road (520/744-7548). (East Side)

### GEPPETO'S TOYS AND DOLLS
**7049 N. Oracle Rd.**
**520/297-1041**

Named, of course, for the old woodcarver who created Pinocchio, this shop carries specialty toys, instructional toys, athletic toys, musical toys—you get the point. Not surprisingly, there's a wide selection of hand puppets, as well as stuffed animals, Madame Alexander dolls, porcelain and vinyl dolls (Lee Middleton, Fazah Asparo, Zook), and bears by Gund, North American Bear, and Boyd Bears. Open Mon–Fri 9:30–5:30, Sat 9:30–5. (West Side)

### MRS. TIGGY-WINKLES
**4811 E. Grant Rd., Suite 151**
**520/326-0188**

Right in midtown Tucson—it's a bookstore! It's a kids' clothing store! It's a specialty yo-yo shop! Located in an upscalish mall (with a household goods store for Mom, a cigar store for Dad, and restaurants and movie theaters for everybody), Mrs. Tiggy-Winkles is above all a fun, hands-on toy shop. It also features Southwestern-themed children's books, toys from around the world, and a huge selection of children's music. (Central-North)

*Colossal Cave Mountain Park, p. 110*

### YIKES! TOYS
**306 E. Congress St.**
**520/622-8807**

At last! A toy store without the latest fad doll or movie tie-in! In fact, you can take your kids into Yikes! knowing that absolutely *nothing* in the store has ever been advertised on Saturday morning TV. Yikes! claims to carry the largest selection of rubber snakes, lizards, and spiders in southern Arizona. Wind-up and gag toys are another specialty, but don't overlook the paper dolls, stickers, cards, educational project toys, and children's books. Simple things popular long ago, like wooden tops and ordinary balls, hold special appeal here. Open Mon–Sat 10–6. (Downtown)

## THEME PARKS

### BREAKERS WATERPARK
**8555 W. Tangerine Rd.**
**520/682-2530**

Off Interstate 10 about a dozen miles north of Tucson, Breakers boasts one of the world's largest wave pools, making waves every 15 minutes, and five hydrotube slides—one of them called "The Black Hole," allowing you to zip through in the dark. Open daily 10–7, Memorial Day weekend through Labor Day. Admission: $9.95 adults, $7.95 kids 4–12. ♿ (West Side)

## JUSTIN'S WATER WORLD
**3551 S. San Joaquin Rd.**
**520/883-8340**

Curving slides, straightaway slides, side-by-side racing slides, gentle slides—all are slicked down for rides wild or mild. They dump you into any of several pools, one of which is for adults only. You'll find plenty of shade and picnic tables for an outside lunch. Open Fri–Sun and holidays 10–5, late May through Labor Day. Admission: $8.50 (free for children 5 and under, and seniors 60 and over). ♿ (West Side)

## OLD TUCSON STUDIOS
**201 S. Kinney Rd.**
**520/883-0100**

Built as a set for the movie *Arizona* in 1939, Old Tucson now lures visitors as a combination film location and Wild West theme park. Few movies are shot here anymore (although you might get lucky and see a TV commercial or Japanese country music video in production), but as a theme park the place is booming. Literally. Staged gunfights break out along the frontier streets at intervals through the day, with stunt men getting into fist fights and blasting each other off the roofs. More sedate visitors may prefer the rides, including one through the haunted Iron Door Mine. Or venture into the Arizona Ruins, with its Native American–themed Storyteller's Theater; or the Young

Riders' Park, a kid-friendly play area. In addition, there are Western wear and curio stores, an old-fashioned ice cream parlor, and a theater showing a history of the Hollywood Western. If you mosey through in October, check out "Nightfall," Old Tucson's nighttime Halloween bloodfest. Open daily 10–6, 9–7:30 in the summer. Admission: adults $14.95, children 4–11 $9.45. ♿ (West Side)

## TRAIL DUST TOWN
**6541 E. Tanque Verde Rd.**
**520/296-4551**

A quick and cheap way to get a taste—but only a very small taste—of the Old Tucson experience is to visit Trail Dust Town. You can wander around the little frontier-façade street free of charge. Two restaurants and a few shops are open for business, including a photo studio where you can get photographed in Western garb, an arcade, an old-style sweetshop, and a couple of curio and apparel dealers. Nightly, on the hour, there's a stunt show/gunfight for an extra charge. You also pay individually to ride the old-fashioned carousel or take a little train trip through a mine tunnel and around the premises. ♿ (East Side)

# PLACES TO PLAY

## BRUNSWICK CAMINO SECO BOWL
**114 S. Camino Seco**
**520/298-2311**

This isn't your father's bowling alley. Friday and Saturday nights feature "Cosmic Bowling," with black light, strobes, fog machines, laser lights, glow-in-the-dark bowling balls and pins, and loud music. Admission is $11 per person. Saturday nights is

*Herb Garden at the Tucson Botanical Gardens, p. 112*

Rock'n'Bowl, which is regular bowling (with the lights on) accompanied by high-volume rock 'n' roll. Admission for R'n'B is $9 per person. The bowling alley is at Broadway Boulevard and Camino Seco, right behind Jeff's Pub. (East Side)

### DISCOVERY ZONE FUN CENTER
**6238 E. Broadway Blvd.**
**520/748-9190**

This large, brightly colored indoor playground was aptly described by one employee as "like the playgrounds at McDonald's, but about five of them stuck together." It also has a full-service diner, facilities for birthday parties and camp-ins, and a laser tag arena. Open Mon–Thu 11–8, Fri–Sat 10–9, Sun 11–7. Children up to 12 pay a few dollars to get in, but admission is free for kids over 12 (and infants under 12 months) with a paying child. (Central-North)

### FUNTASTICKS FAMILY FUN PARK
**221 E. Wetmore**
**520/888-4653**

There's lots to do at this family activity park, including two 18-hole miniature golf courses, go-karts, bumper boats, kiddie rides, and video games. Open Mon–Thu 1–9 (but the miniature golf courses, batting cages, and video arcades open at 10), on Fri and Sat 10–midnight, Sun 10–9. No admission price; you pay per ride or golf round. (West Side)

### GOLDEN PIN LANES
**1010 W. Miracle Mile**
**520/888-4272**

Friday and Saturday nights, 9:30 to 12:30, bring "Kosmic Bowling," with strobes, black lights, and fog machines; hit a strike to "kountry" music on Friday, rock on Saturday. Admission is $8 per person, plus shoe rental. This alley also boasts a laser tag indoor arena. (West Side)

### GOLF 'N' STUFF
**6503 E. Tanque Verde Rd.**
**520/885-3569**

Located on "restaurant row," this family fun center offers plenty of ways to work up an appetite: miniature golf,

# TIP

Teen clubs come and go, sort of like teens themselves. One place that stands a good chance of still being in business by the time you show up is Skrappy's, an all-ages joint that often features live bands (see Chapter 12, Nightlife). During the summer, the Rillito Downz, at the old Rillito Downs Racetrack, Campbell Avenue and River Road, opens Friday nights for music, games, and midnight basketball.

batting cages, bumper boats, a "Li'l Indy" racetrack, laser tag tent, and a large, very noisy video arcade with games for all ages. Open Mon–Thu 10–10 (with the rides opening at 2 p.m.), Fri–Sat 10 a.m.–1 a.m., Sun 10–10. The charge is per ride or golf game. (East Side)

## ICEOPLEX
**7333 E. Rosewood**
**520/290-8800**

This large ice skating center offers skating lessons, figure skating, and ice hockey equipment rental—and the only ice skating rink in Tucson. Public session times are Mon–Fri 9:30–11:30 a.m. and 1:30–5 p.m., and Sat–Sun 1–4 p.m. Evening public sessions are Fri–Sat 7:30–10:15 p.m. Admission is $6.50 for adults, $5.50 for kids 12 and younger. (East Side)

## SKATE COUNTRY
**2700 N. Stone Ave.**
**520/622-6650**

Tucson's two Skate Country roller skating rinks get you off the sidewalk and into blasting tunes. If you haven't brought your own, you can rent equipment here. These family recreation centers have sessions for tiny tots, dancers and figure skaters, plus a mess of public skating sessions. Family skating sessions are Sat 7–noon and 1–10, and Sun 1–8. Admission is $3; skate rental is $1.75. Also at 7980 E. 22nd Street (520/298-4409). (West Side)

## STAGE 35
**Foothills Mall**
**7401 N. La Cholla Blvd.**

Every mall has an arcade, but this is one intense game room. In a carefully cluttered, grunge-chic setting, test your skill with virtual race cars, Jet Skis, and baseballs; aim real basketballs at moving hoops; or just flip and tilt with an old reliable pinball game. This place can be packed, especially on the weekend. Open Mon–Thu 10–9, Fri–Sat 10–midnight, Sun 11–9. Game prices range from 25 cents to $1.25; Tuesday evening it's $10 for unlimited games. (West Side)

© Metro Tucson CVB/Gill Kenny—Tucson Museum of Art

# 7

# MUSEUMS AND GALLERIES

*Let's be honest: In Tucson you won't discover vault after vault of world-famous artistic masterpieces, aside from the splendid collection at the Center for Creative Photography. You will, however, find a context for all those masterpieces, mainly through the historical holdings at the University of Arizona Museum of Art. Even more importantly, you will encounter the full range of contemporary visual art. Not just Western art, which is abundantly represented (one of its leading practitioners, Howard Terpening, resides in Tucson), but the cutting-edge varieties as well. Remember, too, that the city's special strengths reside in its museums of science, history, nature, and ethnography. Alas, the wonderfully quirky yo-yo museum has gone the way of the Hula-Hoop, but there remains an emporium of esoterica for nearly every taste.*

## ART MUSEUMS

### CENTER FOR CREATIVE PHOTOGRAPHY
**UA Fine Arts Complex**
**Park Ave. and Speedway Blvd.**
**520/621-7968**
The center houses one of the leading photography collections in the world, with changing exhibitions on display in the galleries, library, and mezzanine. The archive tucks away more than 50,000 photographs, including the complete oeuvre of Ansel Adams plus works by Richard Avedon, Edward Weston, and more than a thousand others. Unfortunately, the center lacks space for permanent exhibition of its treasures, but its print viewing room allows you to see nearly anything from the archives privately. Viewing room hours are 1–4 Mon–Fri and the first and third Sundays of each month; reservations are required. Regular center hours are Mon–Fri 11–5, Sun noon–5.

The suggested donation is $2. ♿ (Central-North)

## DEGRAZIA'S GALLERY
## IN THE SUN
## 6300 N. Swan Rd.
## 520/299-9191

The late Ted DeGrazia studied with Mexican muralist Diego Rivera, whose style—along with that of Marc Chagall—informs DeGrazia's own paintings of Southwestern and Catholic subjects, usually incorporating Native American figures or imagery. These canvases, as well as bronzes, jewelry, and pieces in other media, are all displayed here. Some people find DeGrazia's work unbearably cute or sentimental, but the artist developed a large international following. He also designed this architecturally intriguing gallery and for a time lived and worked in it; now he's buried on the grounds. Wheelchair patrons must ask for ramps to be put out. Open daily 10–4. Free. ♿ (Central-North)

## TUCSON MUSEUM OF
## ART AND HISTORIC BLOCK
## 140 N. Main Ave.
## 520/624-2333

The city's leading exhibitor of contemporary art has recently undergone a massive expansion. The large interior square-spiral space offers rotating exhibitions and a small gallery of pre-Columbian pieces. The John K. Goodman Pavilion of Western Art features selections from the museum's permanent collection of cowboy 'n' cattle canvases. Also in the TMA compound are several restored former residences from the mid-nineteenth to early twentieth centuries. The 1906 J. Knox Corbett House, for example, holds period arts and crafts, furnishings, and accessories (see Chapter 5, Sights and Attractions). Open Mon–Sat 10–4 (Tue–Sat 10–4 June–August), Sun noon–4. Admission: $2 adults, $1 seniors and students, free for members and children under 12; Tue free for everyone. ♿ (Downtown)

## UNIVERSITY OF ARIZONA
## MUSEUM OF ART
## UA Fine Arts Complex
## Park Ave. and Speedway Blvd.
## 520/621-7567

Old mingles with new in a permanent collection featuring Renaissance and later European and American art,

# Up in Smoke

*The late Tucson artist Ted DeGrazia left a huge number of works for display in his Gallery in the Sun. But he could have left even more. Every few years, DeGrazia called out the news media and publicly burned several of his canvases. He said he was doing it to protect his heirs from confiscatory inheritance taxes. He never seemed inclined simply to paint less.*

including 26 panels of the fifteenth-century altarpiece of the Cathedral of Ciudad Rodrigo and a gallery devoted to 61 plaster and clay models by twentieth-century sculptor Jacques Lipchitz. Spanking-new paintings and installations go up regularly, too. While you're on campus, don't forget to inspect the UA's various small art spaces (see Galleries, below). Open Mon–Fri 9–5 (10–4 May 15 through Labor Day), Sun noon–4. Closed Saturdays and university holidays. Free ♿. (Central-North)

## HISTORICAL MUSEUMS

### ARIZONA HISTORICAL SOCIETY MUSEUM
#### 949 E. Second St.
#### 520/628-5774
Temporary shows share space with permanent exhibits in a museum devoted mainly, but no longer exclusively, to local prestatehood history. Of particular interest to families is "Exploring 1870s Tucson," a hands-on exhibit that re-creates three frontier settings: a ranch house, a Native American dwelling, and a town shop; each allows kids to get physically involved. Similarly, the mining exhibit offers an underground tunnel and an assay office. There are also rooms decorated in Territorial style, a small collection of old weapons, and a fine library available to researchers. Open Mon–Sat 10–4, Sun noon–4. Free, but donations are encouraged. ♿ (Central-North)

### ARIZONA HISTORICAL SOCIETY/ SOSA-CARRILLO-FRÉMONT HOUSE
#### Tucson Convention Center
#### 151 S. Granada Ave.
#### 520/622-0956
Not to be confused with the society's full museum, above, this is an 1858 adobe home once owned by a Territorial governor, among other local notables, and preserved in 1880s style. This is the best way to see how a Tucson family of some means lived a century ago. Special weekday tours conducted in English, Spanish, and several other languages can be arranged by calling the number above. While here, pick up a brochure detailing a self-guided walking tour of downtown. Open Wed–Sat 10–4. Free. ♿ (Downtown)

### FORT LOWELL MUSEUM
#### 2900 N. Craycroft Rd.
#### 520/885-3832
A few melting adobe walls and a couple of restored buildings at the edge of an ordinary, grassy park are all that remain of an army fort that was shut down a century ago. Frontier soldiers led fairly unpleasant lives, as you can tell from "Fort Lowell Archaeology, Architecture and Army Children," a permanent exhibit of hundreds of artifacts excavated at the old post, together with photographs and text. If they're selling hard tack, don't buy it unless you have strong coffee or a good dental plan. Open Wed–Sat 10–4. Free. ♿ (Central-North)

### WHITE DOVE OF THE DESERT MUSEUM
#### Mission San Xavier del Bac
#### 520/294-2624
Take Interstate 19's San Xavier exit, about 10 miles south of downtown, and go west, following the signs a short distance to the mission. The museum's long-term exhibit is "Blackrobes, Grayrobes and the Magnificent White Dove: Three Hundred Years at Bac," examining the early Jesuit (blackrobe) occupation at Bac and the later

Franciscan (grayrobe) residency at the Indian mission village. Exhibits also cover the native people of Bac, mission architecture, and religious artifacts. Open daily noon–4:30. Free; donations accepted. ♿ (West Side)

## NATURAL HISTORY MUSEUMS

### ARIZONA STATE MUSEUM
**University of Arizona**
**University Blvd. and Park Ave.**
**520/621-6302**

This institution devoted to Southwestern anthropology and ethnography occupies two large buildings on opposite sides of University Boulevard, within the UA's main gate. In the north building is a long-term show titled "Paths of Life: American Indians of the Southwest." It combines historic and prehistoric artifacts with displays depicting the origins, history, and contemporary life of ten groups of Native Americans residing in Arizona and Sonora. In the south building, "Ancient Images: Plants and Animals of the Prehistoric Southwest" includes exhibits on prehistoric Native American cultures, featuring mammoth bones, Hohokam arts and crafts, and a re-creation of a Mogollon cliff dwelling. Nearby, "Mexican Masks: Faces of the Fiesta" displays 350 colorful Mexican folk masks. Open Mon–Sat 10–5, Sun noon–5. Free. ♿ (Central-North)

### INTERNATIONAL WILDLIFE MUSEUM
**4800 W. Gates Pass Rd.**
**520/617-1439**

Reviled as the "Museum of Death" by detractors who criticize it as a tax write-off for the big-game hunter who founded it, this museum hangs a good many trophy heads from its pseudo-medieval fortress walls. Although the place does try to make a case for hunting as a valid sport, it also offers information on conservation and ecology, with many of the 300 animal species on display mounted in replicas of their natural habitats. If hunting and taxidermy don't bother you, you're probably also game for the buffalo

*Eleanor Jeck Galleries, p.128*

Eleanor Jeck Galleries

burgers in the museum café. Open daily 9–5, except Thanksgiving, Christmas, and New Year's Day. Admission: $5 adults, $3.75 seniors and students, $2 children 6–12. & (West Side)

## SCIENCE AND TECHNOLOGY MUSEUMS

### ASARCO MINERAL DISCOVERY CENTER
**1421 W. Pima Mine Rd.**
**520/625-7513**

If you dig mining and aren't terminally offended by the ecological damage wrought by strip mines, check out this facility's earth sciences exhibits, historic and modern mining equipment, multimedia theater shows, and tours of ASARCO's Mission open-pit mine. Even if you fantasize about filling this enormous hole with the corpses of ecorapists, it pays to know your adversary, and this is a fine place to get the inside scoop. Open Wed–Sun 9–5. Admission is free, but you pay for tours: $6 adults, $5 seniors, $4 kids 5–12, free for children under 5. & (South Side)

### PIMA AIR AND SPACE MUSEUM
**6000 E. Valencia Rd.**
**520/574-9658**

Dead aircraft don't go to some great hangar in the sky; they're grounded here, on display for all to see. Outdoors you'll find about 100 planes, many of them open to cockpit inspection. More aircraft huddle inside the museum's hangars, including a replica of the first Wright flyer, a B-24, a Mach three-plus SR-71 Blackbird, a Mercury space capsule mockup and, in a special memorial to the 390th Bomb Group and Strategic Missile Wing, a B-17 "Flying Fortress." You'll also find a World War II barracks, a display of officers' uniforms, and lots of technical aircraft information. On a more modest scale, you can inspect an extensive collection of homebuilts, ultralights, and hang gliders. Open daily 9–5 (last admittance at 4); closed Thanksgiving and Christmas and Mon–Tue May–September. Admission: $6 adults, $5 senior citizens and military personnel, $3 kids 10–17, free for children under 10. Combination admission with the Titan Missile Museum costs $10. & (South Side)

### TITAN MISSILE SILO MUSEUM
**Duval Mine Rd. in Green Valley**
**520/625-7736**

Take Exit 69 off Interstate 19 and follow the signs. One thing that used to make Tucsonans sweat, aside from the heat, was that the city was ringed with supposedly secret nuclear missile silos, which meant that Tucson would be a prime target in a nuclear war. Fortunately for everyone, those days are over. By 1987, all of the 54 silos across the nation were dismantled and in many cases filled in—except for this one, which has been opened to the public. Find out what duty was like in the silo's cold, cramped launch control center and rub your hand against an actual, though deactivated, Titan missile. Because of the tight space, reservations are recommended; high heels are not. Open daily 9–4. Admission: $6 adults, $5 senior citizens and military personnel, $3 kids 10–17, free for children under 10. Combination admission with the Pima Air and Space Museum costs $10. & (South Side)

## OTHER MUSEUMS

### FRANKLIN MUSEUM
**3420 N. Vine St.**

# Top Ten Works of Public Art in Tucson
### By David Hoyt Johnson, director of the
### Tucson/Pima Arts Council's public art program

1.  **Pioneer Memorial**, 1920, by Beniamino Bufano and Bernard
    Maybeck, 200 S. Sixth Ave., in front of the Tucson Children's
    Museum. This is the earliest work of public art in Tucson. It was
    created by a distinguished San Francisco architect (Maybeck) and
    artist (Bufano) and transported to Tucson by train. It commemo-
    rates the pioneer settlement of Tucson in a neoclassical style
    intended to complement the neoclassical architecture of the build-
    ing in front of which it was installed, the 1901 Carnegie Library.

2.  **Legend of the Seven Cities of Cibola**, 1955, by Jay Datus, 150 N.
    Stone Ave., in the main lobby of Wells Fargo Bank. These imposing
    murals, which are 11 feet tall and run for approximately 200 linear
    feet, depict the Spanish expedition headed by Coronado to locate
    seven legendary cities of fabulous riches. The murals were commis-
    sioned by Lew Doublas (1894–1974) for the Southern Arizona Bank,
    which first occupied the building.

3.  **El Rio Neighborhood Center Murals**, 1975–1997, by Antonio Pazos,
    David Tineo and others, 1390 W. Speedway, exterior walls and main
    lobby. The earliest murals at this active neighborhood center date
    from the mid-'70s and commemorate the effect of the Chicano
    movement on social consciousness in Tucson. In 1970 several hun-
    dred Mexican American families staged nonviolent demonstrations,
    requesting that land at the site be reserved for a neighborhood
    center. In response, the city built El Rio Neighborhood Center and
    commissioned several exterior murals to enhance it. When the facil-
    ity was expanded in 1997, the city commissioned additional murals
    for the new main lobby.

4.  **Alene Dunlap Smith Garden**, 1985, by Barbara Grygutis, 312 N.
    Granada Ave. This pocket park took the artist five years to complete
    and was named for a resident of El Presidio neighborhood who was
    instrumental in saving many of the neighborhood's historic struc-
    tures. The U-shaped blue tile walkway in the center of the park is a
    metaphor for the nearby river. Glazed stoneware blocks provide
    seating and are also stacked as human-sized totems. The volcanic
    rock in the entry pillars and the bricks in the paths were salvaged
    from the site.

5.  **Sonora**, 1991, by David Black, 101 N. Stone Ave. The abstract forms of
    this painted steel sculpture, according to artist Black, derive from nat-
    ural forms in the Sonoran desert surrounding Tucson. They include the
    serrated peaks of the Tucson Mountains and the cascading stream in
    Sabino Canyon. When the sculpture was installed on the plaza in front

of the austere new main library, it received mixed reviews. Many commentators did not appreciate the abstract references to the desert nor the fanciful contrast to the architecture of the library.

6. **River Paths and Mountain Relics**, 1992, by Roger Asay, Mountain Avenue between Speedway and Grant. The artwork along Mountain Avenue is so well integrated into the overall design of the roadway and sidewalks that many users do not distinguish it from other design features. Everyone agrees, however, that the natural stone sculptures and the meander in the sidewalk make the North-Side commute to the University of Arizona much more interesting, especially for pedestrians and bicyclists.

7. **Santa Cruz Linear Park Plaza**, 1992, by Susan Gamble, west bank of the Santa Cruz River midway between St. Mary's Road and Speedway. The columns and arches of this festive artwork are clad with thousands of mosaic tile tesserae that tell "histories" of the nearby neighborhoods. This public art project was the first of several in linear parks created along Tucson's rivers, washes, and arroyos.

8. **Gila Monsters**, 1993, by Bob Vint, Dan Wilhelm, and Mike Wilhelm, in the median of the Irvington Road bridge over the west branch of the Santa Cruz River. These two 50-foot-long gila monsters were designed by Vint in response to a request by area residents for a distinctive, landmark bridge. They are made of concrete covered with pieces of ceramic tile, porcelain, and mirror glass installed by the Wilhelm brothers. The best view of the gila monsters may be from an airplane approaching Tucson International Airport.

9. **Untitled Ceramic Murals**, 1994, by Cristena Cardenas and Melody Peters, Pima County Minimum Security Facility at Mission and Silverlake Roads. On exterior walls at the southwest corner of this minimum security jail, Cardenas and Peters created two huge ceramic tile murals that portray architectural landmarks and cultural icons of the region, along with representations of civic values relating to family, education, work, and service to the community. The high color, sculptural relief, and distinctive shapes of the tiles are striking.

10. **Sun Circle**, 1994, by Paul T. Edwards, Susan Holman, and Chris Tanz, at Rillito Linear Park, at Roller Coaster Wash between La Cañada Drive and La Cholla Boulevard. The Sun Circle is an archaeo-astronomical "monument" consisting of eight interrupted curving walls that together imply a circle. Six of the wall segments have small ports oriented toward sunrise and sunset at the summer and winter solstice, and during spring and fall equinoxes. On the critical days, light pierces through the wall ports and projects onto the facing wall. The walls also incorporate benches to strengthen the allusion to kivas and to provide a pleasant place to sit.

**520/326-8038**

This small automobile museum specializes in the Franklin, featuring 18 fully restored or original models built between 1910 and 1934. A few other classic American cars dating from 1909 to 1941 are rotated through seasonally. Open Wed–Fri 10–4, September 15 through Memorial Day. Because volunteer staff is hard to come by, actual hours fluctuate—a call ahead is strongly recommended. Donations accepted. (Central-North)

**GADSDEN-PACIFIC DIVISION TOY TRAIN OPERATING MUSEUM**
**Foothills Mall**
**7401 N. La Cholla Blvd.**

**520/790-0337**

Trains opened up the West, and model trains have opened up the wallets of many a parent, not to mention obsessive adult collectors. Here, keep your money pocketed and watch up to four trains at once run on a 200-foot circuit. You can also inspect old full-sized railroad memorabilia. Guided tours are available by appointment. Open daily 10–9. Free. ⑤ (West Side)

**POSTAL HISTORY FOUNDATION**
**920 N. First Ave.**
**520/623-6652**

This little museum houses a nationally important collection of domestic and foreign stamps, and details the history

# Monument to a Murderer?

*Tucsonans have argued heatedly about public art in contemporary styles—the sculptures in front of the downtown library (101 N. Stone Avenue) and at the east end of the University of Arizona (Campbell and Third Street) drew particular derision when they were new. But no piece of art has generated more controversy than a straightforward equestrian statue downtown. It's a likeness of Pancho Villa, whom some hail as a Mexican revolutionary hero and others condemn as a murderous opportunist and war profiteer.*

*Mexican officials donated the statue to the city of Tucson; despite loud local protests, the city fathers feared they'd cause a minor international incident if they turned the statue down. As a compromise, they hid the thing—it sits on a wide grassy median (formally called Veinte de Agosto Park) between Congress and Broadway, in front of the big government office buildings just east of Interstate 10. Despite the area's heavy traffic—or perhaps because of it—the statue is difficult to identify from a moving car, and it's awkward to visit on foot.*

Davis Dominguez Gallery, p. 128

or so of the year. Free, but donations are accepted. ♿ (South Side)

# GALLERIES

*With the University of Arizona offering a training center, downtown providing the bohemian atmosphere, and the urban and natural environments offering inspiration, artists find Tucson conducive to their work. Galleries pop up all over, but those specializing in contemporary work tend to cluster downtown, while Western art spreads out at the city's northern and eastern fringes. The following is a highly selective list of Tucson's best-established or most unusual galleries. The most exciting—if crowded—times to visit the downtown venues are during the weekly self-guided ArtWalks Thursday from 5 to 7 p.m., and during Downtown Saturday Night, the entertainment-filled block party radiating out from Congress Street the first and third Saturdays of each month.*

of postal deliveries from colonial days to the present. It's also a working post office. Open Mon–Fri 8:30–3. Free. ♿ (Central-North)

## RODEO PARADE EQUIPMENT MUSEUM
**4825 S. Sixth Ave.**
**520/294-1280 or 294-3636**
Open only from the first business day in January to the week before the rodeo (usually at the end of February), this hangar complex next to the rodeo grounds (the site of Tucson's original 1919 airport) houses about 130 wagons and buggies, most of them a good century old. Much of the equipment actually rolls in the annual rodeo parade. The collection also features life-size replicas of Old West settings, including a blacksmith's shop, a saloon, and a bunkhouse, plus such curiosities as a white horse-drawn child's hearse, a Chinese rickshaw, and a wagon marked "Doctor Brown's Snake Oil." Gravel outside the building makes wheelchair access tricky. Open Mon–Sat 9–4, only during the first six weeks

## BERO GALLERY
**41 S. Sixth Ave.**
**520/792-0313**
For people who want to go far beyond pretty Polaroids, this gallery of challenging nontraditional contemporary photography is a smart stop. Open Wed 2:30–5, Thu 2:30–7, Fri–Sat 12–5, and during Downtown Saturday Nights. ♿ (Downtown)

## CENTRAL ARTS COLLECTIVE GALLERY
**188 E. Broadway Blvd.**
**520/623-5883**
Anything goes at this experimental gallery, as long as it doesn't compromise the building's structural integrity. Installations and individual

pieces by members are shown most of the year, with time set aside for juried shows and invitationals. Open Tue–Sat 12–4 (until 7 Thu), and during Downtown Saturday Night the first and third Saturdays of the month. & (Downtown)

## DAVIS DOMINGUEZ GALLERY
**154 E. Sixth St.**
**520/629-9759**
Leading contemporary Tucson artists are showcased here in changing exhibitions of paintings, sculpture, drawings, photographs, and fine-art prints. Open Tue–Fri 10–5, Sat 10–4. (West Side)

## DINNERWARE ARTISTS CONTEMPORARY ART GALLERY
**135 E. Congress St.**
**520/792-4503**
Run by a collective of local artists who work in virtually every visual medium, this gallery displays a wide variety of contemporary pieces through the course of a season, although at any one time only three or four artists show. Open Tue–Wed and Fri–Sat 12–5, Thu 12–7; open until 9 the first and third Saturdays of the month. & (Downtown)

## EL PRESIDIO GALLERY
**Santa Fe Square**
**7000 Tanque Verde Rd.**
**520/733-0388**
Southwestern art, bronzes, and ceramics abound at these galleries (the other is in St. Philip's Plaza, 4340 N. Campbell Ave., 520/529-1220), each in an upscale shopping center. Oils by Chuck Mardosz and Sue Krzyston, acrylics by Lawrence Lee, and watercolors by Coleen Bobinack are among the items you're almost certain to find. Open Mon–Sat 10–5:30, Sun 1–4 (no Sun hours June–August or at the St. Philip's Plaza location). & (East Side)

## ELEANOR JECK GALLERIES
**St. Philip's Plaza**
**4280 N. Campbell Ave.**
**520/299-2139**
This long-established purveyor of contemporary art, sculpture, ceramics, and jewelry offers the work of over 40 international and regional artists. Open Tue–Sat 11–4. & (Central-North)

## ETHERTON GALLERY
**135 S. Sixth Ave.**
**520/624-7370**
One of Tucson's most respected galleries, the Etherton offers contem-

# Phantom Galleries

*Tucson's smallest art galleries are open for viewing 24 hours a day—if you can find them. The Tucson/Pima Arts Council operates a "Phantom Gallery" program, displaying work in the windows of empty downtown buildings. Locations shift often, depending on the real estate market, so keep your eyes open, especially as you stroll along Congress Street.*

*Etherton Gallery*

porary paintings, prints, and sculptures, and an impressive array of contemporary and historical landscape and ethnographic photographs, mostly dealing with the Southwest. Open Tue–Sat 12–5 (Thu until 7) and 7–10 the first and third Saturdays of the month. Open by appointment only June–August. (Downtown)

### JOSÉ GALVEZ GALLERY
**743 N. Fourth Ave.**
**520/624-6878**
Pulitzer Prize–winning photojournalist Galvez established this nonprofit space to help record Mexican American culture. He intends to branch out from exhibiting art—by Mexican American artists, or on Hispanic themes—to providing a wide-ranging mini cultural center. Open Wed–Fri 10–4, Sat 11–3, plus 5–8 the first and third Saturdays of the month. Summer hours: Wed–Fri 11–3, Sat 5–8. &c (Downtown)

### MANLEY GALLERY
**2425 E. Fort Lowell Rd.**
**520/321-9705**

High-quality Southwestern photographic images are the specialty here, although scenic and landscape photos from around the world also grace the walls. Open Tue–Fri 9:30–5, Sat 10–2, Sun–Mon by appointment. &c (Central-North)

### OBSIDIAN GALLERY
**St. Philip's Plaza, Suite 90**
**4340 N. Campbell Ave.**
**520/577-3598**
National and, particularly, regional artists present contemporary crafts in clay, fiber, metal, glass, wood, and mixed media. Open Mon–Sat 10–5:30; also Sun 12–5 November through May. &c (Central-North)

### PHILABAUM CONTEMPORARY ART GLASS
**711 S. Sixth Ave.**
**520/884-7404**
One of the city's most unusual galleries, the Philabaum is connected to an infernally hot glass-blowing studio that offers public demonstrations Tuesdays through Saturdays; call for specific times or to arrange a tour. The

gallery itself purveys all manner of magnificent glass items, from paperweights to vases and bowls. Open Mon–Sat 10–5. ♿ (Downtown)

## PRIMITIVE ARTS GALLERY
**Broadway Village**
**3026 E. Broadway Blvd.**
**520/326-4852**
In Tucson's first, and in many respects most elegant, shopping center, this gallery specializes in American Indian, pre-Columbian, and ethnographic art. Open Tue–Sat 10–4 and by appointment; appointments are especially recommended in the summer. (Central-North)

## ROSEQUIST GALLERIES
**1615 E. Fort Lowell Rd.**
**520/327-5729**
Billing itself as Tucson's oldest gallery—established in 1946—the Rosequist features landscapes, still lifes, and other figurative work by contemporary artists of the Southwest. Open Tue–Sat 10–5. ♿ (Central-North)

## UNIVERSITY OF ARIZONA GALLERIES
Smallish gallery spaces cluster mainly in two campus areas, providing glimpses of works by UA art students and faculty. The Arizona Gallery is on the second floor of the Memorial Student Union. Open Mon–Fri 10–4. The Union Gallery lies on the building's first floor and is open during the same hours. Over in the UA's official arts complex is the Joseph Gross Gallery, at the southeast corner of Park Avenue and Speedway. Open Mon–Fri 10–5. Nearby is the Lionel Rombach Gallery, next to the UA art department administrative offices, with identical hours. ♿ (Central-North)

## VENTURE FINE ARTS GALLERY
**Trail Dust Town**
**6541 E. Tanque Verde Rd.**
**520/298-2258**
While soaking up the Western atmosphere at Trail Dust Town—a complex that includes a popular steakhouse, replica Western storefronts, and nightly gunfights—you might as well inspect some authentic Western art, too. Some sculpture and many representational canvases are offered for your consideration. Open Mon–Sat 10–5 and by appointment. ♿ (East Side)

Tohono Chul Park

# 8

# PARKS, GARDENS, AND RECREATION AREAS

*Welcome to Tucson. Now get out.*

*Outdoors, that is. The desert is no wasteland, as you'll see if you spend a few hours tramping around in it. And if you just can't bring yourself to cuddle up with a cactus, green forests lie within a 30-minute drive of town. The city itself hosts a variety of parks and gardens, from conventional little grassy play areas to carefully tended showplaces for desert vegetation.*

*Whether you aim to picnic near a prickly pear or hike into the hills, your destination is only a few minutes away.*

## PARKS

### CHRISTOPHER COLUMBUS REGIONAL PARK
**Silverbell Road, just south of La Cholla Blvd.**

Trees, some of them not yet fully mature, cast shade over the packed-dirt banks of Silverbell Lake, which is stocked with catfish in the summer and trout in the winter. You need a license to fish, and you're not allowed to swim in the lake, but it can be relaxing just to sit and watch the water and observe the waterfowl (ducks, geese, herons). The only drawback is that this is a favored spot, mainly late Saturday mornings, for model boat and model airplane enthusiasts; their activities are confined to the entrance side of the lake, but the buzzing does carry across the water. Open dawn to dusk. (West Side)

### DRACHMAN AGUA CALIENTE PARK
**12325 East Roger Rd.**

*Agua caliente* means "hot water," and a perennial warm spring flows into three ponds in this 101-acre park. Water attracts animals, of course, and this is a pleasant place to see what shows up, including birds. What showed up in 1873 was a ranch and health resort. The ranch bunkhouse, which was built in the 1920s, still stands. Sand-topped trails designed to blend with the surrounding ground provide wheelchair and stroller access throughout the developed portion of the park, which beckons picnickers. Interpretive signs explain the geology and history of the warm spring and the natural and human history of the site. Open daily, sunrise to sunset. (East Side)

## GREASEWOOD PARK
### Southwest corner of Speedway and Greasewood
This modest park has no place to play ball, no grassy expanses, no towering green trees. Instead, it provides tables and grills—some under a ramada, many in the open—in a natural area thick with desert vegetation. You're welcome to venture down into Anklam Wash, the dry, sandy riverbed along the park's western boundary, and hike a bit in either direction, along a natural corridor for coyotes and javelina. Open roughly 7–10:30 daily. (West Side)

## REID PARK
### Bounded by Broadway Blvd. and 22nd St., and Country Club Rd. and Alvernon Way
This sprawling, grassy park right in the middle of the city has all the standard amenities: covered picnic tables, trees, open spaces for running around wildly, shaded spaces for lounging, a lake complete with ducks, a zoo (see Chapter 5, Sights and Attractions), baseball fields, a bandshell, and a one-acre rose test garden. Open daily 7–10. (Central-North)

## RILLITO LINEAR PARK
### Along the Rillito, between Campbell Ave. and La Cholla Blvd.
Clinging to the banks of the usually dry Rillito wash, this park offers pedestrian and bicycle trails, a horse trail, restrooms, public art, a Children's Memorial Park, and an exercise course. Open daily, dawn to dusk. (Central-North)

## SANTA CRUZ RIVER PARK
### Along the Santa Cruz River, between Silverlake Rd. and Grant Rd. and from Irvington Rd. to Ajo Way
Like its Rillito counterpart, this linear park includes pedestrian and bicycle trails, exercise courses, restrooms,

**T I P**

If you're going hiking, it's critical to avoid dehydration. Drink 20 ounces of fluid two hours before you set out, and take a good drink every 15 minutes on the trail. Recent research indicates that cold water is absorbed into the body fastest. Don't rely on soda pop, alcohol, fruit drinks, or caffeinated beverages—they'll *cause* dehydration. (See "Top Five Hikes near Tucson" in Chapter 10, Sports and Recreation.)

You may see signs for, or hear references to, the "Rillito River." This is redundant. *Rillito* means "little river," so "Rillito River" would be translated "Little River River."

ramadas, playgrounds, and art projects. The river park also provides access to the Garden of Gethsemane at Congress Street. (See Chapter 5, Sights and Attractions.) At the Irvington-to-Ajo section, look carefully at the retaining walls; the patterns were created with tire treads. Open daily, sunrise to sunset. (Downtown, West Side)

## GARDENS

### TOHONO CHUL PARK
**7366 N. Paseo del Norte**
**520/742-6455**
This 48-acre desert garden was established in 1984 on formerly private property just west of Oracle Road, off Ina. The grounds feature ethnobotanical, hummingbird, and children's gardens, and demonstrate creative uses of water in desert landscaping. As you'll see, desert plant life includes all manner of shrubs, trees, and wildflowers, in addition to the expected abundance of cactus. There's also a hall exhibiting art of the Southwest and a fine Tea Room (see Chapter 4, Where to Eat). Park tours Tue, Thu, and Sat 8 a.m. and 9 a.m.; birding tours Mon, Wed, Fri, and Sat 8 a.m.; "Art in the Park" tours Tue, Thu, and Sun 2 p.m. The schedule may vary over time, but all tours meet at the entry ramada. Suggested donation: $2. (West Side)

### TUCSON BOTANICAL GARDENS
**2150 N. Alvernon Way**

**520/326-9686**
Five and a half acres of peaceful plant life, much of it large enough to provide shade, blooms in the middle of the city. Desert vegetation is the emphasis, with special attention given to low-water gardening. Guided garden tours are offered weekly. The Tropical Exhibit and Sensory Garden are always in bloom. Peak times for other areas: April–June for the Herb Garden, April–May and September–October for the Backyard Bird Garden, May–August for the Native American crops garden, April–August for the Cactus Garden, March–October for the surprisingly lush Xeriscape (low water) Garden, April for the Iris Garden, March–May for the Wildflower

*Hummingbird Garden at*
*Tohono Chul Park*

Tohono Chul Park

# Cactus Corner

*Here's how to tell which kind of cactus you're about to back into.*

**Barrel:** *Looking more or less like barrels, depending on the variety, these thorny plants adorn themselves with a crown of flowers and fruit, in season. Forget the old story about cutting into one to quench your thirst with the water inside; you'll find a pulpy mass, the liquid from which may well make you vomit.*

**Cholla:** *A many-branched cactus, its cylindrical "joints" rising one from another rather than from a central trunk. Papery sheaths cover a cholla's spines, giving the plant a bright color or glow in the right light. Those spines are easy to avoid, but you should really watch out for the little clusters of tiny barbed spines called glochids, just above the ordinary spines. They're very difficult to get out of your skin.*

**Hedgehog:** *Short-stemmed and ribbed, these little fellas bristle with spines and grow close to the ground. They put out brilliant, showy flowers in the spring.*

**Pincushion:** *Small, round, and furry with little spines, often white. Don't even think about touching one, even though the comparatively large yellow blooms can be very attractive.*

**Prickly pear:** *Constructed like a cholla, except that its branches are flat, fleshy pads. In season, they bear large red or yellowish flowers and plump reddish fruit that resembles radishes. As with the cholla, watch out for glochids, which occur even on the fruit.*

**Saguaro:** *Majestic, human-shaped cactus that rises to 40 feet and sprouts several up-thrusting branches, all from the same level. The plant has a smooth, cool skin, except for the row of spines along each vertical rib. From age 50 or so, the saguaro puts out white flowers in May; what looks like red flowers a few weeks later is really the pulp of burst fruit.*

Garden, and March–October for the Butterfly Garden. Don't forget to sniff out the tropical greenhouse, home to coffee and vanilla plants. Perhaps your visit will coincide with the annual fall chile festival or the December holiday luminaria nights. Picnic area available. Open daily 7:30–4:30. Admission: $4 adults, $3 seniors (over 62), free for children under 12. (Central-North)

## RECREATION AREAS

### CATALINA STATE PARK
**11570 N. Oracle Rd.**
**520/628-5798**
Camping, picnicking, hiking, and birding (more than 150 species flock together here) are the prime distractions at this 5,500-acre high-desert park at the base of the Santa Catalina Mountains. Equestrian and hiking trails wind through the area; the most popular destination is the always-wet Romero Pools. Another, easier endpoint is the Romero Ruin, remains of prehistoric and historic Hohokam settlements; it's a large archaeological site covering most of the low ridge to the right, just as you enter the park. The park offers campsites, picnic tables, grills, drinking water, and restrooms. There is a small per-car admission fee. Entrance is free to people on foot or bike, but it's a bit of a trudge from the parking area outside the entrance to the picnic tables and trailheads. (West Side)

### CORONADO NATIONAL FOREST
**Santa Catalina Mountains, up the Catalina Highway**
There's actually a lot more to Coronado National Forest than what's described here; various regions of it are splattered across southern Arizona. Of greatest interest to people in Tucson is the Santa Catalina Mountain district, which rises from the saguaro-dotted desert floor up through juniper and piñon into tall aspen and pine forests—all in less than an hour's drive from town. Rose Canyon Lake, managed for recreational fishing, is tucked into a stand of mature ponderosa pines between Mileposts 17 and 18, 7,000 feet up. Rainbow trout are stocked May through June and in the autumn. A license is required, as is a parking fee; boating and swimming are prohibited. More than 20 picnic areas are scattered throughout the forest, as are several campgrounds—some fee, some free. The highest and lowest are open only seasonally. An excellent online trail guide may be found at http://www.azstarnet.com/public/nonprofit/coronado/trails.htm. A $5 per car fee is collected at the base of the mountains from anyone not going straight up to the village of Summerhaven or the privately operated Mount Lemmon Ski Valley and straight back. (Central-North, East Side)

*Parrot at the zoo in Reid Park, p. 132*

J. Bongratz

# TRIVIA

Peppersauce Canyon was named by prospector Alex McKay, who, after camping there around 1880, reported that his hot sauce had come up missing. The thief was never found.

## MADERA CANYON
**Take I-19 to the Continental exit, south of Green Valley, and follow the signs**
A lush riparian habitat carved out of the Santa Rita Mountains by Madera Creek, this lovely forested area is called home by vast numbers of birds and not a few mammals (including bears). Dozens of miles of intersecting trails thread through the canyon and up several nearby peaks. There's only one campground, Bog Springs, and it's accessible by car. A useful little map provided by the Friends of Madera Canyon may be available at the campground or at the parking lot at the end of the paved road. If you're up for it, take the 11-mile round-trip hike to the top of Mount Wrightson; from its 9,434-foot vantage point, you can survey the Sonoran Desert to the north and west and the grasslands of Sonoita and Patagonia to the east and south. (South Side)

## MOUNT LEMMON SKI VALLEY
**10300 Ski Run Rd., at the end of Catalina Highway**
Ski-lift rides are offered for fun in the summer (call 520/576-1321); in the winter, it's serious business. This is one of the southernmost ski areas in the United States, and the snowfall is irregular and sometimes disappointing. But when everything works out, the slopes and a good little lodge serve the slalom set. Call the Mount Lemmon

Highway information line (520/749-3329) for current road conditions. For information on weather-related road closures, the Pima County Sheriff's Department road condition information line is 520/741-4991. (East Side)

## PEPPERSAUCE CANYON
**Forest Road 38, 6 miles southeast of the town of Oracle**
Part of Coronado National Forest, this area merits a separate entry because it requires its own approach. Drive north on Oracle Road (U.S. 89) to State Highway 77. Turn right (east) and drive 10 miles to the town of Oracle. Take the first Oracle exit and travel four miles through town to Forest Road 38. Follow FR 38 to Peppersauce Canyon. It's a shallow, tree-filled canyon cut by Peppersauce Creek through foothills covered with grass, oaks, and yucca. Campsites, with drinking water and restrooms, are spread throughout an oasis of gnarly sycamore and walnut trees. Spelunkers, note: Peppersauce Cave lies nearby. Day use of the campground area costs $2.50 per vehicle; camping is $5 per night per vehicle. Trailers are not recommended at these small sites. (Central-North)

## PICACHO PEAK
**Off Interstate 10, 35 miles northwest of Tucson**
It's a dull drive north through Pima County's denuded flatland, used

*Tucson Botanical Gardens, p. 133*

mainly for agriculture. But Picacho Peak, jutting from the desert floor, is worth the trip for two reasons: spectacular wildflowers, briefly in the spring (but only if the weather's been right through the winter), and a very interesting hike to the summit. Portions are steep and exposed, so this could be a good place to confront your fear of heights. However, rails and fencing have been put up along the most difficult stretches of trail. It's really quite fun and not that difficult if you have good lungs and fair upper-body strength with which to pull yourself along occasionally. The whole trip—drive and hike—takes about half a day. (West Side)

### SABINO CANYON
**5900 N. Sabino Canyon Rd.**
**520/749-2861**
This highly popular oasis runs with water through the year. The canyon creek is lined with cottonwood and other trees that would go thirsty just a few yards away. You may spot a variety of birds, deer, snakes, and other critters in the wild, but more likely

you'll just want to relax with a picnic lunch or take an invigorating hike on one of the canyon's several trails. A favorite option is Seven Falls, a complex of cascades and swimming holes that's a four-mile round-trip hike from the shuttle drop-off point. Another is Phone Line Trail, which provides spectacular views of the canyon. Nearly four miles of road snake along the creek, but the pavement is closed to motor traffic. That fee shuttle provides a narrated 45-minute tour or quick transportation to trailheads and picnic spots; it departs about every half-hour. Moonlight rides run three nights per month, April through December; for reservations, call 520/749-2327. Admission is free for hikers and cyclists not using the tram. Otherwise, depending on how far you go on the shuttle, it costs $3 to $5 for adults, $1.25 to $2 for kids 3 to 12. Open daily, dawn to dusk. (East Side)

### SAGUARO NATIONAL PARK EAST
**Rincon Mountain District**
**3693 S. Old Spanish Tr.**
**520/733-5153**

Named for the region's distinctive, giant human-shaped cactus, Saguaro East is dedicated to preserving it and other cacti, desert trees and shrubs, and animals. A 15-minute slide program about the park is presented every half-hour in the visitors center auditorium. Naturalist-guided two-hour night walks in the Sonoran Desert occur on the second and fourth Fridays of each month, beginning at 7. Reservations are required. On your own, you can drive a paved loop road or get out for some substantial hiking (see Chapter 10, Sports and Recreation). Open daily, sunrise to sunset. The visitors center is open 8:30–5, except Christmas. There's a $4 entrance fee per private car. Golden Eagle, Golden Age, and Golden Access Passports are honored and are available for purchase. (East Side)

## SAGUARO NATIONAL PARK WEST
**Tucson Mountain District**
**2700 N. Kinney Rd.**
**520/733-5153 or 733-5158**
Compared to Saguaro East, the western unit of the park, just beyond the Tucson Mountains, sports subtly different vegetation (shorter, pricklier) and shorter trails, appropriate for day hikes. Several picnic areas exist along a well-maintained dirt road, and one is a short hike up a canyon. The Red Hills Visitor Center features an observation deck, exhibits, videos, and a slide program. Open daily, sunrise to sunset. The visitors center is open 8:30–5, except Christmas. Free. (West Side)

## TUCSON MOUNTAIN PARK
**Take Speedway Blvd. west to Gates Pass; the park begins here and spills over the western slope of the mountains onto the desert floor.**
**520/883-4200 or 740-2690**
This 20,000-acre natural preserve holds a magnificent saguaro forest through which you may hike, bike, or go horseback riding. Picnicking and camping are also options. Open 7–10 daily. Down on the desert floor is Gilbert Ray Campground, sporting 130 RV sites with individual 30-amp electrical hookups. It has centrally located water, picnic tables, restrooms, and an RV dumping station. Camping is on a first-come, first served basis; fees are $6 for tents, $9.50 for RVs. Three picnic areas also lie within the park, and Gates Pass Overlook is a popular lookout spot; it's usually crowded at sunset, for good reason. Free. (West Side)

Old Town Artisans

# 9

# SHOPPING

Whether you're looking for a scorpion in a paperweight, exquisite turquoise jewelry, or a topographic map of the Grand Canyon, you're likely to find it in Tucson. A few things, however, are scarce. Upscale tailored men's clothing—Armani, Gucci, and beyond—is as rare as snowflakes in July, simply because the local casual culture doesn't demand it. But you can acquire that elsewhere; if you're going to shop in the Old Pueblo, you really should look for something indigenous, something that will evoke the Southwest no matter where it winds up. And that's one emphasis of the following pages.

## SHOPPING DISTRICTS

### Downtown

Once the only place to shop, downtown Tucson fell into serious decline in the 1970s. When the big department, clothing, and drug stores moved to the malls, there wasn't enough foot traffic to support little shops, and Tucson's two century-old, landmark department stores—Steinfeld's and Jacomé's—closed for good. Revitalization began in the 1980s, and today downtown is home again to oddball specialty shops, galleries, and eateries. Still, the area lacks anchor stores, and merchants restrict their hours because the locals tend not to come downtown in the evening, except for Downtown Saturday Night festivities the first and third Saturdays of each month. So plan your shopping trip for broad daylight.

### ADAMS ETHNIC VARIETY STORE
### 272 E. Congress St.

The Kenyan proprietor, who lounges on the sidewalk chatting with passersby when business is slow, aims for variety, indeed, and the ethnicity in question is African. He's assembled articles from all over that continent: clothing, art, crafts, jewelry, drums, even coral guitars from turbulent West Africa. There's also a good selection of books in English on racial issues. Open Mon–Thu and Sat 10–6, Fri 2–6. (Downtown)

## CRESCENT TOBACCO/ NEWSSTAND

See Notable Bookstores and Newsstands, below.

## HYDRA LEATHER AND MORE
### 145 E. Congress St.
### 520/791-3711

This fetishist wonderland stocks lacy corsets, rubber and vinyl (yes, even in Tucson) skirts and short-shorts, silk lingerie, fur-lined handcuffs, and spiked collars. A walled-off "bondage room" displays more extreme sex toys—restraints, clamps, whips—which you must be 18 or older to inspect. This is no seedy sex shop, but a respectable establishment that caters to the not-so-respectable fantasies of all sorts of people; the owner claims her best customers in the bondage room are lawyers, businesspeople, and secretaries. Body piercing is another specialty, done under sterile conditions. Sure, you can get a needle stuck through your nipple, but mothers also bring their teenage daughters here for routine, safe ear piercings. Open Mon–Sat 11–7. (Downtown)

## OLD TOWN ARTISANS
### 201 N. Court Ave.
### 520/623-6024

Stretching through a block of 1850s adobe buildings surrounding a restful courtyard, this marketplace houses six different but interlinked establishments handling, for the most part, high-quality crafts rather than kitschy curios. One features handmade Southwestern pottery; another, Southwestern-style blouses and dresses. A third, Tolteca, offers gifts from Mexico, Central and South America, and Indonesia. Another specializes in dried flowers, chiles, pottery, and Mexican furniture. There's also a shop devoted to Native American art, jewelry, kachinas, and fetishes, and one purveying pots, gourd art, T-shirts, and the like. If shopping makes you hungry, the complex also contains a fine little restaurant called La Cocina, serving lunch every day and dinner Wednesdays through Sundays. Open Mon–Sat 9:30–5:30, Sun 12–5. (Downtown)

## PICANTE DESIGNS/YIKES! TOYS
### 306 E. Congress St.
### 520/622-8807

Picante itself carries women's clothing and folk art from Mexico, including votive candles, but part of the same store is Yikes!, which probably has the largest selection of rubber snakes, lizards, and spiders in southern Arizona. Wind-up and gag toys are another specialty here, but don't overlook the paper dolls, stickers, cards, educational project-toys, and children's books. Simple things popular long ago, like wooden tops and ordinary balls, hold special appeal here. Open Mon–Sat 10–6. (Downtown)

## SAGUARO MOON ANTIQUES
### 45 S. Sixth Ave.
### 520/623-5393

The Fabulous Fifties live on, thanks to these specialists in chrome and Formica dinettes, *Life* magazines, license plates, and vintage lamps. Actually, four dealers share this space, and one stocks only such items as tablecloths, linens, and cookie cutters. Open Mon–Fri 10:30–5:30; open until 10 the first and third Saturdays of each month. (Downtown)

## TESOROS DE MEXICO IMPORTS
### 262 E. Congress St.
Here's an unpretentious source of rough-hewn Mexican furniture, heavy untempered glassware, colorful ceramics, and precolonial-style decorative items. Hours are irregular; daylight on weekdays is a safe bet. (Downtown)

## WIG-O-RAMA
### 98 E. Congress St.
### 520/882-8003
How this place stays in business is something of a mystery—it's never crawling with customers. Yet it is one of those durable, quirky landmark stores that locals would feel lost without. Wigs for every style and occasion adorn the battered mannequin heads; some of the hairpieces apparently have been there since around 1975 (the Farrah Fawcett look lives!), but that merely indicates the range of stock. You may not realize you want a wig until you've visited Wig-O-Rama. After your visit, you *still* may not want a wig, but your aesthetic horizons will have been broadened. Shoe repair is a sideline. Open Mon–Sat 10–5. (Downtown)

## Fourth Avenue

*This district would like desperately to be part of downtown, but the train tracks, underpass, and a forthcoming stretch of Aviation Parkway create physical and psychological barriers that have required Fourth Avenue to develop its own character. Its funky post-hippie identity makes this the logical location for a huge street fair in the spring and winter. The rest of the time, you'll find bead sellers, re-sale houses, a natural foods co-op, a few attractive and unpretentious restaurants, and a string of interesting gift shops.*

## ANTIGONE BOOKS
See Notable Bookstores and Newsstands, below.

## CREATIVE SPIRIT GALLERY
### 628 N. Fourth Ave.
### 520/792-9910
Owned by people who used to sell jewelry and operate a food-service trailer at Grateful Dead concerts, Creative Spirit offers Middle Eastern and Deadhead clothing and jewelry, drums, Oriental rugs and pillowcases, and even some half–Middle Eastern, half-hippie kids' clothes. Around back is the Casbah Tea House, with organic vegetarian cuisine, Turkish coffee, nightly entertainment, and Friday night belly dancing. Open Mon–Sat 11–6, Sun 12–5. (Downtown)

## DESERT VINTAGE AND COSTUME
### 636 N. Fourth Ave.
### 520/620-1570
So you've gotten yourself into one of those odd vacation situations in which you simply *must* have a flapper dress, or maybe a poodle skirt. After making a mental note to find a new travel agent next time, sort through the racks of Desert Vintage and you'll probably find exactly what you need. The store's definition of "vintage" includes Nehru jackets as well as nineteenth-century clothing. There's also a line of accessories such as hats, purses, and ties; men's clothing, too. Open Mon–Sat 11–6, Sun 12–5. (Downtown)

## HOW SWEET IT WAS VINTAGE CLOTHING AND RENTALS
### 419 N. Fourth Ave.

**520/623-9854**

So you're still looking for that flapper dress, but you'd rather rent than buy. How Sweet It Was can help you out with all manner of rental period costumes—Renaissance, Victorian, 1920s, and '50s through '70s. There are plenty of duds for purchase, too, plus bags, shoes, jewelry, and linens. Open Mon–Sat 10–6, Sun 12–6. (Downtown)

## NATIVE SEEDS/SEARCH
**526 N. Fourth Ave.**
**520/622-5561**

Native Seeds/SEARCH is a nonprofit organization devoted to preserving and disseminating seeds indigenous to the northern Sonoran Desert, and advocating the cultivation and consumption of traditional local foods. Its tidy little shop sells all sorts of dried beans ready for the stewpot, plus packets of wildflower seeds. The organization also supports itself through the sale of such items as inexpensive Tarahumara baskets and bowls, more expensive Tohono O'odham baskets, handmade wooden spoons, Mayo/Yaqui Pascola dance masks, and cookbooks and T-shirts. Open Tue–Sat 10–6, Sun noon–4 (summer hours may be more restricted). (Downtown)

## PINEY HOLLOW
**427 N. Fourth Ave.**
**520/623-4450**

You might expect a bead store established as a jewelry workshop in 1972 to reek of patchouli oil and be staffed by middle-aged people with long straight hair and tie-died T-shirts, but Piney Hollow is so mainstream that its owner has even served on the Tucson city council. Beads of every variety—new, old, Czech, African, wood, glass, strung, and loose—lie

Colonial Frontiers

*Some of the merchandise at Colonial Frontiers, p. 144*

within the display cases. Some odd materials also find their way here, such as python vertebrae. Finished jewelry by local artisans constitutes a major portion of the stock. There's also a gallery displaying historic beads from around the world and pottery from the northern Sonoran Desert. Open Mon–Fri 10–6, Sat 10–5:30, Sun 12–4. (Downtown)

## *North Campbell Avenue*

*From Grant Road north to River, Campbell is a hodgepodge of interesting, eclectic stores and restaurants. The following few entries serve as a merely token introduction to the area. Don't try this on foot; things are a bit spread out, and the scenery isn't that interesting, anyway. The one place that you can explore without driving from door to door is St. Philip's Plaza, at Campbell and River; it's listed under "Major Shopping Malls and Plazas" toward the end of this chapter, but one of its* merchants really deserves a separate listing in this section.

## BAHTI INDIAN ARTS
**Philip's Plaza**
**4300 N. Campbell Ave.**
**520/577-0290**
A reputable establishment passed down from father to son, Bahti specializes in handmade arts from Southwestern and northern Sonoran tribes. You'll find a wide variety of jewelry, pottery, Kachinas, rugs, and baskets. If you're looking for local goods, check out the Yaqui masks, and the baskets of yucca and devil's claw or bailing wire and copper by Tohono O'odham artists. Jewelry by O'odham silversmith Rick Manuel is a shop specialty. Open Mon–Thu 9–6, Fri–Sat 9–9, Sun 12–5. (Central-North)

## KAIBAB SHOPS
**2837 N. Campbell Ave.**
**520/322-0146**
The selection of Native American goods seems nearly as huge as the West itself: 9,000 square feet of jewelry, Southwestern clothing (including moccasins), Nambé food ware, vases, frames, clocks, Navajo rugs, pottery, and basketry. There's also Mexican furniture, folk art and dishes, and books and toys for kids. Fortunately, Kaibab Shops avoids the warehouse feel by displaying its goods in several separate rooms, so it's never overwhelming. Open Mon–Sat 9:30–5:30, Sun 11–5. (Central-North)

## PLAZA LIQUORS
**2642 N. Campbell Ave.**
**520/327-0452**
Here's a logical stop if you'd like to investigate Arizona wines. Plaza has one of Tucson's two most interesting

and rewarding selections of fine wines (the other is the Rumrunner), and its prices are economical. Look into Arizona microbrews while you're here, as well as the astonishing variety of beers from around the world. As you can tell from the paraphernalia decorating the place, the owner is even more likely to get a buzz from *Star Trek* than from booze. Open Mon–Sat 10–10, Sun 11–9. (Central-North)

## *Park Avenue Warehouse District*

*About a mile east of the downtown core, two blocks of brick 1908 warehouses have been transformed into vibrant-colored businesses capitalizing on the art, exotica, and atmosphere of the American Southwest and Mexico. Some of the merchants despairingly referred to the area as the "Lost Barrio Warehouses," because they're a bit off the beaten track, and two years of road construction on Park Avenue have caused potential shoppers to steer clear. But the road work is finished, and, after a decade of getting established, these unique shops are finally coming into their own. Nevertheless, the nickname has stuck.*

## APPARATUS
**299 S. Park Ave.**
**520/791-3505**
Across the street from the main warehouses, this establishment belongs to the same family of businesses, even if it's quite removed from them in spirit. Unlike the stores across Park, Apparatus offers nothing from Mexico. Nearly everything is by local artisans, and some of it is high art (especially the items shown inside). The front yard displays metal

and ceramic garden sculptures (some of them are carved, rusty coffee cans), copper-roofed wooden bird-houses, stained-glass *luminarias*—pieces that aim to be expressive rather than pretty. Open Tue–Sat 10:30–5. (Central-North)

### AQUÍ ESTÁ
**204 S. Park Ave.**
**520/624-3354**

Step into this warehouse store and it's like making a trip to Mexico without the nuisance of a border crossing. Hand-painted tile and sinks, and handmade furniture, are the principal attractions, but lots of its little accessories are just begging to become gifts. Open Mon–Sat 9:30–5:30. (Central-North)

### COLONIAL FRONTIERS
**244 S. Park Ave.**
**520/622-7400**

This gallery carries antique furniture, folk art, and accessories from around the world—meaning locales as far-flung as China, Portugal, and the Amazon. If you happen to be vacationing in a truck, you might also consider lugging home a teak door, old wrought iron, a column, or some other architectural piece. Open Mon–Sat 10–5. (Central-North)

### MAGELLAN TRADING
**228 S. Park Ave.**
**520/622-4968**

Breaking from the Southwestern and Mexican items favored by the other warehouse stores, Magellan lives up to its navigator namesake by drawing items from around the world: African folk art, Balinese weavings and carvings, Indonesian furniture, and, of course, items from Latin America. Open Mon–Sat 9–5. (Central-North)

### RUSTICA
**200 S. Park Ave.**
**520/623-4435**

Distinctive Mexican-style furniture and accessories abound here, with an emphasis on custom wood and wrought-iron furniture. Among the other fixtures looking for homes are iron window grilles, kitchen pot racks, chandeliers, and table and floor lamps. The staff is happy to give estimates for building wood or iron furniture to your own design. If you're looking for something more portable, check out the Mexican knickknacks. Open Mon–Fri 9:30–5:30, Sat 10–5:30, Sun 11–4. (Central-North)

### VAQUEROS DE LOS ARTES
**242 S. Park Ave.**
**520/670-1186**

High-quality items from the Mexican states of Oaxaca and Michoacán fill this space. Many pieces are old, some are new. You'll find elaborate mirror frames, skeletal Day of the Dead figurines, abundant carved-wood furniture (from antique tables to new entertainment centers), and a great variety of chair designs. Open Mon–Sat 10–5. (Central-North)

## OTHER NOTABLE STORES

### THE ANTIQUE MALL
**3130 E. Grant Rd.**
**520/326-3070**
From china and silver to cowboy items, all sorts of old collectibles are purveyed by 110 dealers with individual displays, booths, and showcases. Readers of the *Tucson Weekly* voted the Antique Mall best antique store in Tucson three years in a row, and hometown shoppers ought to know. Open Mon–Sat 10–5:30, Sun 11–4:30. (Central-North)

### ARIZONA GAMEROOM FURNISHINGS
**Foothills Mall**
**7401 N. La Cholla Blvd.**
**520/797-8029**
The noisy, gaudy, utilitarian stuff you used to find in any bar and youth hangout is now collectible entertainment equipment. Here you'll discover old and recent arcade video games, pinball machines, slot machines, movie posters, jukeboxes, neon signs, and vintage Coca-Cola gear, plus various unclassifiable nostalgic items. Open Mon–Sat 10–9, Sun 11–5. (West Side)

### ARIZONA HATTERS
**3600 N. Stone Ave.**
**520/292-1320**
You've come out West; you owe yourself a cowboy hat. This is the place to get the authentic article, if you're willing to pay the price for carefully blocked felt headgear. Arizona Hatters sells its own label as well as Stetson, Resistol, and Bailey hats. There's a good selection of belts, men's Western shirts, hatbands, and Pendleton jackets and blankets. Open daily 9–6. (Central-North)

### BERTA WRIGHT
**Foothills Mall**
**7401 N. La Cholla Blvd.**
**520/742-4134**
Highly attractive folk and high art from around the world and around the block lines these shelves. Also peruse the stock of jewelry, clothing, stone and fossil carvings, fetishes, geodes, masks, Paolo Soleri wind chimes, pottery—you name it. After several years, Berta Wright closed her downtown location, and the remaining store's continued tenancy in Foothills Mall is questionable as the once-struggling mall continues to reinvent itself. But the gallery is sure to continue somewhere in town and is well worth the effort to look it up in the phone book. (West Side)

### BIG KIDS (TOO) COMICS
**8791 E. Broadway Blvd.**
**520/290-5080**
For kids who simply want to keep up with the latest comic books, and adult collectors who want to reclaim their youth by creating their own private pop-culture shrines, Big Kids Too specializes, as you would anticipate, in comic books—Marvel, DC, Image, and smaller press publications. If two dimensions won't suffice, you can opt for the action figures (*Spawn*, original and new *Star Wars* items) and Beanie Babies. Open Mon–Tue 12–6, Wed 12–7,

Thu–Fri 11–6, Sat 10–6, Sun 12–4. Also at 3930 W. Ina Road (520/744-7548). (East Side)

## BOOKED UP
See Notable Bookstores and Newsstands, below.

## BUFFALO EXCHANGE
**2001 E. Speedway Blvd.**
**520/795-0508**
Used clothing, yes. Thrift store, not on your life. Buffalo Exchange is a most discriminating establishment, buying and selling mainly current styles and some vintage apparel for men and women. There's also some new garb here, and the total stock runs the gamut from dresses and trousers to scarves, belts, shoes, handbags, and jewelry. What started as a hip little Tucson resale house in 1974 has become a Southwestern empire, but this is still the seat of power. Open Mon–Fri 10–8, Sat 10–7, Sun 11–6. Also at 7045 E. Tanque Verde Road (520/885-8392). (Central-North)

## CORRAL WESTERN WEAR
**4525 E. Broadway Blvd.**
**520/322-6001**
Both traditional and chic Western apparel for men, women, children, and even infants can be rustled up here—not just pearl-snap shirts and jeans, but belts, jewelry, and boots by Stewart, Justin, and Tony Lama. Open Mon–Tue 10–6, Wed–Fri 10–9, Sat 10–6, Sun 12–5. (Central-North)

## DESERT ARTISANS' GALLERY
**La Plaza Shoppes**
**6536-A E. Tanque Verde Rd.**
**520/722-4412**
This co-op gallery shows the work of more than 30 artists. You'll find abstract and realistic paintings, pottery, and realist and abstract sculpture large and small. There's also a selection of utilitarian ceramics, handmade pins, key rings, cards, and small laser-reproduction paintings. Open Mon–Sat 10–5, Sun 10–1:30. (East Side)

## DESERT SON
**4759 E. Sunrise Dr.**
**520/299-0818**
Moccasins are handmade right on the premises; brought in from elsewhere are Indian jewelry, baskets, Navajo rugs, Hopi kachinas, Zuni fetishes, and a variety of other Native American crafts, belts and buckles, books, and pottery. Open Mon–Sat 9–5:30. (Central-North)

## DISCOUNT AGATE HOUSE
**3401 N. Dodge Blvd.**
**520/323-0781**

Strip malls—those little rows of small stores lining every major boulevard in the West—may look tacky, but they often contain emporia of offbeat, or at least useful, moderately priced goods. To cruise the strip malls of Tucson, your best bets are Speedway between Campbell and Wilmot, Broadway between downtown and Wilmot, and Oracle Road between Miracle Mile and Magee.

One of the few places in Tucson where you can legally get stoned, Discount Agate House offers minerals, agate, petrified wood, bookends, fossils, carbachons, spheres, and egg- and obelisk-cut stones. There's also sterling silver and turquoise Indian jewelry, and such silversmithing and lapidary supplies as pliers, files, diamond wheels, dremels, polishing machinery, and 250 types of cutting materials. Open Mon–Sat 9:30–5:30. (Central-North)

## GEPPETO'S TOYS AND DOLLS
**7049 N. Oracle Rd.**
**520/297-1041**
Named, of course, for the old woodcarver who created Pinocchio, this shop carries specialty and instructional toys, athletic toys, musical toys, and so on. A wide selection of hand puppets accompanies stuffed animals, Madame Alexander, porcelain, and vinyl dolls (Lee Middleton, Fazah Asparo, Zook); and bears by Gund, North American Bear, and Boyd Bears. Open Mon–Fri 9:30–5:30, Sat 9:30–5. (West Side)

## INDIAN TERRITORY
**5639 N. Swan Rd.**
**520/577-7961**
Few other places stock the class of Native American goods that includes weaponry—knives, tomahawks, and beaded hatchets. You'll also encounter ceremonial regalia and the more usual run of old and new Native American arts and crafts: Hopi kachinas; Hopi, Jemez, and Casas Grandes pottery; Zuni fetishes; jewelry; and men's war shirts, women's dresses, and children's items. Open Tue–Sat 10–7, Sun 12–6. (Central-North)

## LORI'S COLLECTABLES
**6121 E. Broadway Blvd.**

**520/790-6668**
For those who obsessively acquire little things, this is a must stop. The shop sells Hummel figurines, Lilliput Lane and David Winter cottages, DeGrazia gift items, Fontanini figures, gnomes, Disney stuff, and plenty more. Open Tue–Fri 10–6, Sat 10–5. (East Side)

## MAC'S INDIAN JEWELRY
**2953 E. Grant Rd.**
**520/327-3306**
Navajo rugs, pottery, squash blossom necklaces, Hopi and Navajo kachinas, knives, sand paintings, dream-catchers, artifacts, flutes, Yaqui masks, porcelain dolls with Native American costumes and hair, and all sorts of jewelry fill this shop, which also takes on repairs and custom work. Open Mon–Sat 9–6. (Central-North)

## MORNING STAR TRADERS
**2020 E. Speedway Blvd.**
**520/881-2112**
Older Indian art, particularly from the 1930s and '40s, is the specialty in this converted old home. Baskets, rugs, and jewelry dominate the first building; the second contains an antique furniture gallery. By "antique," they mean predominantly Spanish Colonial– and '30s Spanish Colonial Revival–style goods. Open Mon–Sat 9–6. (Central-North)

## MUNSON'S TUCSON DATE CO.
**52 E. Roger Rd.**
**520/887-2731**
The *medjool* date is king at Munson's, where you can buy ordinary boxes and fancy gift baskets of plain dates, candied dates, date pecan loaves, desert honeys, Arizona shelled pecans and pistachios, and cactus and citrus jellies and candies. The

store also sells a small selection of souvenirs and Southwestern cookbooks. Nearly all these delectable items are produced either on the Munson property or somewhere in southern Arizona, so these are ideal indigenous souvenirs and gifts that you won't have to dust. Munson's will ship from the shop, too. Open Mon–Sat 9–5. (West Side)

### PDQ RECORDS AND TAPES
**2342 N. Dodge Blvd.**
**520/881-2681**
The staff, with some notable exceptions, is notoriously surly. Yet PDQ is worth a visit for anyone seeking a truly gigantic selection of used recordings—vinyl as well as CD. Most of the trade is in rock and pop, but all sorts of music find their way into the store, including rare European pop imports, plenty of classical, and a stunningly huge selection of Latin American music. Because the staffers don't always understand the value of some of the stock, a few items are ridiculously overpriced—and others are absolute steals. Open Mon–Sat 9–8, Sun 10–7. (Central-North)

### PINK ADOBE GALLERY
**6538 E. Tanque Verde Rd.**
**520/298-5995**
This gallery sells work by more than 100 artists. The styles are colorful, often whimsical, and contemporary or folklike (yet not rustic) in spirit. It's hard to know what will be in stock any given month—wood sculptures, handmade backpacks, paintings, drawings, bowls, and vases are safe bets. Call ahead to be sure. Open Mon–Sat 10–5, Thu to 8. (Downtown)

### RUMRUNNER WINE AND CHEESE CO.
**3200 E. Speedway Blvd.**

**520/326-0121**
South and east of Tucson is a little patch of valiant wineries. A few other vintners operate in this state, too, and some of their products are available at the elegant Rumrunner. This store's main business revolves around its collection of fine wines from California and Europe, plus excellent cheeses and a very few other select items of interest to the connoisseur. Open Mon–Sat 10–10, Sun 11–7. (Central-North)

### SONORAN DESERT MARKETPLACE
**1333 N. Oracle Rd.**
**520/624-4018**
If it has anything to do with the Sonoran Desert and its surroundings and cultures, it's here—regional books, ethnic books, gems and minerals, T-shirts by Tohono O'odham artists, Zapotec rugs, Mata Ortiz pottery, Zuni fetishes, Native American sterling silver and turquoise jewelry, specialty foods, and gifts of both museum and tourist quality. Open Mon–Sat 10–5:30. (West Side)

### SUMMIT HUT
**5045 E. Speedway Blvd.**
**520/325-1554**
Here's a very good stock of outdoor products mainly for hikers, campers, and climbers, with lines a bit more upscale (and sometimes pricier) than those you'll find at chain stores like Popular. Gear, clothes, sunglasses, climbing equipment, freeze-dried food, excellent walking sticks, boots, books, and topographic maps are the main attractions. The store also rents packs, tents, and boots, and the staff generously dispenses free advice about where to use it all. Open Mon–Fri 9–8, Sat–Sun 10–6:30. (Central-North)

Don't overlook the gift shops at various Tucson attractions and museums. At the Saguaro National Park West visitors center, for example, you'll find many nature-oriented children's books as well as the usual range of plant and astronomy guides. The Tucson Museum of Art shop offers cards, posters, and some very nice pieces of decorative art. The Tohono Chul Park gift shop is stocked with jewelry, baskets, and odd items (rain sticks, good luck charms) from the Southwest and Latin America. It never hurts to take a peek before moving on to your next destination.

### TANQUE VERDE GREENHOUSES
**10810 E. Tanque Verde Rd.**
**520/749-4414**

It may seem like you're driving halfway to the East Coast to get here, but Tanque Verde Greenhouses is worth a little excursion for its 1,500 types of cacti and succulents. Don't expect to take packets of seed back with you; these plants start much better from clippings, which is what you'll find here, as well as more mature plants ranging in price from 85 cents to $100 or more. Open Mon–Sat 9–5. (East Side)

### TEISSEDRE GALLERY
**4937 E. 29th St.**
**520/745-9700**

In any Mexican-influenced building, you'll find yourself treading on tile. That's largely what you'll discover here, without even glancing down at your feet: ceramic tiles, tiles for hot plates, tile clocks, even custom tile designers. You'll also encounter sculpture, pottery, framed prints, wall hangings, and other Southwestern gifts. Open Mon–Fri 8–4:30, Sat by appointment. (South Side)

### TUCSON MAP AND FLAG CENTER
See Notable Bookstores and Newsstands, below.

### UNIQUE ANTIQUE
**500 E. Speedway Blvd.**
**520/323-0319**

In an increasingly popular arrangement, this is a mall setup of 70 or 80 dealers, each with his or her own booth or showcase. Glass, furniture, pottery, silver jewelry, and military items are plentiful. Open Mon–Sat 10–6, Sun 11–5. (Central-North)

### ZIA RECORD EXCHANGE
**3370 E. Speedway Blvd.**
**520/327-3340**

This statewide chain features mostly CDs, mostly but not exclusively used. Mainstream popular music is the bread and butter here, but the bins hold everything from classical to world beat music. Finding something specific can be a bit of a hunt sometimes, but the staff is enthusiastic or, at the very least, helpful. Open daily 10–midnight. Also at 7191 E. Speedway Boulevard (520/290-2443) and 3655 N. Oracle Road (520/887-6898). (East Side)

## NOTABLE BOOKSTORES AND NEWSSTANDS

### ANTIGONE BOOKS
**411 N. Fourth Ave.**
**520/792-3715**

Specializing in books by and for women, this store has fared much better than its Sophoclean namesake. It has expanded over the years to include cards, music, journals, calendars, and jewelry. But still, books are the heart of this establishment: feminist essays, women's studies, lesbian (and gay) material, and classic and contemporary novels and poetry by writers who happen to be female. Male customers are entirely welcome, by the way. Open Mon–Thu 10–6, Fri–Sat 10–9, Sun 12–5. (Downtown)

## BARNES & NOBLE BOOKSELLERS
### 5130 E. Broadway Blvd.
### 520/512-1166
Some people object to big chain stores like Barnes & Noble and Borders on principle, but it's hard to ignore the lure of the gigantic stock of books—a few new titles and staff-picks deeply discounted—plus abundant magazines, CDs (generally *not* discounted), and coffee. The Broadway store is a bit hard to spot; it's at the corner of Broadway and Rosemont, sitting well off the street, and there's an unrelated restaurant more or less in front of it. Open daily 9 a.m.–11 p.m. Also in the Foothills Mall, 7325 N. La Cholla Blvd., 520/742-6402. (Central-North)

## BOOKED UP
### 2828 N. Stone Ave.
### 520/622-8238
This store stands apart as Tucson's leading source of rare books on every subject, including art, animals, music, mystery, and general fiction and literature. There's a fair number of signed and first-edition volumes, too, plus a small selection of *objets d'art*. Perhaps the store's greatest point of interest is its owner: Pulitzer Prize–winning novelist Larry Mc-

Murtry (*Lonesome Dove*, *The Last Picture Show*). Don't count on seeing the proprietor behind the counter, though; McMurtry has novels to write, and two, larger Booked Up stores to run in Archer, Texas, and Washington, D.C. Open daily 10–6. (West Side)

## BOOKMAN'S
### 1930 E. Grant Rd.
### 520/325-5767
A veritable supermarket of used books, Bookman's is housed in a large former grocery store. The huge selection of pre-read tomes is neatly categorized, and it's a good idea to consult the maps at the ends of most shelves if you're looking for a specific genre. Rare books occupy a small niche; far larger sections are given over to used CDs and LPs, new and used magazines (an especially impressive stock), and computer games. You can get either cash or credit for the goods you bring in, provided they meet the store's standards of resellability (what the clerks do and do not accept can sometimes seem quirky). Open daily 9

*Arizona Avenue at Tucson Mall, p. 153*

Tucson Mall

a.m.–10 p.m. Also at 3733 W. Ina Rd., 520/579-0303. (Central-North)

## THE BOOK MARK
**5001 E. Speedway Blvd.**
**520/881-6350**

This beloved bookstore was the Tucson bibliophile's Mecca until the big chains came to town. Nonetheless, the Book Mark is still managing to compete, with more than 200,000 new books in just about every imaginable category. The choice of periodicals is decent but limited by the standards of the chains and Bookman's (above); the children's room, though, is especially wide-ranging. Non-fiction and novels about the southwest occupy an admirable amount of shelf space, too. Best of all, this still *feels* like a bookstore, rather than an antiseptic department store devoted to books— the shelves are tall and full and fairly close together, and the staff is tremendously helpful and friendly but unobtrusive. Open Mon–Sat 9–9, Sun 11–5. (Central-North)

## BORDERS BOOKS & MUSIC
**4235 N. Oracle Rd.**
**520/292-1331**

Not much sets Borders apart from its major chain competition in Tucson, Barnes & Noble, except that, subjectively, Borders' periodical selection seems more limited and its CD selection seems more abundant. Also, it's more aggressive in booking special events, like author signings and mini concerts. Otherwise it's the standard story: lots of books and hot java. Open Sun–Thu 8–11, Fri–Sat 8–midnight. (West Side)

## CLUES UNLIMITED
**Broadway Village Center**
**123 S. Eastbourne Ave.**
**520/326-8533**

Known under its former owners as Footprints of a Gigantic Hound, Clues Unlimited devotes its entire 5,000-book stock to mysteries—drawing room puzzlers, police procedurals, and hard-boiled detection, classic and contemporary. The selection is mainly paperback, both mass-market and trade, but new items are often stocked in hardcover, and there's a selection of signed and othewise collectible cloth-bound books. It's a tiny store, and the person at the counter knows her stuff. The only drawback is that, given the nature of its holdings, Clues Unlimited is too tidy and organized; it ought to be cramped and musty, with a devious poisoner just around the corner. Open Mon–Fri 10–6, Sat 9–5, Sun 12–4. (Central-North)

## CRESCENT TOBACCO/
## NEWSSTAND
**216 E. Congress St.**
**520/622-1559**

Since 1908 this smoke shop and newsstand has been a downtown fixture. It offers the same-day *New York Times* and the Sunday editions of papers from all over the nation, and an admirable selection of magazines, from girlie rags to literary journals. There's also a variety of tobacco products (including cigars) and accessories. This comfortingly traditional old place never came close to being a head shop, although, incongruously, it does now carry several forms of incense. Open Mon–Sat 9–7, Sun 9–5. (Downtown)

## TUCSON MAP AND FLAG CENTER
**3239 N. First Ave.**
**520/887-4234**

If you're on the road trying to find yourself, you'll undoubtedly know your location once you visit this fas-

## TIP

For teenagers going to Tucson malls, traditional good manners just don't suffice anymore. Not only are teens not allowed to run, shout, spit, operate boom boxes, sit on the floor, or put their feet on the benches, security officers may eject them if they are skulking around in feral packs of four or more. Merely wearing a bandana may be sufficient reason to be thrown out—bandanas and certain sports team clothing are branded as gang wear. Kids probably will not be hassled if they dress like Pee Wee Herman—and spend money.

cinating shop. There are topo maps covering nearly every square inch of the United States and Mexico; wall maps of Tucson, the Grand Canyon, and other Southwestern points of interest; Forest Service maps; hiking maps and books; street atlases; world maps; maps of every state; globes; travel guides; aeronautical maps; compasses; and hand-held GPS units. As if that weren't enough, you can buy flags from every state and most nations. Open Mon–Fri 8–5:30, Sat 9–5:30. (Central-North)

## MAJOR SHOPPING MALLS AND PLAZAS

### BROADWAY VILLAGE
**Broadway Blvd. and Country Club Rd.**
Built in 1939 according to a design by architect Josias Joesler, Broadway Village was Tucson's first modern shopping center and to this day remains the city's most alluring. Not that the retailers and restaurateurs offer anything that can't be found elsewhere; it's the look of the place, the vine-covered brick walls in Spanish Colonial style, that holds special appeal. The shops themselves, though fairly few by contemporary standards, hold fine browsing potential in an atmosphere that does, indeed, resemble that of a well-to-do village. Specialties include clothing, Native arts, personal accessories, and household accent furnishings. Among the shops: Angel Threads, Thunderbird Shop, Aroma Tree, Primitive Arts, Whimsey Designs, Patania's Sterling Silver Originals, Coyote's Voice, and Zocalo (Colonial-style furniture). (Central-North)

### CROSSROADS FESTIVAL
**Grant and Swan Rds.**
Clothing claims most of your attention at this stylish strip mall. Mills Touché purveys fine wear for men and women; Draper's and Damon's, as well as Eileen of Tucson, cater exclusively to ladies. Other stores, large and small, include Little Outlet (men's shoes and apparel), Hall of Frames, Bed Bath and Beyond, Mrs. Tiggy-Winkle's (an outstanding toy store), Anthony's Cigar Emporium, Paper Warehouse, Ski & Sports, and SAS Factory Shoe Store. (Central-North)

### EL CON MALL
**3601 E. Broadway Blvd.**

**520/327-8767**

The city's first enclosed mall remains one of its two best. Stores include Robinsons-May, JC Penney, Dillard's, Montgomery Ward, Pacific Swimwear, Arizona Outfitters Western Wear, Lerner New York, The Limited, Victoria's Secret, Things Remembered, Zarfa's Luggage and Gifts, Radio Shack, Software Etc., Indian Arts and Crafts, Blockbuster Music, and Payless Shoesource. (Central-North)

### PARK MALL
**5870 E. Broadway Blvd.**
**520/748-1222**
Most of the exterior trees that gave this mall its name in the mid-1970s have been removed, revealing a façade of depressing banality. The interior, too, is beginning to show its age (although the indoor trees still look young); the whole place, while trendy 20 years ago, now seems small and slightly faded compared to Tucson's other malls. Still, it holds a good range of the usual mall stores, including The Gap, The Limited, Victo-

*Plaza Palomino*

Plaza Palomino

ria's Secret, Millers Outpost, Walgreens, May's, Dillard's, Sears, A Taste of Arizona, Radio Shack, Daniel's Jewelers, Native Treasures, Sam Goody, Florsheim Shoes, and Naturalizer Shoes. (West Side)

### PLAZA PALOMINO
**2970 N. Swan Rd.**
**520/795-1177**
Wrought-iron gates, quiet fountains, and abundant foliage (by desert standards) mark this latest Spanish Colonial complex of elegant shops and galleries. Locally owned shops purvey contemporary clothing, jewelry, antiques, Native American and Southwestern arts and crafts, home accessories, and various unusual gift items. Note: These stores close at 6 p.m. daily, and many don't open at all on Sunday. (Central-North)

### ST. PHILIP'S PLAZA
**4380 N. Campbell Ave.**
**520/886-7485**
"Elegant fashions, dining and pampering" are promised at this tree-shaded, flower-graced complex built around a grassy courtyard. Much truth lies in that advertising. The half-dozen locally owned clothing stores (some catering to men as well as women) offer sophisticated, reasonably upscale fashions and accessories. Small leather goods huddle in a couple of individual shops. Elsewhere in the facility may be found contemporary art, Native American crafts and jewelry, and three of the city's best restaurants—Café Terra Cotta, Daniel's, and Ovens (see Chapter 4, Where to Eat). (Central-North)

### TUCSON MALL
**4500 N. Oracle Rd.**
**520/293-7330**
This two-level facility stands as Tucson's busiest shopping mecca; of all

the city's malls and shopping plazas, the Tucson Mall has maintained the greatest vitality. Stores include Sears, Macy's, Mervyn's, Dillard's, Robinsons-May, JC Penney, The Gap, Guess, Eddie Bauer, Ann Taylor, Banana Republic, Frederick's of Hollywood, Victoria's Secret, the Body Shop, Disney Store, the Nature Company, Sunglass Hut, Warner Bros. Studio Store, Radio Shack, Sam Goody, and "Arizona Avenue"—a collection of Southwestern gift shops. (Central-North)

## FACTORY OUTLET CENTERS

**FOOTHILLS MALL**
**7401 N. La Cholla Blvd.**
**520/742-7191**
Architecturally the most appealing of Tucson's four malls, Foothills came late to the game and has spent its first decade struggling to survive. Its latest tactic is to transform itself into an outlet-and-entertainment center. The mix of outlet stores and regular retailers includes Off 5th, Desert Digs Furniture and Doodads, Donna Karan, Bugle Boy, Nike, Quicksilver, L'eggs/Hanes/Bali/Playtex, Samsonite, Black & Decker, and E & J's Designer Shoe Outlet. (West Side)

**VF FACTORY OUTLET/FACTORY STORES OF AMERICA**
**5120 S. Julian Dr.**
**520/889-4400**
You'll find bargains here but not a hint of atmosphere. Vanity Fair, Lee, Jantzen, and Van Heusen clothing sprawl through this complex's largest space. Individual shops offer American Tourister items, housewares by EKCO and Rubbermaid, plus remaindered books, liquidated toys, and discontinued fragrance and cosmetics. (South Side)

# 10

# SPORTS AND RECREATION

*If you really want to understand Tucson, head outdoors. True, this is not a particularly wise course of action on a summer afternoon, unless you're hoping to sweat off a few pounds. Even so, the early hours of a summer morning are pleasant enough for a short hike or run. And the rest of the year, the desert sun is your friend; few are the days that are so cold or windy or damp that you'll be able to resist the call of the outdoors.*

*People who tend to be spectators rather than participants can find action in a number of athletic venues. The biggest draws are University of Arizona sports, particularly the men's basketball team and its coach, Lute Olson, whom the locals esteem as highly as Christ and the Apostles.*

## PROFESSIONAL AND COLLEGE SPORTS

### Auto Racing

**SAGUARO NATIONAL SPEEDWAY**
**4300 E. Los Reales Rd.**
**520/574-7526**
This facility, with seating for 4,000 and a new ⅜-mile clay oval track, races sprint cars, midgets, modifieds, late models, and sportsman classes year-round. Racers are mostly from Arizona and elsewhere

around the Southwest, although East Coast racers take a few turns during the winter. Adult admission $8–$12, depending on event; $2–$3 off for seniors; free for kids under 11. (South Side)

**SOUTHWESTERN**
**INTERNATIONAL RACEWAY**
**11300 S. Houghton Rd.**
**520/762-9100**
This newly opened quarter-mile drag-racing facility at the Pima County Fairgrounds offers racing January

through November, plus six major events, including the American Drag Bike Association Southwest Nationals Harley Top-Fuel Showdown in May, and the Super Chevy Show in March. Top Fuel Dragsters and Nitro Funnycar champions from around the country stop by to test out their rigs before the Winter Nationals in Pomona. The facility has concession stands and permanent restrooms. To reach the place, take Exit 275 off I-10 and drive one mile to the fairgrounds. General admission ($8 general, free for kids under 12) gets you entrance to the racing pits, where you can talk to the drivers. (East Side)

### TUCSON RACEWAY PARK
**12500 S. Houghton Rd.**
**520/762-9200**
Here it's NASCAR stock car racing, billed as the "fastest ⅜-mile (track) in the West." In December and January it's the site of Winter Heat racing, televised on ESPN II. Regular racing is every Saturday night, April through October. Located next to the Pima County Fairgrounds (see directions in entry above), this facility has lots of free parking. Adult admission costs $9 (Winter Heat price is $10); seniors (over 65), juniors (12–17), and military are $6; kids 11 and under are free. (East Side)

## Baseball

### COLORADO ROCKIES SPRING TRAINING
**Hi Corbett Field, at Reid Park**
**520/327-9467**
Spring training games run late February through late March. The park is bounded by Broadway Boulevard on the north, 22nd Street on the south, Country Club Road on the west, and Alvernon Way on the east. Adult admission to the games costs $4–$12,

depending on seating area. Kids under 2 are free. (Central-North)

### TUCSON SIDEWINDERS
**Tucson Electric Park (at Kino Boulevard and Ajo Way)**
**520/325-2621**
Sandwiched between blocky Kino Community Hospital and the dour Pima County Juvenile Court Center is the clumsily named (yet brand-spanking-new) Tucson Electric Park. It's home to the Tucson Sidewinders, a Pacific Coast League baseball team formerly known as the Tucson Toros. Sidewinders games are played April through September. Adult admission is $4–$8, depending on where you choose to sit; kids get in for $3. (South Side)

## Dog Racing

### TUCSON GREYHOUND PARK
**2601 S. Third Ave.**
**520/884-7576**
Tucson's home for the sport of Joe Six-Pack offers year-round greyhound racing. Live dog races are Wednesday and Friday nights, and all day and into the night Saturdays and Sundays. Seven days a week, noon to 6, the park broadcasts horse-racing simulcasts and dog-track simulcasts from seven other tracks around the nation. Take the Fourth/Sixth Avenue exit from I-10, then look for the green neon–outlined dome. General admission is $1.25; children are welcome if accompanied by an adult. (South Side)

## Ice Hockey

### TUCSON GILA MONSTERS
**Tucson Convention Center Arena**
**260 S. Church Ave.**
**520/791-4266**
Ice hockey in the desert? Given the

# TRIVIA

There used to be a big post-Christmas college football game in Tucson called the Copper Bowl. Over the years, sponsorship deals appended various commercial names to the event, but the vessel remained Copper—until 1997, when a Phoenix-area computer-tech company essentially bought it and named the game after itself: the Insight.com Bowl. Outrage among local bowl fans, not to mention changing sponsorships, may eventually bring back the copper sheen.

environment, it's not too surprising that the embryonic Gila Monsters, which enjoyed their first full season of play in 1997, filed for bankruptcy late that year. By the time you get to Tucson, the ice may have melted—or the puck may be flying again. West Coast Hockey League games run October through March. Adult admission costs $6–$12, with $1 discounts for students with ID, military personnel, or seniors 55 and older. (Downtown)

## UNIVERSITY OF ARIZONA ATHLETICS
**Various locations around Tucson, mainly on the UA campus**
**520/621-2287**
Not professional sports, but a number of the UA teams are just as exciting. The University of Arizona Wildcats men's basketball team won the 1997 National Collegiate Athletic Association championship, and the women's softball team was also a national champion. Other Wildcat athletic offerings include women's basketball, football, golf, gymnastics, tennis, soccer, swimming—and the ever-popular, ever-rowdy Icecats hockey club, which plays at the downtown Tucson Convention Center. (Central-North, Downtown)

## RECREATION

### Bowling

## BRUNSWICK CAMINO SECO BOWL
**114 S. Camino Seco**
**520/298-2311**
Friday and Saturday nights, 9:30 to midnight, feature way-cool "Cosmic Bowling"—think black light, strobes, fog machines, laser lights, glow-in-the-dark bowling balls and pins, loud music. Admission is $11 per person. Saturday nights is Rock'n'Bowl, meaning regular bowling (with the lights on) accompanied by high-volume rock 'n' roll. Admission for R'n'B is $9 per person. The bowling alley is located at Broadway Boulevard and Camino Seco, right behind Jeff's Pub. (East Side)

## GOLDEN PIN LANES
**1010 W. Miracle Mile**
**520/888-4272**
Home of the "Tucson Open," which is on the Pro Bowlers Tour, Golden Pin Lanes offers mere mortals colored-pin bowling (get a strike with a colored pin and you can win prizes, free game passes, etc.), Fridays at 9 a.m. for everyone and Wednesdays at

1 p.m. for seniors only. Friday and Saturday nights, 9:30 to 12:30, is "Kosmic Bowling," complete with strobes, black lights, and fog machines. (Note: Friday night Kosmic Bowling plays country music only.) Admission is $8 per person, plus shoe rental. This alley, located down the street from an exotic-dancing club, an automobile scrap yard, and an assortment of modest (or immodest, depending on how you look at it) adult motels, also boasts a laser tag indoor arena. (West Side)

## Biking: On the Road

### OLD SPANISH TRAIL/SAGUARO NATIONAL PARK EAST
Set off from the corner of Broadway Boulevard and Old Spanish Trail, it's a slightly curvy climb up Old Spanish Trail—nearly 300 feet over about 6 miles—but at least the paved bike path is separated from the street. You'll find yourself at the entrance to Saguaro National Park, where you will pay $2 and continue along a fun, hilly, paved 9-mile loop. Drinking water and benches are available along the way. (East Side)

### RANCHO VISTOSO/CATALINA
Here's a long ride—32 miles—but not a terribly difficult one. Start at the corner of Oracle and Magee Roads and follow Oracle north (the traffic should be much thinner here than it is to the south). You'll be going pretty much up, but slowly, over hills that shouldn't cause excessive panting. After you pass the Sheraton El Conquistador Resort (3.7 miles along) and descend to the Cañada del Oro wash, turn left on First Avenue. Keep going north, and you'll find yourself in the retirement burg of Rancho Vistoso. After a total of 11.8 miles of gentle

climbing, the road meets up again with Oracle. If you're up for another four miles or so (and four more back), head north again on Oracle to the little town of Catalina. If, from Catalina, you go straight back down Oracle without the Rancho Vistoso detour, your round trip will be only 28 miles. (West Side)

### RILLITO LINEAR PARK
A linear park is not a place to walk your snake, it's a strip of land along a wash, landscaped and paved for walkers, cyclists, and in-line skaters. The park along the Rillito extends from La Cholla Road in the west (just north of River Road) to Campbell Avenue in the east (just south of River Road). The path lies along the north bank; the unpaved south bank path is for equestrians. The Rillito stands dry much of the year, so don't expect a gentle river scene (but don't worry about mosquitoes, either). It's an easy, pleasing, flat ride, except for the underpasses at the major cross streets. One-way distance is about five miles, and there are benches and a few drinking fountains along the way. (Central-North)

### SABINO CANYON
Because this recreation area swarms with visitors, cyclists may ride the paved road only from dawn to 9 a.m. and 5 p.m. to dusk. It's four miles uphill to the end of the canyon, but only the last mile is steep. Along the way you'll see some lavish landscape, fed by the creek that the road crosses nine times (and the creek does flow over the road during the rainy season). It's an easy coast back to the entrance, but the 15 m.p.h. speed limit is strictly enforced. For directions to Sabino Canyon, see the day hiking section, below. (East Side)

## SANTA CRUZ RIVER PARK

Hugging both the west and east banks of the Santa Cruz wash, this linear park offers about four miles, one way, of peaceful, scenic riding on pavement. Underpasses cross each intersection, except for the east bank at Congress. Landscape varies from a grassy kiddie park to fine desert landscaping (the sage emits a wonderful aroma after a rain), and there are good views of the downtown skyline and Sentinel Peak. You'll pass a few drinking fountains, a couple of restrooms, and, at Congress, the Garden of Gethsemane sculpture park (see Chapter 5, Sights and Attractions). The Santa Cruz Park extends from Grant Road on the north to Silverlake Road on the south. After

---

# Bicycle Races

*With its fine weather and varied terrain, Tucson is a perfect place for a bicycle race. (Well, the weather has been awful for one or two races, but we don't want competitors to get complacent, do we?) Several annual events draw competitors from around the world.*

*The Tour of the Tucson Mountains, held the Sunday after Easter since 1987, is a 100-kilometer event that circles the jagged mountains on the city's West Side. Circling doesn't mean you avoid hills.*

*In April there's the Speedway Bikes Tucson Bicycle Classic, a three-day stage race featuring an international field and a wide span of ages and abilities. One stage is the Gates Pass Road Race, where racers are treated to at least one grueling climb up the (west) side of the pass; the elite men race for 101 miles and climb the pass three times, and the top women race for 61 miles, climbing Gates Pass twice. A second event is a circuit race in which competitors race for a varied number of laps on a 5.6-mile loop of roads in the Tucson Mountain foothills.*

*El Tour de Tucson, launched in 1983, is a more challenging 111-mile race clockwise around the city's perimeter. The winner usually comes in after roughly four and a half hours of balmy November biking. The race begins and ends downtown, at Congress and Granada. Four-mile and quarter-mile events are offered to kids downtown, and adults who aren't up for the grueling 111-mile circuit may start elsewhere in the city for 75-, 50-, and 25-mile courses.*

a one-mile break, there's also a little section between Ajo Way and Irvington Road. (West Side, Downtown)

## Biking: On Mountain Bike Trails

### CHIVA FALLS

Go to the end of Tanque Verde Road, then follow the dirt Reddington Road about 4.5 miles to the trailhead. You'll find yourself mostly on Jeep roads, meaning rutted, rocky going on a path you may have to share with four-wheel-drive vehicles. It's 4.3 miles to the falls. You'll encounter four junctions along the way; just remember the pattern right, left, right, left (this last one comes after you've crossed the wash, which may or may not be running). It's a two-hour round trip for experienced riders; beginners may find themselves pushing their bikes at a few points. (East Side)

### SAGUARO NATIONAL PARK EAST
### 3693 S. Old Spanish Tr.

The short, lovely Cactus Forest Trail is the sole off-road path open to cyclists in this park. It takes you by some lovely desert scenery lush with plant life (at least by local standards) and not crawling with people. Trail maps are available at the main entrance. $2 admission fee. (East Side)

### STARR PASS TRAIL
### Near Starr Pass Golf Resort
### 3645 W. Starr Pass Blvd.

The best way to find the trailhead is to take Anklam Road west to the resort, turn left into it, and continue to the first stop sign. Hang a right on a dirt road just beyond the intersection. Keep right at the fork and eventually you'll come to the marked trail (but don't take off on the David Yet-

man hiking trail that shoots off to the right). Signs will direct you to the proper two-hour loop trail, which is a bit rocky (and, when it crosses a wash, sandy) and lined with prickly plant life. Sometimes rough but not exceptionally difficult. (West Side)

## Birding

### AUDUBON NATURE SHOP
### 300 E. University Blvd.
### 520/629-0510

When you think desert, the only birds that probably flutter into your mind are roadrunners, cactus wrens, and hawks (maybe also buzzards, of which there are none in Tucson's immediate vicinity). Yet 450 species of birds travel through the area annually. The enthusiastic volunteers at the Audubon Nature Shop will point you toward the prime birding areas, which vary somewhat according to time of year. Audubon also offers some guided field trips. Birders beyond serious should occasionally check the "Rare Bird Alert Hotline" (520/798-1005) for word on the latest unusual sightings. (Central-North)

### MADERA CANYON
### Take I-19 25 miles south to the
### Continental exit, then follow the
### signs.

Hummingbirds, flycatchers, summer tanagers, the luminescent varied bunting, and dozens of other birds hang out in this forested canyon, criss-crossed with hiking trails. You're on your own here; bring hiking boots, field glasses, and your life list. (South Side)

### RAMSEY CANYON
### Near Hereford (off Highway 92,
### south of Sierra Vista)

**Want to get away from it all without going too far?** Drive west on Speedway into the Tucson Mountains and over Gates Pass (where the road briefly becomes narrow and winding on its way down to the next valley; don't try it with an RV). Park in the lot at the foot of the mountains and tramp around the quiet desert trails for a while. You'll be close to Old Tucson, the Arizona–Sonora Desert Museum, and the International Wildlife Museum.

**520/378-2785**

A Nature Conservancy preserve, Ramsey Canyon is a sort of Club Med for hummingbirds. From April to September, as many as 13 species of hummers wile away the hours in the canyon. If, after the 90-mile drive out here, you don't feel like tramping around looking for them, the Conservancy has thoughtfully (for human and bird alike) set up a feeder area to make it easier to mingle with our fine feathered friends. Several other bird species migrate through the canyon, too. It's much easier for them than for us. Human admission is extremely limited, and reservations are required on weekends. Call the number above—preferably before you even arrive in Tucson. (East Side)

### Camping/Backpacking

#### SAGUARO NATIONAL PARK EAST; RINCON MOUNTAINS
**Just south of intersection of Old Spanish Trail and Freeman Road**
**520/733-5153**

The park rises from desert scrub through four different types of plant communities, finally ascending to mixed conifer forest at the summits of the Rincon Mountains. You can take day hikes with no hassle, but backcountry camping is allowed only at designated sites, and permits must be obtained before you set out at the park's visitors center (where you should also pick up a free map). Two campgrounds lie within six miles of a trailhead: Juniper Basin is approached via the Tanque Verde Ridge Trail, which takes off from the southernmost point of the park's paved loop road. You must approach Douglas Spring from the Douglas Spring Trail, which takes off from the east end of Speedway Boulevard (not from the loop road area). The park also contains three more-distant campgrounds and 75 miles of intersecting trails, some leading to peaks that rise above 8,000 feet. (East Side)

#### SAGUARO NATIONAL PARK WEST
**Off Kinney Road, just east of Sandario Road**
**520/733-5153 or 733-5158**

You can't actually camp within Saguaro West, but you may spend so much time surveying the desert terrain and climbing into the scrub-covered Tucson Mountains (high point: Wasson Peak, 4,687 feet) that you'd like to spend the night at the Gilbert Ray Campground, just a couple of miles south of Saguaro West in Tucson Mountain County Park (it's accessible by vehicle). Saguaro West's trails are fairly short, but most involve some elevation gain. Don't wander off the trails, or you could find yourself plummeting down an abandoned mineshaft. (West Side)

## SANTA CATALINA MOUNTAINS
**Take Tanque Verde Road east to Catalina Highway.**
**520/576-1321**
Part of Coronado National Forest, the Catalinas offer hiking through everything from saguaro-lined canyons to wildernesses of boulders, warm juniper and piñon forests, and a cool pine-shaded lake district. Several campgrounds pop up along the Catalina Highway, at least one in every vegetation zone, and none more than 45 minutes from the city. No permits are required to hike or camp here, but you must pay to use some of the campgrounds. A tollbooth at the base of the mountains collects an additional fee as your car begins its ascent. (Central-North, East Side)

## SANTA RITA MOUNTAINS/ MADERA CANYON
**Take I-19 to the Continental exit, south of Green Valley, then follow the signs.**
Because it's farther from Tucson, Madera Canyon doesn't often echo with the tread of armies of hikers. It's a popular spot, though, because dozens of miles of intersecting trails thread through the lovely forested canyon and up several nearby peaks (high point: Mount Wrightson, 9,453 feet). There's only one campground, Bog Springs, and it's accessible by car. A useful little map provided by the Friends of Madera Canyon may be available at the campground or at the parking lot at the end of the paved road. (South Side)

## Casinos

## CASINO OF THE SUN
**7406 S. Camino de Oeste**
**520/883-1700**
The self-proclaimed home of "500 of Arizona's loosest slots" has been newly renovated. In addition to one-armed bandits, the casino (operated by the Tohono O'odham Indian Nation, and therefore alcohol-free) offers live bingo, and keno, video poker, video blackjack, come-hither all-you-can-eat lunch and dinner buffets, and a couple of games called Megabucks and Quartermania. Open 24 hours, seven days a week. You must be at least 18 to enter. Take Interstate 19 to the Valencia exit, then drive five miles west on Valencia to the casino turnoff, marked by signs. (West Side)

## DESERT DIAMOND CASINO
**7350 S. Nogales Hwy.**
**520/294-7777**
This casino, too, prohibits alcohol, and anyone under 18, from the premises. No floor shows, either. All you do here, aside from accepting the occasional complimentary beverage or grabbing something from the snack bar, is gamble. You can contribute to the financial development of the Native Americans by pouring your money into hundreds

*Hiking near Tucson*

© Metro Tucson CVB/Gill Kenny

of quarter and dollar slot machines, video blackjack, craps, poker, and roulette, live poker and keno, or high stakes bingo. Open 'round the clock the entire year. If you're coming from Tucson's East Side, take the Kolb Road extension to Valencia Road. Drive past Tucson International Airport, then turn left on Old Nogales Highway. If you're coming from Tucson's West Side or Green Valley, take I-19 to the Valencia Road exit, drive east on Valencia, then turn right on the Nogales Highway. (South Side)

## Fishing

*Although it's a desert region, southern Arizona does have its share of lakes, all of which are regularly stocked to benefit fishing enthusiasts. Anglers will need to visit the Arizona Game & Fish Department (520/628-5376) to procure a general state fishing license, which costs $12. Those who want to fish for trout will also need a $10 trout stamp. (One-day fishing licenses cost $8.) Fishing inside Tucson city limits also requires a license—a $12 urban fishing license, which is also good for trout. The urban fishing lakes that are regularly stocked with catfish in the summer and trout in the winter are Silverbell Lake at Christopher Columbus Regional Park (West Side), and lakes at Kennedy Park (West Side) and Lakeside Park (East Side). Avid anglers might want to try the waters listed below.*

### PARKER CANYON LAKE
### Coronado National Forest
### 520/455-5847
This juniper- and oak-surrounded lake is close to the Mexican border, just west of Sierra Vista, Arizona. It is stocked with trout, bass, and bluegill.

Take Interstate 19 to State Highway 82 and follow the signs.

### PATAGONIA LAKE STATE PARK
### Patagonia, Arizona
### 520/287-6965
In addition to catfish, bass, bluegill, crappie, and trout, this large desert lake offers water- and Jet-Skiing, a good boat ramp and launch, and a designated swimming area. Take Interstate 19 south from Tucson for about an hour and follow the signs.

### ROSE CANYON LAKE
### Santa Catalina Mountains
### 520/749-8700
There's no boating and no swimming in this little lake near Mount Lemmon, but it does feature a relaxing pine-forest ambience, camping areas, and some great trout fishing. Take Tanque Verde Road east to the Catalina Highway, and continue on up the Mount Lemmon Highway toward, but not all the way to, the summit.

## Fitness Centers

### BALLY TOTAL FITNESS
### 4690 N. Oracle Rd.
### 520/293-2330
Energy is high in this cavernous, neon-bedecked gym. It offers a little of everything: free weights, weight machines, stationary bikes, and stair-steppers, plus a variety of extras: pool aerobics, wet and dry saunas, a Jacuzzi, an indoor track, and child-care. You may even find inspiration by watching through a glass-block wall as the aerobics classes do their thing. Open Mon–Fri 5 a.m.–midnight, Sat–Sun 6 a.m.–8 p.m. $10/day. (West Side)

### FITNESS AND HEALTH
### INSTITUTE OF TUCSON (FIT)
### 110 S. Church Ave.

# Top Five Hikes near Tucson

By Pete Cowgill, founder of the Arizona Hiking Club,
co-author with Eber Glendening of *The Trail Guide to the
Santa Catalina Mountains* (describing, with maps, nearly
100 trails and routes), and author of *Back Roads and Beyond
in Southern Arizona* (describing 20 mostly four-wheel-drive
roads, covering about 500 miles, that lead to great places
for hiking, camping, and hunting).

1. **Wasson Peak via King Canyon.** This is a seven-mile round-trip hike gaining 1,800 feet in elevation to the high point in the Tucson Mountains. This is a fall, winter, and spring hike.

    Drive west on Speedway or Anklam Road over Gates Pass and go right on Kinney Road to an unsigned dirt parking lot on the north side of the road, just beyond the signed entrance to the Arizona–Sonora Desert Museum. About 100 yards north of the parking lot is a gate with a sign-in register and map showing the route to the top of Wasson Peak.

    The first mile is an old mining road, lined with saguaro and palo verde. Where the road drops into King Canyon, bear right up the wash to where it forks. Go left and pick up the Wasson Peak Trail. It meanders eastward at first on an easy grade. It steepens and becomes more rocky, going into Sweetwater Saddle.

    Go left, climbing the ridge. The trail is good but fairly steep in places. Just east of the high saddle, go right ³⁄₁₀ mile to the top of Wasson Peak, elevation 4,687 feet. The 360-degree view is great.

2. **Romero Canyon Pools, Santa Catalina Mountains.** Many permanent pools, great for warm-weather swimming and diving, are 2.8 miles from the trailhead in Catalina State Park. The final two miles are steep and rocky. This is a hike for spring and fall.

    Drive Oracle Road (Arizona 77) north to the signed entrance to Catalina State Park. There is an entrance fee. Drive to the end of the road and the large parking area. The signed trail starts near the end of the turnaround. It crosses Sutherland Wash and swings around a low hill to the base of a rocky ridge. Here, the trail heads west, swinging around a couple of ridges into a saddle. It drops a short distance and then goes around the north side of a knob with views of several pools in the canyon below. The trail drops into the low divide between Romero and Montrose Canyons, and then comes to Romero Canyon.

    The major pools start about 100 feet downstream. Some are 20 or more feet deep. This is a popular destination for hikers in the warmer months of the year.

3. **Seven Falls in Bear Canyon, Santa Catalina Mountains.** These falls are probably in the most spectacular setting in southern Arizona. It is an eight-mile round trip on good trails, with about 700 feet of elevation. This is a fall, winter, and spring hike.

Drive on Sabino Canyon Road four miles north of Tanque Verde Road into the paved parking area at the signed Sabino Canyon Visitor Center. Park at the far east end of the lot. Hike due east on a wide trail and then a paved road. After crossing a second bridge over Sabino Creek, either follow the road to the right or take the signed Bear Canyon–Seven Falls Trail. The road ends at a rock restroom where the original Seven Falls Trail starts.

The wide trail parallels Bear Canyon, crossing it seven times. Water is in the canyon up to six months of the year. In the spring, wildflowers are abundant. After the last crossing, the trail switchbacks to about 200 feet above the canyon and heads to a sharp left bend in the canyon. Seven Falls is in this bend. A side trail goes to the falls. Many of the pools below the falls have permanent water. Experienced trail runners make a 16-mile loop going up Bear Canyon by Seven Falls and then coming back down Sabino Canyon.

4. **Aspen Trail–Marshall Gulch Loop, Santa Catalina Mountains.** This 3.7-mile loop is one of the most popular high-elevation hikes in the summer. The Aspen Trail climbs 700 feet. The trails are good and the route is signed. Drive up the Mount Lemmon Highway (a fee is charged) through Summerhaven to the Marshall Gulch Picnic Area, elevation 7,500 feet. On weekends, parking spaces are in short supply. This loop goes clockwise from the parking area.

   The Aspen Trail starts on the west side of the parking area and climbs steadily south. It soon wanders through a thick stand of quaking aspen trees, which turn a brilliant yellow in the fall. The trail follows a ridge northwest, circles the flattish, wooded Marshall Peak, and comes into Marshall Saddle, a five-way trail intersection. Many loops are possible using these trails.

   To complete this loop, bear right in the saddle and head down into Marshall Gulch, which has permanent water. The trail crosses the creek several times. Bigtooth maple trees abound. The trail climbs to about 100 feet on the north side of the creek and heads back down to the parking lot.

5. **Mount Wrightson (Old Baldy), Santa Rita Mountains.** This is the most popular peak climb in southern Arizona. It is 10.5 miles, and the 3,900 feet of elevation qualifies it as moderately difficult. The trail to the top of 9,453-foot Mount Wrightson is good but steep and rocky.

   Drive I-19 south to the Continental exit at Green Valley and follow the signs to the Madera Canyon Recreation Area. Drive to and park at the end of the road at Roundup. From the parking area, follow the old road up Madera Canyon to the signed start of the Mount Wrightson Trail. It climbs steadily to Josephine Saddle and then more steeply by Bellows Spring, where water can normally be obtained, to 8,800-foot Baldy Saddle. Backpackers occasionally camp here.

   Steep, rocky switchbacks on the north and south sides lead to the summit, the site of an abandoned lookout cabin. The view from the top is unsurpassed in southern Arizona. Summer lightning and thunderstorms are frequent.

**520/623-6300**

This is the site of a physician-owned cardiac rehab program as well as a regular gym. Free weights and machines; a variety of cardio equipment, such as Nordic tracks, rowing machines, and Versaclimbers; racquetball courts; wet and dry saunas; Jacuzzi; and an indoor pool are available. Nearby parking garage is at Stone Avenue and Jackson Street. Open Mon–Fri 5:30 a.m.–8:30 p.m., Sat 9–5, Sun 10–2. $5/day. (Downtown)

## METRO FITNESS
### 520/297-8000 or 751-0303

Whether you're on Tucson's West Side or East Side, you're probably fairly close to one of the Metro Fitness centers. They have free weights, weight machines, lots of cardio equipment, aerobics and water aerobics classes—as well as yoga, massage, tanning beds, childcare services, and personal trainers available for immediate hire. Open Mon–Fri 5 a.m.–11 p.m., Sat–Sun 7 a.m.–8 p.m. $8/day. (Central-North, West Side)

## WORLD GYM
### 1240 N. Stone Ave.

**520/882-8788**

If you're a serious lifter (or just want to steer clear of thongs and other fitness-center frippery), this is the gym for you. World Gym has a wide selection of well-maintained machines, sweat-producing cardio equipment, and, of course, a generous assortment of free weights. Gym etiquette, such as re-racking your weights, is strictly enforced. Open Mon–Thu 5:30 a.m.–10 p.m., Fri 5:30 a.m.–9 p.m., Sat 8 a.m.–7 p.m., Sun. 9 a.m.–5 p.m. $8/day. (Central-North)

## YMCA (DOWNTOWN-LOHSE FAMILY)
### 60 W. Alameda
### 520/623-5200

Several YMCAs around town have small workout facilities, but the two-story downtown branch offers the best selection. It has free weights, weight machines, cardio equipment including bikes and treadmills, aerobics classes, racquetball courts, and a semicovered, and heated pool. Childcare is available at this family-oriented facility. $7/day. Park on the street if you can or in the nearby county parking garage. Open Mon–Fri 6 a.m.–9 p.m., Sat 8–5, Sun 11–3. (Downtown)

Looking for a place to run without getting run over? Pima Community College, 2202 W. Anklam Road (West Side), has a fine, easy-on-the-knees track that's available to the public much of the time. Sabino Canyon, at the north end of Sabino Canyon Road (East Side), is a wonderful natural area. The asphalt road that crosses the creek nine times as it rises into the canyon is closed to vehicular traffic, and is a favorite path for joggers and walkers.

## Golf

*The major pastime in Tucson, aside from sweating, is golfing. It can be tough to get a tee time that perfectly suits your schedule, but there are plenty of courses to check into. Fees vary widely, not only from course to course but from season to season, and visitors pay a bit more than residents. Generally, green fees at municipal courses run between $10 and $20; the resorts and country clubs charge around $50 in the summer, double that in the winter. This section focuses on courses that are intended mainly for the general public, rather than country club members and resort guests.*

### ARTHUR PACK DESERT GOLF COURSE
**9101 N. Thornydale Rd.**
**520/744-3322**

"Desert" doesn't mean there's no lake at this par-72, 6,887-yard course, and local golfers have nothing but praise for how well the 18 greens are maintained. (West Side)

### DORADO GOLF COURSE
**6601 E. Speedway Blvd.**
**520/885-6751**

Dorado offers 18 holes, 3,751 yards, par 62. The Executive course features ten par-3 holes and eight par 4s, on bentgrass greens. You also get fine mountain views for your money. (East Side)

### EL RIO MUNICIPAL GOLF COURSE
**1400 W. Speedway Blvd.**
**520/623-6783**

If you think the flat terrain looks too easy, consider that the greens are small and the fairways are tight at this 18-hole, 6,418-yard, par-70 course. Plenty of trees and a couple of modest lakes drive off thoughts of the desert,

if that's what you hope to accomplish. The course opened in the 1930s as part of a country club and was the original site of the Tucson Open. It's been a public facility since 1968. (West Side)

### FRED ENKE MUNICIPAL GOLF COURSE
**8251 E. Irvington Rd.**
**520/296-8607**

Think desert. Think sand traps. Some pretty serious ones lie in wait at this par-72, 6,809-yard, 18-hole course. And the ninth hole—4,555 yards, par 4—has brought good golfers to tears. (East Side)

### THE LINKS AT CONTINENTAL RANCH
**Between I-10 and the Santa Cruz River, a mile north of Ina Road**
**520/744-7443**

Designed to look, feel, and play like a windy, seaside golf course in Scotland, this is a new 18-hole, 6,950-yard, par-72 course. The thick heather and gorse of Scottish fairways has been replaced in out-of-play areas by such native drought-resistant Southwest flora as curly mesquite grass and purple three-awn. Bermuda grass is used on the fairways, with over-seeding of rye grass in the winter. Another Scottish-inspired feature is the chain-like, end-to-end layout. One more bit of Scotland: The Links is windswept about 60 to 70 percent of the time. (West Side)

### RANDOLPH MUNICIPAL COURSES
**600 S. Alvernon Way**
**520/325-2811**

There are two 18-hole courses at this facility. The north course (6,902 yards, par 72) is the site of the PING Welch's LPGA Open, with all that implies. The south course (6,229 yards, par 70) is to

*Golf among the saguaros*

golf what the bunny slope is to skiing: smooth, quick, straightforward, and not a source of frustration to beginners. Both are in a lovely park setting in the middle of the city. (Central-North)

### RAVEN GOLF CLUB AT SABINO SPRINGS
**9777 E. Sabino Greens Dr.**
**520/749-3636**

This gorgeous new facility in the Catalina foothills, designed by Robert Trent Jones Jr., hugs the natural contours of the saguaro-guarded desert—not that several elevated trees and bent-grass greens don't pose more traditional challenges. You'll find 18 holes on this par-71, 6,776-yard course. (East Side)

### SANTA RITA GOLF COURSE
**16461 S. Houghton Rd.**
**520/762-5620**

If you're visiting during hot weather, make the trek out to this par-71, 6,396-yard, 18-hole course. It's a thousand feet above the city and a few degrees

cooler. You also get great views, and after a post-game visit to the Santa Rita Country Club's Desert Dove Restaurant, you won't have to listen to your stomach growl on the ride back to town. (East Side)

### SHERATON EL CONQUISTADOR RESORT AND COUNTRY CLUB
**10000 N. Oracle Rd.**
**520/544-1770**

The rolling nine-hole, 2,788-yard, par-35 Resort Course wraps around the resort itself. This means, of course, that the fairways are unforgivingly slender, and the greens are compact. Watch out for the cactus along the way. The Sheraton's 18-hole, par-72 Sunrise and Sunset courses give priority tee times to country club members; it can be tough for non-members to squeeze in, but it is possible, in theory (520/544-1800). (West Side)

### SILVERBELL MUNICIPAL GOLF COURSE
**3600 N. Silverbell Rd.**
**520/743-7284**

# Top Ten Athletes From Tucson
## By Greg Hanson, *Arizona Daily Star* sports columnist

1. **Sean Elliott.** Homegrown, NCAA basketball Player of the Year, twice an NBA All-Star for the San Antonio Spurs.

2. **Fred W. Enke.** Believe it or not, he was the last former UA quarterback to play steadily in the NFL, from 1948 to 1955. He was also Arizona's last three-sport athlete of note, a football, basketball, and baseball standout. His father, Fred Enke, won 523 games as the UA's basketball coach from 1931 to 1960.

3. **Terry Francona.** Manager of the Philadelphia Phillies. He was the NCAA baseball Player of the Year for the UA, winning the 1980 National Championship.

4. **The Bates Brothers.** Take your pick: Michael, Mario, and Marion were all-state football players at Amphi High School. Michael went on to win the bronze medal in the 200 meters at the 1992 Summer Olympics and has twice been an All-Pro kick returner for the Carolina Panthers. Mario, a tailback for the New Orleans Saints, was a 1,000-yard rusher at Arizona State.

5. **Crissy Ahmann.** From nearby Benson, of all places, Crissy earned a swimming scholarship at the UA and in 1992 won two gold medals and two silvers in the Summer Olympics in Barcelona, Spain.

6. **John Fina.** He was a 210-pound senior at Salpointe Catholic High School in 1987, later a standout tackle at the UA. Now he is a seven-year starter for the NFL Buffalo Bills, at almost 300 pounds. Oh, yes, he has two Super Bowl rings.

7. **Annika Sorenstam.** She is the world's best female golfer, No. 1 on the LPGA money list in 1997, twice the Women's Open champion, and a former NCAA champion while playing for the Arizona Wildcats.

8. **Rodney Peete.** While at Sahuaro High School, Peete led the Cougars to state titles in baseball and basketball, then led USC to a Rose Bowl title before making millions as an NFL quarterback.

9. **Steve Kerr.** No other Tucsonan is more popular than Kerr, the former Arizona Wildcat who led his team to the 1988 Final Four. His jump shot with three seconds left in the 1997 NBA Finals gave the Chicago Bulls another world championship.

10. **Kerri Strug.** Our courageous, 88-pound gymnast crept into the hearts of Americans with her gold medal–clinching vault in the '96 Summer Olympics.

The view—of the Tucson and Catalina Mountains—is far hillier than the course. The fairways may be spacious, but the par-5 17th hole has a killer reputation. You may give up and go fishing in the park immediately north of the course.But that's not an option in any of the golf course's nine lakes. The 18-hole Silverbell Course is par 72 and 6,824 yards; watch out for the wind and the strategically placed trees. (West Side)

## STARR PASS GOLF CLUB
**3645 W. Starr Pass Blvd.**
**520/670-0400**
One of Tucson's newer courses, this one—par 71, 6,910 yards, 18 holes—hosts the Northern Telecom Open, a stop on the PGA Tour. The fairways are Bermuda grass, the greens (many of them elevated) are bent-grass, but much of the rest of the landscape bristles with cacti and rocks. The course is nestled into the foothills of the Tucson Mountains, a beautiful desert setting. (West Side)

## VENTANA CANYON GOLF COURSES
**7000 N. Resort Dr.**
**520/299-2020**
Two Tom Fazio–designed 18-hole courses await you here. The Canyon Course (6,818 yards, par 72) winds through Esperero Canyon with a magnificent mountain backdrop. You may have to concentrate too hard to enjoy the scenery on the much more difficult Mountain Course (6,926 yards, par 72), which employs parts of the natural desert landscape as formidable obstacles. (East Side)

## Horseback Riding

*Forget those images of Indians astride fiery steeds racing across the desert sands. Today's riding stables offer safe, single-file rides that even the most timid non rider can handle. Many of them are clustered along Tucson's far East and West Sides and offer guided "group rides" that are really more like "group sits." (But at least you don't have to worry about getting saddled with a wild runaway horse.) Among the city's many riding stables are those below.*

## COLOSSAL CAVE MOUNTAIN PARK STABLES
**16600 Colossal Cave Rd.**
**520/647-3450**
This stable offers guided trail rides, with horses walking in single file, through desert at the base of the Rincon Mountains. It also features hayrides, stagecoach rides, and an overnight camp trip for $120/person. Prices for group rides: one hour, $20/person; 90 minutes, $30/person; two hours, $40/person. Children under 5 can ride on the same horse as their parent or guardian for $5. Open daily. (East Side)

## DESERT-HIGH COUNTRY STABLES
**6501 W. Ina Rd.**
**520/744-3789**
This stable provides leisurely guided horseback rides that wind through the foothills of the Tucson Mountains and Saguaro National Park West. Prices: one hour, $15/person; 90 minutes, $18/person; two hours, $20/person; half-day, $40/person; full day, $60/person. Horse-drawn wagon rides are also available for $6 per person over age 7, $3 for kids 3–6. Fully catered campfire meals can also be arranged. (West Side)

## PUSCH RIDGE STABLES
**13700 N. Oracle Rd.**
**520/825-1664**

Trails through more than 10,000 acres of desert and mountain land, in Catalina State Park and Coronado National Forest, lie before your rented steed's hooves. The stables offer outings for both advanced and novice riders with all sorts of interests: sunset rides, steak rides, breakfast rides, moonlit rides, a "lovers' retreat," overnight trips, and hayrides. Prices vary widely according to the nature of the ride. (West Side)

## TANQUE VERDE GUEST RANCH
**14310 E. Speedway Blvd.**
**520/296-6275 or 800/234-DUDE**
If you want to immerse yourself in the horse experience, this 640-acre former cattle ranch (which has been a guest ranch since the 1920s) may be just the ticket. It has more than 100 horses for guest use, three group rides daily, riding lessons, and walking rides for beginners. Also available: hiking, biking, tennis pros. Prices vary according to season; call for details. (East Side)

## WALKING WINDS STABLES
**10811 N. Oracle Rd.**
**520/742-4422**
Offers single-file, walking guided trail rides through scenic Catalina State Park, as well as private rides for experienced riders. Prices: one

hour, $15/person; two hours, $28/person; three hours, $55/person; 90-minute sunset rides, $23/person. (West Side)

### *Helicopter Tours*

## PAPILLON HELICOPTERS
**1921 E. Flight Line Dr.**
**520/573-6817**
A 30-minute buzz of the city, Saguaro National Park West, and the Catalina foothills costs $80 per person, with a two-person minimum. A 60-minute tour that additionally crosses over the Catalinas' high point (Mount Lemmon) and continues to Biosphere 2 and back costs double that. A 30-minute "City Lights" night tour runs $80 per person, with the same two-passenger minimum. (South Side)

### *Hot-Air Ballooning*

## BALLOON AMERICA
**520/299-7744**
Hot-air balloon rides with views of the Catalina and Rincon Mountain ranges, piloted by FAA-certified commercial pilots, are on the menu here. Self-billed as "Tucson's only full-time professional balloon company," Balloon America has operated here since 1980. It is the only company permitted to launch from a

---

**T** **I** **P**

If you're an in-line skating enthusiast but couldn't fit your gear into your luggage, don't despair. You can rent skates and protective equipment from *Peter Glenn Ski & Sports* (520/745-4514), *Play It Again Sports* (520/795-0363 and 296-6888), or the *Sports Authority* (520/292-6955).

*Horseback riding*

© Metro Tucson CVB/Gill Kenny

private area on the East Side of town. Its "Desert Sunrise" hot-air balloon tour costs $135 per person. Enjoy a champagne mimosa toast after the flight. (East Side)

### A SOUTHERN ARIZONA BALLOON EXCURSION
**520/624-3599**
This outfit offers hot-air balloon rides with FAA-certified commercial pilots. Balloonists can ride along the West Side Tucson Mountains/Interstate 10 corridor daily in the winter, unless it's raining or very windy. The balloon gondolas can carry from two to ten people. Rides last from one hour to 90 minutes, and culminate in a cele-bratory orange juice/champagne toast. The cost is $125 per person. (West Side)

## Rock Climbing

### ROCKS AND ROPES
**330 S. Toole, Suite 400**
**520/882-5924**
This indoor climbing gym offers

personalized instruction, equipment rental, and several 35-foot-high simulated-rock walls for practice. It has 8,000 square feet of climbing space. Gym admission is $8 a day; equipment rental costs $6 a day. A first-time package for beginning climbers goes for $30. Reservations recommended for groups of six or more. Rocks and Ropes also offers guided instruction for rock-climbing visits to nearby Mount Lemmon. (Downtown)

### WINDY POINT OVERLOOK
**Santa Catalina Mountains, via the Catalina Highway**
A popular destination for outdoor rock-climbing enthusiasts. If you're a novice climber (or have only climbed at indoor gyms), professional instruc-tion is essential before attempting Windy Point. The Summit Hut, which sells mountain and rock-climbing equipment, is a good place to seek tips on local climbing associations and other climbing destinations (520/325-1554). (East Side)

## Skating

### BLADEWORLD
**1065 W. Grant Rd.**
**520/624-1234**
Billed as "Arizona's premiere in-line hockey facility," Bladeworld offers roller hockey leagues, lessons, clinics, and camps. Daily admission is $10 plus tax. Full equipment (including a hel-met, facepiece, elbow pads, and a hockey stick) is required. (West Side)

### ICEOPLEX
**7333 E. Rosewood**
**520/290-8800**
This large ice skating center has a family atmosphere and offers skating lessons, in-house youth and adult

hockey leagues, figure skating, and ice hockey equipment rental. It's the only ice skating rink in Tucson. Public-session times are Mon–Fri 9:30–11:30 a.m. and 1:30–5 p.m., and Sat–Sun 1–4 p.m. Evening public sessions are Fri–Sat 7:30–10:15 p.m. Admission is $6.50 for adults, $5.50 for kids 12 and younger. (East Side)

### SKATE COUNTRY
### 2700 N. Stone Ave.
### 520/622-6650

Yes, Virginia, people do still roller skate. And in Tucson, they do it at one of two Skate Country rinks—replete with cement floors, blasting tunes, and, of course, rental equipment for the skateless. Admission is $3; skate rental is $1.75. Public skating sessions are Tue 8–10:30 p.m. (adults only); Sat 7–noon, 1–10; Sun 1–8. Also at 7980 E. 22nd Street (520/298-4409). (West Side)

## *Skiing*

### MOUNT LEMMON SKI VALLEY
### Mount Lemmon, via the Catalina Highway
### 520/576-1321

With a ski school, skiing, and snow-boarding only an hour's drive from Tucson, Mount Lemmon's only major drawback is that it may not have enough snow for good skiing conditions. It pays to call the Snow Report line (520/576-1400) before venturing up the mountain. The ski center is open daily 9–4. Lift tickets: $28 for adults, $12 children. Equipment rentals: $15 adults, $10 children.

## *Swimming Pools*

*If you visit Tucson during the summer, at least one trip to a pool is almost essential. You'll find them at hotels,* *motels, and resorts of all calibers; most YMCAs around town (520/795-9725); and at plenty of public schools and parks. Make sure to use sunscreen. In the wintertime public pools are closed, but you'll still find lots of indoor pools (such as the large, heated, partially indoor pool at the Downtown-Lohse Family YMCA; 520/623-5200). For a full listing of public pools, check the phone book Blue Pages under "Tucson City Government—Parks & Recreation Department—Swimming Pools." Here are the prime public swimming holes:*

### CATALINA HIGH SCHOOL POOL
### 3645 E. Pima St.
### 520/791-4245 (Central-North)

### OURY PARK POOL
### 600 W. St. Mary's Rd.
### 520/791-4186 (West Side)

### SUNNYSIDE HIGH SCHOOL POOL
### 1725 E. Bilby Rd.
### 520/791-5167 (South Side)

*Tennis in Tucson
(Is that a saguaro in the background?)*

© Metro Tucson CVB/Gill Kenny

**UDALL POOL**
**7200 E. Tanque Verde Rd.**
**520/791-4004 (East Side)**

## Tennis

**FT. LOWELL PARK**
**2900 N. Craycroft Rd.**
**520/791-2584**
This centrally located park has eight
lighted tennis courts. Use costs $1.50
per person per half-hour of play.
(Central-North)

**HIGH SCHOOL TENNIS COURTS**
Tennis courts are available, after
hours, at several local high schools,
notably Catalina High (3645 E. Pima
St., Central-North) and Rincon High
(422 N. Arcadia, East Side). There is
no charge to use them.

**HIMMEL PARK**
**1000 N. Tucson Blvd.**
**520/791-3276**

Another centrally located park with
eight lighted tennis courts. It also
costs $1.50 per person per each half-
hour of playing time. (Central-North)

**PIMA COMMUNITY COLLEGE**
**WEST CAMPUS**
**2202 W. Anklam Rd.**
The lighted courts are available free
to the public whenever they're not
being used by the community college.
They're especially convenient for
people staying downtown or just
west of that district. (West Side)

**RANDOLPH TENNIS CENTER**
**100 S. Alvernon Way**
**520/791-4896**
The city's largest public tennis center, located in Reid Park, has 25
lighted tennis courts and 10 racquetball courts. They are assigned on a
first-come, first-served basis. Each
person pays $1.50 per half-hour of
play. (Central-North)

# 11

# PERFORMING ARTS

*In Tucson, the wild and the mild of local culture both call into the night. Rarely, one howl attempts to drown out the other. But usually the two voices sing out in a mildly dissonant counterpoint, quite independent of each other. Shoestring theater companies loudly confront questions of race, rights, and sexuality, while more entrenched institutions uphold the standards of venerable Western culture. Such is the cultural climate of Tucson, which is both a conservative retirement mecca and a progressive college town. The experimental younger set and the older guardians of high culture largely ignore one another, although the arts groups they support undoubtedly would appreciate more intermingling at the box office.*

*More constructive audience participation would make the local arts even stronger. The traditional arts institutions' core audience and donor group is discriminating enough to expect a certain level of professionalism but rarely pushes innovation in programming. Meanwhile, the little alternative theater and dance groups are driven by visionary leaders and attended by small audiences. These companies rarely achieve the critical mass of filled seats and solid bank accounts that permit full professionalization. So you pays your money and you takes your choice: polished, mainstream, thoughtful presentations of the classics, or rougher, provocative presentations of new work. Either way, chances are good that you'll happen upon a performance that is in some way compelling.*

## THEATER

**ARIZONA REPERTORY THEATRE**
**UA Marroney Theatre and**
**Laboratory Theatres**

**Speedway Blvd. and Park Ave.**
**520/621-1162**
Though it features UA drama students, this entity showcases young actors ready to be unleashed upon

the theater world and gives them the benefit of fine production values. Recent shows have included classics by Molière and Shakespeare, old chestnuts like *Arsenic and Old Lace*, and such new work as Robert Schenkkan's massive, Pulitzer Prize–winning *The Kentucky Cycle*. (Central-North)

## ARIZONA THEATRE COMPANY
**Alice Holsclaw Theatre**
**Temple of Music and Art**
**330 S. Scott Ave.**
**520/622-2823**

The state's official theater company, ATC opens its shows in Tucson, then carries them to Phoenix, for about a one-month run in each municipality. Although ATC may occasionally lavish its attention on a questionable play, the acting, directing, and production will usually please patrons accustomed to the best regional theaters and Broadway. The six-production season recipe calls for one classic (often Shakespeare), a twentieth-century standard or two, a musical revue, and recent plays by the likes of August Wilson, Athol Fugard, and Steven Dietz. Another good reason to patronize ATC is to get a good look at the Temple of Music and Art, a lovely Southwestern-style hall built in the late 1920s (see Chapter 5, Sights and Attractions). (Downtown)

## BORDERLANDS THEATER
**Pima Community College**
**Proscenium and Black Box**
**Theaters**
**2202 W. Anklam Rd.**
**520/882-7406**

Although Borderlands sometimes juxtaposes material and actors that are highly professional with those that are faintly amateurish, the company is always up to something interesting, exploring the collisions of culture and gender. The material tends to be new, although the company has reached back as far as Spanish Golden-Ager Lope de Vega. (West Side)

## GASLIGHT THEATRE
**7010 E. Broadway Blvd.**
**520/886-9428**

Over-the-top parody and melodrama pack this house night after night. Western adventure, pirate tales, science fiction, and '50s suburbia are all fair game for the Gaslight's punning, slapstick treatment, complete with musical numbers stolen from the grave of midcentury pop radio. Hissing the villain is mandatory. The Gaslight is also the closest thing Tucson has to a

You can pay $3 or more above the face price of a ticket if you order through certain box offices. Dillard's and TicketMaster, for example, apply service charges to all their transactions. You can avoid most of these charges if you buy tickets directly from the producers of the performance (the individual dance company, the Tucson Symphony, etc.). Or go straight to the venue's own box office. For instance, the Centennial Hall box office sells tickets for all sorts of things as part of the Dillard's network, and slaps a service charge onto each transaction—*except* for tickets to events in Centennial itself.

*Arizona Theatre Company's 1997-98 production of* Five Guys Named Moe

dinner theater; patrons sit at tables, munch free popcorn, and have the option of buying pizza, sodas, beer, and ice cream. But be prepared for disappointment: Shows may sell out weeks in advance. (East Side)

### INVISIBLE THEATRE
**1400 N. First Ave.**
**520/882-9721**
Once Tucson's only cutting-edge theater company, IT is easing into middle age with seasons heavy on romantic comedy, cabaret, and musical revue. Founder and artistic director Susan Claassen may have her eye on increasing the box office receipts, but she hasn't lost her social conscience. IT still presents new plays that sharply comment on the plight of outsiders in Western culture. Productions have a particular physical immediacy—the little theater seats fewer than 100. (West Side)

### THEATER LEAGUE
**Tucson Convention Center**
**Music Hall**

**260 S. Church Ave.**
**520/888-0509**
Big musicals of a certain vintage, plus more recent sure winners like *Cats*, are mounted—often starring TV actors of a certain vintage—and put on the road, with Tucson as one of a half-dozen stops. The standards tend to be high, except on those few nights when travel fatigue sets in. (Downtown)

## CLASSICAL MUSIC AND OPERA

### ARIZONA EARLY MUSIC SOCIETY
**520/889-4310**
Music composed before 1750 is the bread and butter of this presenting organization, which brings in established but not superstar performers, such as harpsichordist John Gibbons and the Baltimore Consort, as well as up-and-coming vocal and instrumental ensembles from around the world. Concerts are held at the attractive St. Philip's in the Hills Episcopal Church, 4440 N. Campbell Avenue, built in the 1930s in a modified Mission style (see Chapter 5, Sights and Attractions). The acoustics are good, but the sight lines are as unsatisfactory as in any church. Fortunately, a picture window behind the altar provides a grand view of desert vegetation and the Catalina Mountains. (Central-North)

### ARIZONA FRIENDS OF CHAMBER MUSIC
**520/298-5806**
For half a century this group has brought to Tucson such luminous ensembles as the Beaux Arts Trio and the Emerson String Quartet, as well as groups of lesser renown but high quality. The main series presents seven concerts each season; the "Piano and

Friends" series offers four programs by unknown but promising young pianists, often in the company of a string player. The Friends also sponsor the Tucson Winter Chamber Music Festival in early March, a week of concerts featuring a well-known anchoring ensemble and the same musicians you'd find at festivals in Santa Fe or La Jolla—with similarly high standards and interesting programming ideas. All performances are in the acoustically dry but intimate Tucson Convention Center Leo Rich Theatre. (Downtown)

### ARIZONA OPERA
### 520/791-4836

The company mounts five operas each season in Tucson, then packs them off to Phoenix for additional runs. Repertory is very conservative—*Turandot* (1924) is the most recent work presented in the past 15 years. This is not to say that Arizona Opera relies exclusively on war-horses; Gounod's *Roméo et Juliette*, Ponchielli's *La Gioconda*, Delibes' *Lakmé* and a complete Wagner *Ring* cycle have found their way into the mix. With the recent retirement of general director Glynn Ross, formerly of Seattle Opera, things may—or may not—change. As is the case with regional companies, the singers vary from wobbly to excellent, with the majority operating at the high end of the scale. Scenery and stage direction look like high school work on a bigger budget, but the orchestra can be wonderful, especially when the Phoenix Symphony guests in the pit (usually for Wagner, Strauss, and Mozart). (Downtown)

### TUCSON SYMPHONY ORCHESTRA
### 520/882-8585

Founded in 1929 as a determined but probably scrappy group favoring light classics and German symphonists, the Tucson Symphony has grown into a highly capable band with a $2.2 million annual budget. Since his 1996 appointment, music director George Hanson has been refining the orchestra's sound and bringing increased vitality to performances in the Tucson Convention Center Music Hall. The season is built around nine classical programs for full orchestra, trimmed with a four-concert pops series, and sprinkled with a four-concert chamber orchestra series and several chamber music recitals. These latter two groups of events are usually held at the Pima Community College Center

## TRIVIA

The Tucson Symphony Orchestra's gala 50th anniversary concert in the 1979–80 season included a second-half laser show to accompany Scriabin's *Prometheus*. But the display was delayed about 15 minutes. The laser projector's water-coolant system couldn't be activated; during intermission, water pressure in the TCC Music Hall had plunged because of all the flushing toilets. Since then, the Music Hall's plumbing has been fortified, with the benefit of additional restrooms hidden away on the lobby's mezzanine.

# Buying Tickets for Tucson Events

*Most of the organizations listed in this chapter sell admission to their own events by phone. Tickets to many performances are also available through one or more of these central box offices:*

**Berger Performing Arts Center information line:** *520/770-3690*
**Dillard's:** *800/638-4253*
**Pima Community College Center for the Arts:** *520/884-6988*
**TicketMaster:** *520/321-1000*
**Tucson Convention Center main box office:** *520/791-4266*
**University of Arizona Centennial Hall:** *520/621-3341*

---

for the Arts, 2202 W. Anklam Road. (Downtown, West Side)

## UNIVERSITY OF ARIZONA MUSIC FACULTY
### 520/621-1162

Most Monday nights during the school year, UA music professors prove that they can perform as well as teach, in the school's midsized but resonant Crowder Hall or in the smaller and even more echoey Holsclaw Recital Hall. They're both in the music building south of the East Speedway pedestrian underpass, east of North Park Avenue. Tickets go for bargain prices, and, of course, the school's students may be heard in free recitals many other nights of the week. The UA also presents orchestral and band concerts and opera productions a few times each semester. (Central-North)

## DANCE

### BALLET ARIZONA
### 602/381-1096 or 888/3-BALLET

This Phoenix-based classical ballet company sends most of its shows south for Tucson runs. Recent productions have ranged from the inevitable *Nutcracker* through an evening of pieces choreographed by George Balanchine to artistic director Michael Uthoff's setting of *Alice in Wonderland* to music by Bach and the Red Hot Chili Peppers. Performances are either in the lovely, intimate Pima Community College Proscenium Theatre or the larger, generic Tucson Convention Center Music Hall. (Downtown, West Side)

### BALLET ARTS FOUNDATION
### 520/623-3373

The semipro organization has recently specialized in repertory programs of short classical works, as well as its own holiday *Nutcracker*. (Downtown)

### ORTS THEATRE OF DANCE
### 520/624-3799

Tucson's leading modern dance ensemble, led by Anne Bunker, never shies away from the quirky—much of the group's recent work has been

*Tucson Latin Jazz Orchestra*

done on trapezes. Bunker is also increasingly devoted to multimedia presentations, collaborating with writers, videographers, fiber artists, and such musicians as Navajo-Ute flutist R. Carlos Nakai. (West Side)

## SOUTHWEST DANCE
### 602/482-6410
This presenting organization brings in classical, modern, jazz, and ethnic dance companies from around the world. Traditional ballet hasn't been selling well in Tucson, so the offerings these days are more likely to involve Latin American folk dance than *Swan Lake*, although the Stars of the Kirov were a well-attended 1997 attraction. (Downtown)

## TENTH STREET DANCEWORKS
### 520/795-6980
As modern dance companies go, Tenth Street Danceworks is rather more conventional than Orts (above), but the company does present a

steady stream of new work. (West Side)

## TUCSON REGIONAL BALLET
### 520/886-1222
Here's a group populated by community dancers rather than hotshot ballerinas on the fast track to New York. Programs tend to mix classical and contemporary pieces; recent years have also brought Christmastime mountings of *The Nutcracker* in a Southwestern setting. Performances are usually in the smallish Tucson Convention Center Leo Rich Theatre. (Downtown)

## UNIVERSITY OF ARIZONA DANCE DIVISION
### 520/621-4698
The entire gamut of dance, aside from the full-length classical staples, is offered in the UA's Ina Gittings Building, once known dully as Women's P.E. The faculty members are quite accomplished and may be seen on the stage

almost as often as their students. Teachers and students alike provide the choreography. (Central-North)

## JAZZ

### TUCSON JAZZ SOCIETY
### 520/743-3399
Jazz would be a feeble thing in Tucson if left to the bar owners, so the Tucson Jazz Society stands as one of the city's most essential concert sponsors. The group presents formal but outdoor shows in the spring, early summer, and fall at St. Philip's Plaza, 4830 N. Campbell Avenue. The mix includes locals and visiting musicians of national repute, often playing together. There's some emphasis on Latin jazz, but it is by no means an obsession. The Jazz Society also presents a big free show, Jazz Sundae, on one Sunday afternoon in October at Reid Park. Its springtime Primavera concert, at Pima Community College, showcases women in jazz. (Central-North)

## CONCERT VENUES

### BERGER PERFORMING
### ARTS CENTER
### Arizona State Schools for
### the Deaf and the Blind
### 1400 W. Speedway Blvd.
### 520/770-3690
This 500-seat hall, wider than it is deep, has become a popular home for community orchestras, local unaligned chamber musicians, and various presenters of pop and folk music. Acoustically, Berger has proved to be quite satisfactory, even though it's a new hall in an era of bad acoustic design. The one problem is parking. You cannot drive into what looks like the main campus entrance; you must either park in the lot at the west end of the school, which is right next to the auditorium, or, if it's full (and it fills fast), turn around and park in the lot at the east end (closest to the freeway) and thread your way on foot through the school complex. (West Side)

### CENTENNIAL HALL
### University of Arizona
### Park Ave. and University Blvd.
### 520/621-3341
The city's largest concert hall—not counting stadiums and arenas—this 2,400-seat auditorium is excellent for symphonic, dance, and amplified music programs, but can dwarf acoustic ensembles and puts mush in the mouths of actors without microphones. The university's UA*presents*

## TRIVIA

Two favorite concert venues in Tucson are Episcopal churches: St. Philip's in the Hills, 4440 N. Campbell Avenue (at River Road), and Grace St. Paul's, 2331 E. Adams Street (four blocks north of Speedway, between Campbell Avenue and Tucson Boulevard). Tucson Episcopalians apparently enjoy natural gluteal padding, judging from their hard pews; you may wish to carry a cushion.

series offers about 10 different event packages, including classical music (pianist André Watts, the New York City Opera, and Vladimir Ashkenazy and the German Symphony Orchestra of Berlin have been recent guests), touring Broadway shows, world music, performance artists, cutting-edge dance, and jazz. All events are offered separately, of course, and only the biggest celebrities (violinist Itzhak Perlman, for example) tend to sell out. (Central-North)

## PIMA COMMUNITY COLLEGE CENTER FOR THE ARTS
**2202 W. Anklam Rd.**
**520/884-6988**

It doesn't look promising from the street—a boring square building rising from one end of a community college campus—but the PCC Center for the Arts contains the city's finest small theater and two other quite serviceable little venues. The Proscenium Theatre is graced with excellent acoustics; there's not a single bad seat in the house, not even the boxes along the side. (Watch your step, though; the stairs in the back area are steep.) The Black Box Theatre, used almost exclusively for plays, and the Recital Hall are less remarkable but workable spaces. The facility has quickly become popular not just with college faculty and students, but with such discriminating larger organizations as the Tucson Symphony. (West Side)

## RIALTO THEATER
**318 E. Congress St.**
**520/740-0126**

A wonderful old movie house dating from the vaudeville era, when such venues were also equipped with stages, the Rialto fell into disrepair and disrepute in the 1970s and '80s.

Jennifer Girard

*River North Dance Co. presented by Southwest Dance, p. 180*

Now, though, it is being gradually revived and renovated as a theater for live performances—largely, but not exclusively, touring blues artists. The murals are getting spruced up, the balcony is being brought up to code, and the place is regaining its decadent allure. Until recently, the entrance has been easy to miss amid the storefronts; it's on the south side of the street, roughly across from Hotel Congress. (Downtown)

## TUCSON CONVENTION CENTER
**260 S. Church Ave.**
**520/791-4266**

This complex, completed in the early 1970s, would stand as Tucson's civic cultural center if its programming were more coherent and some of the major arts groups weren't operating in their own buildings a few blocks away. The 2,200-seat TCC Music Hall serves as the performance base for the Tucson Symphony Orchestra and Arizona Opera, and hosts various visiting productions requiring lots of flyspace or plentiful seating. The lower balcony offers the best sound, but you might want to bring opera glasses for a better look at what's on stage. The Leo Rich Theatre, about a quarter the Music Hall's size, was designed for actors rather than musicians, so the sound is dry. These days, the Arizona Friends of Chamber Music and presenters of visiting folk and ethnic musicians book Leo Rich more than anyone else. The TCC Arena, as you might guess, is the venue of choice for anything expected to draw crowds 10,000-strong, from Reba McEntire to Barney to the Ice Capades. Performances are also sometimes mounted in the Grand Ballroom, or, more rarely, in one of the two exhibition halls or underground meeting rooms. (Downtown)

# 12

# NIGHTLIFE

*Maybe people used to raise hell in Tucson all night long, but now most nightspots lock up around 1 a.m. And another thing—even though this is the West, if you wander into a bar or club, you're more likely to hear alternative rock than country-western music. So much for stereotypes. The good news is that if you plan ahead and know where to look, you can usually find whatever sort of entertainment you desire and still be in bed by a decent hour. You can, indeed, get your country kicks, dine while a mariachi trumpeter blares in your ear, sip wine to soft jazz, knock back a few designer coffee drinks, or catch the latest Eastern European art film. Maybe all in the same evening.*

## MUSIC CLUBS

### *Jazz*

### CAFÉ SWEETWATER
**340 E. Sixth St.**
**520/622-6464**
On the corner of Sixth Street and Fourth Avenue, this sleek restaurant leaning toward seafood and pasta is also one of the few reliable jazz venues in town. Sometimes the sounds are Latin, sometimes standards, but they almost always can

be heard on Friday and Saturday 9:30 to 12:30. No cover. (Downtown)

### CASCADE LOUNGE
**Loews Ventana Canyon Resort**
**7000 N. Resort Dr.**
**520/299-2020**
Soft jazz for dancing is offered at this elegant resort lounge. A long-time standby here is excellent Tucson vocalist Martha Reed, with her trio. Fri–Sat 9:30–midnight. There's also live piano music Sun–Thu 10–midnight. No cover. (East Side)

## Blues

### BOONDOCKS LOUNGE
### 3306 N. First Ave.
### 520/690-0991

The place with a big concrete wine bottle out front—it started out as a Continental restaurant—is the only joint in Tucson where you can expect to hear blues (from the likes of ex-Tucsonan Sam Taylor) on a regular basis. Reggae and other styles do sneak in, though, via groups like Neon Prophet. Live music Friday and Saturday 9 to 1. Cover usually about $3. (Central-North)

## Latin/Mariachi

### EL MARIACHI
### 106 W. Drachman St.
### 520/791-7793

Nobody patronizes El Mariachi just for the food, which is entirely ordinary. The draw, instead, is the restaurant's house band, International Mariachi America, a large ensemble (depending on how many members have been siphoned off to play at weddings and parties) and one of the city's best. The group plays in a supper club atmosphere, with several sets per night, extending occasionally into the wee hours of the morning. As for that food, it sticks mainly to Sonoran standards (tacos, *burros*, *chimichangas*, enchiladas, and the like), with the occa-sional detour into something unusual, like jumbo shrimp flambéed in tequila. Open for lunch, dinner, Sunday brunch. No cover. (Central-North)

### LA FUENTE
### 1749 N. Oracle Rd.
### 520/623-8659

The food is not spectacular, but it's quite dependable and served in a charming atmosphere replete with murals, Mexican handicrafts, and nightly mariachi music. Those mariachi musicians, if rather loud, are indeed a big draw here. Listen while you consume such Sonoran standards as enchiladas and chiles rellenos, Mexican-style steaks, and a couple of more exotic dishes involving chicken, chiles, and chocolate. Open for lunch, dinner, Sunday brunch. No cover. (Central-North)

### ¡TOMA!
### 6310 E. Broadway Blvd.
### 520/745-1922

There's a live flamenco guitarist here Tuesday and Thursday 6:30 to 8:30, a salsa band on Friday 9:30 to 1, and some sort of Latin music, live or recorded, the rest of the time. Cover usually $3. (East Side)

## Rock

### CLUB CONGRESS
### Hotel Congress

Most of the cybercafés that opened in Tucson in the mid-1990s quickly folded, but one that's stayed online is the Library of Congress. No, not the institution in D.C., but a corner of the popular Club Congress in the hotel of the same name, at 311 E. Congress Street. The Library of Congress boasts a T-1 connection to the Internet for its Power Macs and PCs. It's a bar, too, and music's being generated a few steps away every night.

**311 E. Congress St.**
**520/622-8849**
All manner of alternative rock, rocka-
billy, and barely classifiable bands
play on an unpredictable schedule,
with the occasional nouveau lounge
act or burlesque show thrown in for
curiosity value. National acts (like the
Rev. Horton Heat), local bands, and
DJs all hold forth, with something happening every night, from around 9 to 1.
Although it's on the ground floor of a
historic hotel, Club Congress is anything but stuffy; it's a must-stop for
Those Who Would Be Hip. Cover $3 or
$4; three or four times that amount for
some touring bands. (Downtown)

**O'MALLEY'S**
**247 N. Fourth Ave.**
**520/623-8600**
No-nonsense live rock and blues blast
through O'Malley's Thursday through
Saturday 9 to 1. The rest of the time,
it's an ordinary bar that happens to be
situated on cool Fourth Avenue. Cover
usually $3. (Downtown)

*The brewing facilities at Gentle Ben's*
*Brewing Company, p. 190*

Gentle Ben's Brewing Company

**THE OUTBACK**
**296 N. Stone Ave.**
**520/622-4700**
One cover charge gains you access to
four clubs under a single roof. Most of
the time, DJs spin conventional hits,
but on two or three nights each week,
local bands or '70s revival acts (criti-
cally reviled but strangely popular)
hold forth. Cover $3. (Downtown)

**THE ROCK**
**136 N. Park Ave.**
**520/629-9211**
This university-area bar the size of a
small barn has changed identities almost as often as it's changed hands,
which has been fairly frequently. Most
recently, it's delivered exactly what the
name implies, live, on Monday, Friday,
and Saturday from 9 to 1. A good many
touring alternative rock bands hit The
Rock for a night. When the musicians
are local, the cover is usually about $3.
(Central-North)

**SKRAPPY'S**
**3710 N. Oracle Rd.**
**520/408-9644**
Exactly what or when something will
happen here is anybody's guess, but
when Skrappy's gets its act together
and presents a live band, usually on
Friday and Saturday nights, it's usually
an alternative or punk-revival show in
an atmosphere designed for all
ages—meaning a space without alcohol that accommodates teenagers.
Cover usually $3. (West Side)

### Country and Western

**BUSHWACKER LOUNGE**
**4635 N. Flowing Wells Rd.**
**520/887-9027**
An unpretentious bar free of hokum,
the Bushwacker serves the working
class residents of the Flowing Wells

area with live music 8:30 to 12:30 Friday and Saturday, and often Wednesday and Thursday, plus a jam session Sunday. Early in the week, it's karaoke. No cover. (West Side)

## DURANGO SALOON & DANCE HALL
### 1302 W. Roger Rd.
### 520/888-1331

Local country bands play Wednesday through Sunday 9 to 1 in this slightly out-of-the-way space designed for people who want to kick up their heels—cowboy boots not required, but welcome. Country karaoke reigns early in the week. No cover. (West Side)

## LAST TERRITORY STEAKHOUSE
### Sheraton El Conquistador Resort
### 10000 N. Oracle Rd.
### 520/544-1738

If you're staying at the resort, which is a bit removed from town, and don't want to drive all over tarnation looking for a steakhouse and country music, just mosey on in to the Last Territory. It's a little too swank to be authentic, but if you wanted authenticity, you wouldn't be staying at a resort. Live music, often a lone singing guitarist, fills the air Friday and Saturday 6:30 to 9:30, Sunday through Thursday 6 to 9. No cover. (West Side)

## LI'L ABNER'S STEAK HOUSE
### 8501 N. Silverbell Rd.
### 520/744-2800

For years, the lineup has held steady: Dean Armstrong and the Arizona Dance Hands play authentic Western music (as opposed to more commercial country music) Friday and Saturday 8 to 10:30. Armstrong has been in the music business for more than 50 years, so that could be sufficient reason to make a pilgrimage to the out-of-the-way Li'l Abner's. Titan Valley Warheads, a highly accomplished and extremely popular local bluegrass band (named for the Titan missile silos that used to ring Tucson), usually plays Sunday 6 to 9. No cover. (West Side)

## THE MAVERICK
### 4702 E. 22nd St.
### 520/748-0456

The Maverick has long been a reliable country nightclub for folks who aren't obsessed with big-name acts or, for that matter, a unique atmosphere. It's closed on Sunday and karaoke on Monday, but live music from the house band—it's been Troy Olsen and Overdrive for a while—can be had 8 to 1 the rest of the week (it starts at 7 on Friday). No cover. (South Side)

## NEW WEST
### 4385 W. Ina Rd.
### 520/744-7744

It's honky-tonk heaven, even if the country-oriented New West is only one component of a three-clubs-in-one facility; there's also the rock-flavored Gotham and Screwy Louie's Sports Grill. The New West is the big draw, though. Three thousand patrons can mingle comfortably throughout the total 45,000 square feet, which include an 8,000-square-foot racetrack-style dance floor, a photo salon, a souvenir store, and pool tables and video games. The sound and light system get high marks, but some patrons complain that sight lines to the stage aren't so great—not when there's a sea of cowboy hats in front of you. Something's always happening here, but the main purpose of the New West is to bring in well-known acts like Eddie Money, Mark Chesnutt, Chris LeDoux, and Asleep at the

Wheel. What you'll pony up at the door varies widely. (West Side)

## Other Spots

### COTTONWOOD CLUB
**60 N. Alvernon Way**
**520/326-6000**

No, it's not the Harlem Renaissance all over again; this establishment is snuggled back behind the Cottonwood Café, an excellent New Southwestern restaurant. The elegant Cottonwood Club offers some sort of entertainment 9 to midnight every night but Monday. This could involve West Coast swing dancing, funky jams, postmodern lounge acts, or cabaret shows, though it's most likely to be a jazz band. At press time, the Cottonwood was becoming a dinner and entertainment club. Cover varies. (Central-North)

### STELLAR CELLAR
**3335 E. Grant Rd.**
**520/881-7559**

So maybe you want to get into the act. Well, two nights a week this otherwise ordinary bar sets up a microphone and waits to see who'll use it. Here's your chance. Acoustic music is expected 8 to 12 Fridays; at 7:30 Mondays, it's open-mike night for poets. No cover. (Central-North)

## PUBS AND BARS

### BERKY'S
**5769 E. Speedway Blvd.**

# Tucson Bands

*You've seen the sights of Tucson; now it's time to check out the city's best sounds. The following homegrown bands are well established, popular, and innovative, often in some warped way. To find out where they're playing, scan the nightclub and concert listings in the Friday* Arizona Daily Star *or the* Tucson Weekly.

*The Mollys meld Irish and Mexican traditions. The Bad News Blues Band is just what it claims, except the news is really pretty good. Shoebomb is a pop-rock band with a big following. Doo Rag plays mutant blues and sells its own line of kitschy accessories.*

*Giant Sand offers alternative rock with some echoes of country and jazz, while the Sand Rubies purvey highly accomplished pop rock. For a twisted honky-tonk sound, try Al Perry and the Cattle.*

*The Fells is Tucson's leading garage-punk band; Stefan George and Songtower come through with urban folk originals; and Greasy Chicken sells finger-lickin' good bop, post-bop, and progressive jazz.*

520/296-1981

Berky's has never tried to be chic; it's simply a classic dive, a watering hole for people who want to drink a little, talk a little, maybe hear a good local blues or Motown band once in a while (which does make talking a bit difficult). The location on Speedway—the prime east-west drag—makes Berky's a convenient stop along the way to or from dinner or some other evening activity (unless it's downtown). (Central-North)

### THE BUM STEER
**1910 N. Stone Ave.**
**520/884-7377**

Built in the 1970s, the Bum Steer was the first of several local and chain establishments to borrow decorating ideas from the nearest junkyard. It's a casual restaurant with cold drafts, juicy burgers, and a vaulted ceiling from which hangs anything and everything, from airplanes to cannons. The barnlike building also contains several bars, a dance floor, and a video arcade. (West Side)

### CUSHING STREET BAR AND GRILL
**343 S. Meyer Ave.**
**520/622-7984**

Until 1997, Cushing Street was a nice bar in an intriguing location (right

between the Tucson Convention Center and the historic barrio) serving lousy bar food. Under new ownership, the place has retained its barrio-swank atmosphere and added a classy part-bar, part-bistro menu, running the gamut from bacon cheeseburgers to spinach provolone tortellini. The bar end of the operation offers more than 20 wines and eight microbrews. (Downtown)

### FAMOUS SAM'S
**4801 E. 29th St.**
**520/748-1975**

It started out as a little joint near the air base called Sam's Tavern (the owner's name is actually Jerry). Now, Famous Sam's is a franchise operation with two dozen locations around the Southwest—about half of them in Tucson. Each is an independently owned, comfortable, pleasant sports bar with the requisite pool tables and a menu of tasty, generously portioned fried food and sandwiches—including at least one vegetarian option. The address above is for the mother bar; for the rest, check the phone book. Generally, food is served 10 a.m. to 12:30 a.m.; breakfast is also served beginning at 6:30 at a few locations. (South Side)

*The Library of Congress, the cybercafé at Hotel Congress, p. 185*

Stacey Halper

## GENTLE BEN'S BREWING COMPANY
**865 E. University Blvd.**
**520/624-4177**

In 1997 Gentle Ben's transformed itself from an ordinary, longtime University of Arizona student hangout to a UA student hangout that's also a microbrewery. Gentle Ben's moved into a nicely renovated building next to a new development of retail shops, losing whatever seediness it may have taken on at its old location. The microbrewery has a 30-barrel or 930-gallon capacity—enough to keep even UA students satisfied. There's also a burger-oriented menu and a fine outdoor seating area. (Central-North)

## THE SHANTY
**401 E. Ninth St.**
**520/623-2664**

Opened in 1937 as a hangout for railroad workers, The Shanty has changed location and character over the years. Now it's an upscale watering hole for downtown employees and local politicians (in 1992, Bruce Babbitt stopped by to announce his presidential candidacy). Students also flock here on Friday and Saturday nights. One of the main draws is the beer list, announcing 350 imports from around the world, including China. Don't let the address confuse you; The Shanty is on Fourth Avenue, just north of the underpass. (Downtown)

## THE SHELTER COCKTAIL LOUNGE
**4155 E. Grant Rd.**
**520/326-1345**

Built in 1961 as a bomb shelter to shield Tucsonans from an atomic blast, The Shelter now allows people to get blasted inside. The place is a museum of kitsch, with black velvet paintings and sunburst clocks; a shrine to the Kennedy brothers and Martin Luther King Jr.; a jukebox stocked with Dick Dale, the Ventures, and Henry Mancini; and an old TV above the bar that sometimes shows 1960s television series. Oh, yes—it serves alcohol, too. (Central-North)

## DRINKS WITH A VIEW

### FLYING V BAR & GRILL
**Loews Ventana Canyon Resort
7000 N. Resort Dr.
520/299-2020, ext. 5280**
The view of the golf course won't do you much good at night, but this is also a great vantage point for gazing upon the city lights. Twelve draft beers, 28 tequilas, and several specialty margaritas stand among the beverage choices. The grill also offers menus inspired by Southwestern and Latin American cuisine. (East Side)

### LOOKOUT BAR & GRILLE
**Westward Look Resort
245 W. Ina Rd.
520/297-1151**
To accompany happy hour or a nightcap, the elegant Lookout Bar & Grille provides live dance music Thursday through Saturday, plus a superb view of the city lights. All this without a long drive into the foothills. (West Side)

## COFFEEHOUSES

### BENTLEY'S HOUSE OF COFFEE AND TEA
**1730 E. Speedway Blvd.
520/795-0338**
A favorite haunt of University of Arizona students and professors, Bentley's offers a fine range of hot and iced coffee and espresso drinks, plus several teas, excellent desserts, and wholesome light fare (soups, quiche, and such). The place is often packed, but nobody will scold you for settling in for a long session with a newspaper and a cup of something black. (Central-North)

### CAFÉ PARAISO
**Geronimo Complex
820 E. University Blvd.
520/624-1707**
Not the raucous place you'd expect so near the university. Coffee and tea become comfort foods in the reassuring surroundings of wood floors, dark green walls, and classical music. Open 7–11 daily. (Central-North)

### CAFÉ QUEBEC
**121 E. Broadway Blvd.
520/798-3552**
A Generation X favorite, Quebec serves up JFK memorabilia, local art, and such surreal touches as a naked doll in a birdcage, along with a modest but interesting line of java and

---

For some teenagers, Saturday nightlife means cruising. If you're curious about low-rider action—some of these cars can be pretty impressive—check out the scene on Sixth Avenue from 22nd Street to I-19, between about 8 and midnight. You'll be safe in your car, but don't get involved in any trouble on the sidewalk, because a few of these kids are armed. If you're just interested in slow traffic, the other prime cruising strip is Speedway between Campbell and Wilmot. If you're in a hurry, avoid both streets.

*Patio at The Shanty, p. 190*

vegetarian dishes. Open Tue–Sun 11–midnight. (Downtown)

### COFFEE ETC.
**2830 N. Campbell Ave.**
**520/881-8070**
This and its counterpart at 6091 N. Oracle Road offer a bracing variety of coffees from North and South America, Hawaii, Africa, and Southeast Asia 24 hours a day. Only a few varieties are liquid at any one time, but you can buy all the others as beans or grinds. An extensive food menu, including some vegan options, offers you something to soak up all that coffee with. There's also a selection of mugs, coffee- and tea-related items, T-shirts, honeys, cards, and gifts. (Central-North)

### COFFEE PLANTATION
**845 E. University Blvd.**
**520/628-4300**
This Phoenix-based chain has set up shop in Tucson with a variety of coffee-flavored beverages and bagged coffee beans, sandwiches, salads, soups, pastries, and desserts. The iced espresso mocha

and cappuccino have earned plenty of fans for their balance and smoothness. The shop also features Italian sodas with flavored syrup, and, in the University location, a juice bar. The UA shop also provides live music of the singer-songwriter genre 8 to 11 Friday and Saturday, and 7 to 10 Sunday, Wednesday, and Thursday. No cover. Open 6 a.m.–11 p.m. weekdays, 6 a.m.–midnight weekends. Also at 4500 N. Oracle Road. (Central-North)

### CUP CAFÉ
**Hotel Congress**
**311 E. Congress St.**
**520/798-1618**
Pink-haired leather enthusiasts mingle with mild-mannered government workers at this little café just off the hotel lobby. The Cup roasts its own coffees, bakes its own desserts, and whips up Italian, Mexican, and Thai-tinged entrées. Open 8 a.m.–1 a.m. daily. (Downtown)

### CUPPUCCINO'S
**3400 E. Speedway Blvd.**

# Top Ten Movies Filmed in or Around Tucson

By Renée Downing, *Arizona Daily Star* film critic

1. *The Wild Bunch* (1969). Sam Peckinpah shot much of his ultraviolent masterpiece at Old Tucson.

2. *Tombstone* (1993). Val Kilmer's unforgettable turn as Doc Holliday is all the tastier for being correctly situated geographically. Finally, a shootout in a broad arroyo under big cottonwoods and sycamores.

3. *Speed* (1994). The tunnel scenes were filmed near the University of Arizona's McKale Center. Please note that Sandra Bullock's character is a Wildcat fan.

4. *The Outlaw Josey Wales* (1976). Considered to be one of the last of the great classic Westerns, this Clint Eastwood revenge epic was filmed at Old Tucson.

5. *Tin Cup* (1996). Kevin Costner plays a ne'er-do-well pro golfer in a likable sports romance from Ron Shelton (*Bull Durham*). Largely filmed in and around Tucson, and near Tubac.

6. *Desert Bloom* (1986). Tucson stands in for Las Vegas in this affecting, little-seen film about a '50s family living under the shadow of an A-bomb test. Jon Voight, JoBeth Williams, Ellen Barkin, and Annabeth Gish star.

7. *Rio Bravo* (1959). A big, rootin'-tootin' John Wayne vehicle that was filmed . . . nah, you guess.

8. *Boys on the Side* (1995). Whoopie Goldberg, Drew Barrymore, and Mary-Louise Parker experience female bonding mostly on the east side of Tucson.

9. *Alice Doesn't Live Here Anymore* (1973). Ellen Burstyn and Kris Kristofferson star; Martin Scorsese directs. Various glimpses of the Old Pueblo; most memorably, a very young Jodie Foster shoplifting from the Chicago Store downtown.

10. *Tank Girl* (1994). The desert between Tucson and Green Valley stands in for a desiccated future landscape in an adaptation of the popular comic book; starring Lori Petty and Malcolm McDowell.

**520/323-7205**

Cuppuccino's is loud and hectic at the counter, rather like a coffeehouse version of McDonald's, but the service is friendly and quick, the pastries are seductive, and the place is near the Loft Cinema, so it's often full of people parsing the latest art film. Cuppuccino, by the way, describes the house beverage: double espresso infused with steamed milk and topped with frothed milk and cinnamon or chocolate. Open Mon–Wed 7 a.m.– 11 p.m., Thu–Sat 7 a.m.–midnight, Sun 7 a.m.–10 p.m. (Central-North)

### LE CAFFE
**4695 N. Oracle Rd.**
**520/888-6878**

It's not open in the evening, and—at least during its first year of operation, in 1997—the coffee was weak. So why care about this coffeehouse? Because it's open the rest of the day, the coffee may be improving, and everything else about this family-owned business is so satisfying, especially the great soups and made-to-order sandwiches. Open Mon–Sat 9–6. (West Side)

## COMEDY CLUBS

### LAFFS COMEDY CAFFE
**2900 E. Broadway Blvd.**
**520/32-FUNNY**

The city's sole comedy club usually books a headliner from Comedy Central or any number of cable TV comedy shows, and finds local stand-ups to open. One or two shows are offered Wednesday through Sunday, and sometimes Tuesday. If the jokes get lame, you can distract yourself with pool or foozball. The show schedule varies, so call ahead to find out what's going on. (Central-North)

## MOVIE HOUSES OF NOTE

### EL CON THEATERS
**3601 E. Broadway Blvd.**

Scheduled to open sometime in 1998, this 20-screen complex is intended to be a corrective to the Incredible Shrinking-Screen Multiplexes found elsewhere in town: stadium seating, wall-to-wall screens, love seats, and a café featuring gourmet coffee and

*Live music at the Cottonwood Club, p. 188*

Cottonwood Club –Tucson

baked treats. But will your feet still stick to the floor? (Central-North)

## THE LOFT CINEMA
### 3233 E Speedway Blvd.
### 520/795-7777

It started out in the 1960s as a little upstairs theater near the university specializing in soft-core porn. Soon it became Tucson's treasured purveyor of foreign and independent American films. Today the Loft occupies a large building with a big, old-fashioned screen downstairs and a postage stamp–sized screen upstairs. Two or three recent, off-the-beaten-track movies are always showing; and even after 20 years, *The Rocky Horror Picture Show* still screens at midnight every other Saturday. The Loft's snack bar introduced gourmet coffee to Tucson theaters. The overall decor goes through phases of shabbiness, but once the lights are down, you're in a different world, and it ain't Planet Hollywood. (Central-North)

## THE SCREENING ROOM
### 127 E. Congress St.
### 520/622-2262

The room is tiny and the sound is tinny, but this theater brings us older films too obscure for the video stores, new films too obscure for even the Loft, recent work by film school students, and classic movies grouped into mini festivals. (Downtown)

© Metro Tucson CVB/Gill Kenny

# 13

# DAY TRIPS FROM TUCSON

## Day Trip: Willcox Area

### Distance from Tucson: 105 miles

The town of Willcox is not so much a destination as an interesting turn-around point; a couple of prime attractions lie along the road between there and Tucson.

Your first visit will be just outside the town of Benson, which is off Interstate 10 about 45 miles east of Tucson. The **Singing Wind Bookshop** (520/586-2425) is well stocked with volumes devoted to Western literature and the history and nature of the Southwest. The irrepressible Winifred Bundy runs both the store and the working cattle ranch to which it's attached, so you should call ahead to make sure she'll be there and to get specific directions (the store is tricky to find the first time, and you'll have to remember to close a certain gate behind you to prevent cattle escapes).

If you're prepared for a longer ride and have made reservations ahead, the **San Pedro & Southwestern Railroad** (800/269-6314) will call you aboard for a four-hour train ride through the scenic San Pedro Riparian Area. Take I-10 east to Exit 303/Highway 80 (Benson), go 3.5 miles south to Country Club Drive, and left one block to the depot.

Further along the way to Willcox, pull off I-10 at the Dragoon Exit and drive a mile east, following the signs, to the **Amerind Foundation and Museum** (520/586-3666). If you want to learn about Native Americans in the West, this is the best place to pick up the info. Founded in 1937, the museum displays historic (and prehistoric) artifacts, as well as more recent craft items and fine art. (You may also purchase fine new baskets and pottery in the museum's gift shop.) The Spanish Colonial–style building

# TUCSON REGION

**Daytrips from Tucson**

1 Ghost Towns
2 Nogales, Sonora, Mexico
3 Sonoita and Patagonia
4 Tombstone and Bisbee
5 Tubac and Tumacacori
6 Willcox Area

N

Willcox
6
186
10
Dragoon
Benson
80
90
Sunizona
181
191
Pearce
PEARCE RD
Courtland
Gleeson
1
GLEESON RD
4
Tombstone
82
90
Sierra Vista
83
Elgin
Sonoita
3
83
3
Patagonia
Patagonia Lake
State Park
Tubac Presidio
State Historic Park
Tubac
5
Tumacacori
National
Historic
Park
Tumacacori
19
77
Tucson
Green Valley
82
Nogales
2
Nogales, Sonora

Pirtleville
80
Bisbee
4
ARIZONA
SONORA
Naco
92
Mule Mountains

Parker
Canyon
Lake
UNITED STATES
MEXICO

Saguaro
National
Monument

Saguaro
National
Monument

★ — PLACE OF INTEREST

0        25
KILOMETERS
         25
MILES

provides pleasures of its own, but don't get too distracted from the displays of beadwork, weavings, pottery, and other items from generations past. A separate art gallery presents work by a few contemporary Native American artists, as well as pieces by Frederick Remington and his fellow observers of Native life.

Once you finally reach Willcox, you may well be hungry. The town is surrounded by **orchards and farms** that sell cider, pie, and whatever fruits and vegetables are in season. Billboards point the way to the major locations. Also worth a visit is the **Rex Allen Arizona Cowboy Museum** (520/384-4583). Allen, a singing cowboy whose music career peaked in the 1940s and '50s and whose voice is familiar from Walt Disney nature programs, was born in Willcox, for which the town is forever grateful. The museum, at 150 North Railroad Avenue, contains such Allen memorabilia as posters, guitars, saddles, and the like.

*Getting there: Follow Interstate 10 east about 45 miles from Tucson to Benson and the jump-off point for the Singing Wind Bookshop. To reach Willcox, continue on I-10 another 40 miles east. The Dragoon turnoff—Exit 318—to the Amerind Foundation is about 12 miles east of Benson.*

# Day Trip: Ghost Towns

### Distance from Tucson: 130 miles

When a Western town dies, it doesn't go to Hollywood heaven. Its ghost is not only rooted to the earth, it melts into the earth. Real ghost towns don't look like their movie impostors—Old Tucson before business hours, tumbleweeds blowing down the street, the half-unhinged saloon doors creaking in the wind. Real ghost towns release their adobe walls back into the soil and surrender their bricks and wood to scavengers. They're also a nuisance to find in southern Arizona, except for a nest of three along a dusty road linking Tombstone to Highway 191 (called 666 on older maps).

Moving east out of Tombstone, 13 miles of dirt will get you to **Gleeson**. Indians had mined turquoise for centuries before white men started working copper, lead, and silver claims here in the 1870s. In the 1890s, their camp, called Turquoise, was moved to a lower site to improve the water supply and renamed for a successful local miner, John Gleeson. The town thrived into the 1920s, but it was in serious decline by the late '30s. Today a very few people still live among the ruins, and they keep the handful of crosses in the cemetery nicely whitewashed.

Gleeson's old saloon remains standing in dowdy dignity. The hotel, though, is nothing but a solid foundation surrounding a pit. A plastered red-brick building, its corrugated roof peeling off, may have been a blacksmith's shop. Down a side road are the old jail and schoolhouse. The jail, a tough, blocky, two-room concrete structure, is intact except for its bars and windows. The school, once a substantial two-story building, is in worse shape.

Two classical columns still rise at what used to be the entrance; an impressive arch once connected them, but it collapsed years ago.

Four more miles of dirt road lead to **Courtland**, a 1909 boom town that once held 2,000 residents, most of whom were employed by the area's four mining companies. Courtland went bust by World War II. The town snuggles up against the Dragoon Mountains, a place thick with mesquite that shades the occasional cow. Today only a jail—identical to Gleeson's—and a few roofless concrete and stone structures and several foundations remain here.

About 5 miles farther on is **Pearce**, founded in the 1890s and once home to a population of 1,500. When the local mine closed in the 1930s, most of the townsfolk moved on. Several people still live in Pearce, and a big, modern school serves the area, but the town's main tourist attraction closed a few years ago. That was the Pearce Old Store, an 1893 conglomeration of adobe, stucco, wood, and tin. In recent years it served as a general store, curiosity shop, and museum of Old West paraphernalia. The building's still there, locked up tight, and if anybody ever reopens it, the place should be worth a look.

You can't get into any of Pearce's other abandoned but still-usable buildings, either, which is probably just as well for safety's sake. Besides the possibility of a wall falling on you, these old structures may now be home to rattlesnakes, bats, and bees, none of which are especially hospitable to intruders. In Pearce you can see, from the outside only, some very modest old houses, a post office, the remnants of the Commonwealth Mine and Mill operation dominating a hill, and a church with junk cars surrounded by barbed wire. More accessible is the dilapidated old marshal's office and a cemetery in which Abraham Lincoln's bodyguard supposedly rests.

*Getting there: Take Interstate 10 east about 45 miles to Benson's Exit 303; go through town and pick up Highway 80 south, traveling about 25 miles south to Tombstone. In Tombstone, watch for an eastbound road marked as leading to the towns mentioned above, or to Sunsites, or to Highway 191. To return to Tucson from Pearce without retracing your steps, keep following the same road a very short distance to Highway 191, then go north to Interstate 10 and head west.*

# Day Trip: Nogales, Sonora, Mexico

### Distance from Tucson: 65 miles

If you've never set foot off U.S. soil, this is your big chance. Mexico lies a mere one-hour drive south of Tucson. Now, the border town of Nogales, Sonora (another Nogales mirrors it on the Arizona side of the line), won't deliver the natural beauty, colonial elegance, or tropical chic of other regions of Mexico. It's a frontier city, and northern Mexico has always been rather neglected by the central government and disparaged by residents of the Federal District. Not only is it a frontier city, it crowds up against the border, which means its economy depends heavily on one-day visits from

U.S. tourists who come down for lunch and a few souvenirs. So Nogales, at least that portion within easy walking distance of the customs office, can seem to be one curio shop after another. This can be fun, as long as you're ready for it. And you don't need a passport unless you're venturing beyond the town.

The first thing you should do is park your car on the U.S. side of the border. Mexican urbanites drive, shall we say, improvisationally, and the traffic is thick and frazzling within the first couple miles of the border. It will take far longer to re-enter the United States in a vehicle than on foot. If you do drive into the country, obtain Mexican auto insurance beforehand because even minor traffic accidents (and moving violations) can lead to great unpleasantness without it. A half-dozen parking lots dot the American side of the border, with daily rates ranging from $3 to $4. Of course, you should not leave any valuables in your car. And be sure to learn what time your lot closes; you may find yourself on the wrong side of a locked gate as early as 7 or 8 p.m.

Most of the prime Nogales shopping lies along the main drag, **Avenida Obregón**. Shop owners will try to lure you in to examine their wares. In these shops (as opposed to the larger department stores), you should never pay the asking price for anything. You will be expected to dicker, and you will generally be able to negotiate in English. Even if the shopkeeper pretends this is an innovation, he really does anticipate bargaining with you and will usually come down 15 to 30 percent (the quickest way to get a price concession is to head for the exit). Prices are generally posted in U.S. dollars, but if some look astronomically high, they're surely in pesos, which are also represented by the dollar sign. U.S. currency is welcomed in all border shops, and Visa and MasterCard are frequently accepted. Just remember that you may return with no more than $400 worth of goods per person, per trip; for alcohol, the limit is one liter per person over 21.

Not everything you find will be a bargain, or even desirable. Cut-rate luxury items like Rolex watches are usually fakes. "Pure" vanilla extract sells for low prices, but it may actually be cut with coumarin, an anticoagulant and flavor mimic. Coumarin is supposedly banned from Mexican vanilla, but U.S. authorities have their doubts about enforcement. You can rely, however, on the quality and authenticity of leading liquor brands, which are deeply discounted.

What you should really look for in Nogales are leather goods, handblown glass, ceramics, folk art, wrought iron, furniture (if you have a way to get it across the border and home, or can work something out with the seller), and whatever trinkets tickle your fancy. Along Avenida Obregón, stop by **Firenze** for perfumes, cosmetics, or crystal. Across the street, check out the **Continental** for a selection of enameled wood boxes and chests from Michoacán, and ironwood carvings that may or may not be from the Seri Indians. Decorative strings of fat red chiles hang at the nearby **Maya de Mexico**. East across the railroad tracks is Calle Elias,

*Street vending in Nogales*

where you'll happen upon **Antigua de Mexico**, a rambling store full of interesting furniture, glass, and stone carvings. Nearby, **El Changarro** offers everything from inexpensive Christmas ornaments to pricey chandeliers and hand-carved chests, all well chosen. If you're searching for folk art, try the selection of *santos* at **Baz-Art**, on Elias closer to the border.

Other favorite stores are the **Lazy Frog** (57 Calle Campillo), with an excellent variety of fine folk art, especially pottery and wood carvings; and **El Sarape** (161 Avenida Obregón), which offers sterling silver jewelry, pewter frames, and handmade clothing.

Drug stores offer great bargains, too. Retin-A is deeply discounted in Mexico, and prescription drugs tend to be far cheaper than in the U.S. Just be sure to carry your prescription with you, so the pharmacist will understand exactly what you want and so U.S. customs officials won't give you trouble—because otherwise, they will. The pharmacies preferred by many visitors from the U.S. are **Farmacia Galeno**, on Avenida Obregón, and **La Campana**, at Obregón and Diaz.

As for food, the old rule about eating in Mexico is to avoid water, ice, and uncooked vegetables. Today the larger restaurants catering to tourists aren't likely to serve up much gastric distress, unless you simply can't handle spicy food. Still, more cautious visitors may prefer to order a nice, well-cooked enchilada rather than ceviche, and scrape off the shredded lettuce. Good restaurants near the border are the moderately priced **Café Elvira**, on Obregón near the customs office, and the slightly more expensive **La Roca**, occupying an elegant stone building on Elias. Both serve savory Mexican specialties, and not just the tacos and burritos you find at American fast food joints. **El Greco** and **El Cid**, both on Obregón, also offer moderately priced traditional Mexican dishes, as well as steaks and seafood.

*Getting there:* Take Interstate 19 south about 60 miles almost to its terminus, getting off at Exit 4 and following the signs through Nogales, Arizona, to the border.

# Day Trip: Sonoita and Patagonia

**Distance from Tucson: 60 miles**

About 2,000 feet higher and 10 degrees cooler than Tucson, Sonoita lies in a lovely, rolling, mesquite-dotted valley between the green Santa Rita and brown Patagonia Mountain ranges. Until the late '90s, Sonoita was the wine capital of Arizona. Things have not been going well for the area's vintners recently, though, and oenophiles may prefer to check out the newer wineries in Willcox. Still, you never know how things will turn out from one season to the next, so you may want to stop by for a tasting at **Sonoita Vineyards**, or the **Santa Cruz Winery**, or whatever other vintners you may find along Highway 82 between Sonoita and the tiny town of Elgin, just to the east. (The most highly regarded house, Callaghan, is no longer open to the public at this writing.) Two superb restaurants may be found in Sonoita: **Karen's Wine Country Café** (520/455-5282) and the Roman-style Italian **Er Pastaro** (520/455-5821). Reservations are an absolute must.

Birders must make a pilgrimage to the **Patagonia Sonoita Creek Preserve**, owned by the Nature Conservancy. Wander along the trails that thread through the tall, old cottonwood trees and watch for some of the 250 bird species that drop by through the year, especially March through September. Because this is a privately held preserve dedicated to the welfare of the abundant plant and animal life (javelina, coyotes, deer, mountain lions, and rattlesnakes knock about here, generally out of sight), this is not the place to splash around in the water or even picnic. Just amble through slowly and keep your eyes and ears open.

For more hands-on recreation, you could go to **Lake Patagonia** or **Parker Canyon Lake**, 14 and 40 miles, respectively, from the town of Patagonia. Be warned that these are not pretty, high-forest lakes; the surroundings can look bare to people accustomed to mountain lakes. **Patagonia** itself is home to a few galleries featuring the work of local artists.

*Getting there:* Take Interstate 10 east about 20 miles, then turn south on Highway 83; continue another scenic 27 miles south to Sonoita. When you hit town, turn right on Highway 82 and drive 12 miles to Patagonia; Elgin lies in the opposite direction.

# Day Trip: Tubac and Tumacacori

**Distance from Tucson: 40 miles**

These two modest villages could have become the real seat of power and culture in southern Arizona if Spanish Colonial politics and religious policy had turned out a little differently in the seventeenth and eighteenth centuries. Tubac is Arizona's oldest town, at least from the European era, and had been inhabited by the Hohokam for more than a thousand centuries before that. Now, Tubac is an artists' colony, with about 80 interesting little crafts shops dotting every street. That doesn't count the town's 40 or so art galleries. Most of these establishments feature local work, although imports from Latin America are also common. The town's Chamber of Commerce provides a handy, free map, as do many of the shopkeepers. Two shops that stand out from the rest, simply because they purvey less common goods, are **Tortuga Books**, a fine little bookstore specializing in but not limited to tomes about anything Southwestern, and **Chile Pepper**, a store featuring gourmet Southwestern foods.

More historically oriented visitors should stop at the **Presidio Museum** in **Tubac Presidio State Historic Park**. Here you'll learn about the area under its successive waves of Native American, Spanish, Mexican, and Anglo settlers. The museum also sells a very inexpensive pamphlet guiding you on a walking tour of the old town. Or, still in the park, take a look at the ruins of the original 1751 Spanish fort—not much is left, but it's more than you'll find of Tucson's own fort constructed a few years later.

The 4.5-mile **Juan Bautista de Anza National Historic Trail** leads you past some archaeological ruins and across (several times) the San Pedro River; water-resistant shoes are a good idea, but you won't likely do any serious wading unless it's been raining. The trail winds up at **Tumacacori National Historical Park**, which is also accessible by car. You need know only two things about Tumacacori. First, the name is accented on the third of its five syllables. Second, it holds the romantic

*Shopping in Tubac*

© Metro Tucson CVB/Gill Kenny

ruins of a once-important mission church built in the late eighteenth century. Its adobe walls are 6 feet thick; displays tell about the building process and the daily life of the Native Americans under the supervision of the missionaries.

**Getting there:** *Take Interstate 19 south about 40 miles to Exit 34.*

## Weekend Getaway: Tombstone and Bisbee

**Distance from Tucson: 95 miles**

**Tombstone**, in case you ditched American Popular Culture 101, was the site of the gunfight at the **O.K. Corral**, pitting the more or less law-enforcing Earp brothers and Doc Holliday against the Clanton and McLaury brothers. The corral still stands on Allen Street, between Third and Fourth Avenues, and gunfire still blazes there—but it's only stunt men shooting blanks. Tombstone was a tough, wild, wicked, thriving silver-mine boom town in the late nineteenth century, for a while boasting a population much larger than Tucson's—in fact, in the 1880s it was the biggest metropolis between St. Louis and San Francisco. The place thrives now mainly as a tourist attraction, very well preserved but necessarily a little artificial.

The old **Court House**, on Toughnut Street between Third and Fourth, is now a museum exhibiting nineteenth-century clothing, household accessories, cattlemen's and lawyers' paraphernalia, and even a hangman's platform. The **Museum of the West**, 109 South Third Street, plunges you even more thoroughly into daily life a century ago. Lay your hands on a butter churn, an old washing machine, and even more primitive appliances. Oddly, the facility also displays a lock of hair purportedly trimmed from the scalp of George Washington, who never made it this far from Virginia.

*Witness a gunfight in Tombstone.*

The **Bird Cage Theatre**, on Allen east of Fifth Avenue, was a notorious nightspot catering to outlaws and other unsavory types. The name is derived from the 14 cagelike compartments suspended from the ceiling in which prostitutes tended their customers. Upstanding modern citizens may wish to quench their thirst at the **Crystal Palace Saloon**, investigate whatever family-oriented entertainment may be offered at the 1881 **Schieffelin Hall**, or browse the various shops proffering antiques or Native American arts and crafts. All of these places are easy walking along or just off Tombstone's main drag.

For information on the limited motels and B&Bs in Tombstone, contact the town's Chamber of Commerce at 520/457-9317. But consider moving on to **Bisbee** for the night. There, the B&Bs are more quaint (and plentiful), and the **Copper Queen Hotel** (800/247-5829) offers typical Old West lodgings: no-nonsense rooms over an ornate lobby and restaurant. Call the Bisbee Chamber of Commerce at 520/432-5421 for more information on bed-and-breakfast inns.

The real reason to visit Bisbee, though, is for its atmosphere. Less touristy than Tombstone, Bisbee offers attractions that are generally more subtle. Hugging the slopes of the Mule Mountains, the old part of Bisbee looks rather like a San Francisco that never quite made it. Phelps Dodge mined copper here from 1881 to 1975, and the flat portion of the municipality does show all the marks of a company town. But the hilly oldest portion— most of it dating from around 1910, rebuilt after a devastating fire—remains utterly charming. The homes and public buildings have been neatly restored or are in the process of being spruced up. This is a wonderful town for strolling, if the inclines don't leave you breathless. Artists and craftspeople pretty much took over the place from Phelps Dodge, and the town is full of little shops and cafés. Just remember that nearly everything closes at night; be prepared to hole up in a quiet room with a good book.

The first mining in Bisbee took place in shafts, which you can sink into courtesy of the **Queen Mine Tour**. Don a raincoat and hard hat (both provided by the tour operators), and ride with a veteran miner-guide through the 47-degree tunnels, learning each step of how copper was wrested from the earth (520/432-2071). Eventually, the mines switched to the less expensive but more ecologically destructive open-pit technique, an example of which you may inspect on the **Lavender Pit Open Mine Bus Tour** (520/432-2071), leaving at noon daily from the Queen Mine Building.

If you're not up for such outings, or if you are and just can't get enough mining history, check out the **Bisbee Mining and Historical Museum**, which displays local minerals, historic photographs, and clothing of early settlers. A facility devoted more to private life in the Old West is the **Mulheim Heritage House Museum**, a restored 10-room home built in stages between 1898 and 1915.

While you're in the area, you might make a detour to the **Arizona Cactus Botanical Gardens**, six miles south of Bisbee, off Border Road. It features a free tour of a high-desert garden with hundreds of cacti and other succulents (520/432-7040).

*Getting there:* Take Interstate 10 east about 45 miles to Benson's Exit 303; go through town and pick up Highway 80 south, traveling about 25 miles south to Tombstone. Bisbee huddles another 25 miles further south.

## IMPORTANT PHONE NUMBERS

### Emergency

Police, Fire, Ambulance, 911

### Major Hospitals and Emergency Medical Centers

**El Dorado Hospital**, 886-6361
**Kino Community Hospital**, 573-2800
**La Frontera Psychiatric Health Facility**, 746-0260
**Northwest Medical Center**, 742-9000
**Palo Verde Mental Health Services**, 324-4340
**St. Mary's Hospital**, 622-5833
**St. Joseph's Hospital**, 296-3211
**Tucson General Hospital** (osteopathic), 318-6300
**Tucson Heart Hospital**, 696-2328
**Tucson Medical Center**, 327-5461
**University Medical Center**, 694-0111
**Veterans Administration Medical Center**, 792-1450
**Westcenter** (addiction and behavioral health crisis call line), 795-0952

## VISITOR INFORMATION

### TUCSON CONVENTION AND VISITORS' BUREAU

**130 S. Scott Ave.**
**520/624-1817**
http://www.arizonaguide.com/clients/MMTCVB/000000/001.html

**City of Tucson visitors' Web page**
http://www.ci.tucson.az.us/visit.htm

## CITY MEDIA

### Daily newspapers

*Arizona Daily Star* (morning)
*Tucson Citizen* (afternoon)

### Suburban and weekly publications

*Daily Territorial*
*Desert Airman* (Davis-Monthan Air Force Base)
*Desert Leaf*
*Green Valley News & Sun*
*Oro Valley Explorer*
*Tucson Weekly*

### Magazines

*Tucson Guide Quarterly*
*Tucson Lifestyle*
*Tucson Magazine*

### Ethnic publications

*Arizona Jewish Post*
*El Imparcial*
*El Monitor Hispano*

### Broadcast television stations

KGUN channel 9 (ABC)
KHRR channel 40 (Telemundo)
KMSB channel 11 (Fox)
KOLD channel 13 (CBS)
KTTU channel 18 (UPN)
KUAT channel 6 (PBS)
KVOA channel 4 (NBC)

### Radio stations

KCUB 1290 AM/country
KFFN 1490 AM/sports, talk
KFLR 88.5 FM/Christian

KFLT 830 AM/Christian
KFMA 92.1 FM/alternative rock
KGMS 97.1 FM/Christian rock
KGVY 1080 AM/big bands
KHYT 107.5 FM/rock
KIIM 99.5 FM/country
KLPX 96.1 FM/rock
KMRR 1330 AM/country
KMXZ 94.9 FM/adult contemporary
KNST 790 AM/news, talk
KOHT 98.3 FM/Hispanic music
KQTL 1210 AM/Hispanic music
KRQQ 93.7 FM/contemporary hits
KSAZ 580 AM/'40s–'60s pop
KSJM 97.5 FM/contemporary hits
KTCZ 1450 AM/Hispanic
KTKT 990 AM/news, talk, sports
KTUC 1400 AM/talk, sports, news
KUAT 1550 AM/jazz, public affairs
KUAT 90.5 FM/classical
KUAZ 89.1 FM/jazz, public affairs
  (NPR)
KVOI 690 AM/Christian talk
KWFM 92.9 FM/rock oldies
KXCI 91.3 FM/community radio
KXEW 1600 AM/Tejano
KZLZ 105.3 FM/Hispanic contem-
  porary
KZPT 104.1 FM/adult contemporary

## BOOKSTORES

**Antigone Books** (feminist)
411 N. Fourth Ave., 520/792-3715
**Arizona Bookstore** (college)
815 N. Park Ave., 520/622-4717
**Arizona–Sonora Desert Museum
and Bookshop**
2021 N. Rinney Rd., 520/578-3008
**B. Dalton Bookseller**
Park Mall, 5870 E. Broadway,
  520/747-0330
El Con Mall, 3601 E. Broadway,
  520-/327-4294
Tucson Mall, 4500 N. Oracle Rd.,
  520/293-7666

**Barnes & Noble**
5130 E. Broadway, 520/512-1166
7325 N. La Cholla Blvd., 520/742-6402
**Book Mark**
5001 E. Speedway, 520/881-6350
**Borders**
4235 N. Oracle Rd., 520/292-1331
**Jonathan's Educational Resources**
  (children's)
3100 N. Stone Ave., 520/628-1108
5633 E. Speedway, 520/885-9112
**Kids Center** (children's)
1725 N. Swan Rd., 520/322-5437
**La Casa Del Libro** (Spanish
  language)
2802 E. 22nd St., 520/881-2489
**Minds in Motion** (children's)
3400 E. Speedway #102, 520/
  795-0676
**Teaching Tools** (children's)
405 E. Wetmore Rd., 520/888-1223
**University of Arizona Bookstore**
University of Arizona, 520/621-2426
**Waldenbooks**
Park Mall, 5870 E. Broadway,
  520/747-0066
**Waldenbooks Waldenkids**
Tucson Mall, 4500 N. Oracle Rd.,
  520/293-6799

## MAJOR POST OFFICES

Small stations and annexes are scattered through the city; these are the
principal offices in each area.

**Casas Adobes Branch**
6281 N. Oracle Rd.
Tucson, AZ 85704
800/297-5543
**Cherrybell Station**
1501 S. Cherrybell Strav.
Tucson, AZ 85726
520/388-5175
**Downtown Station**
141 S. Sixth Ave.

Tucson, AZ 85701
800/275-8777
**Kino Station**
2051 N. 13th Ave.
Tucson, AZ 85703
800/275-8777
**Mission Station**
315 W. Valencia Rd.
Tucson, AZ 85706
800/297-5543
**Rincon Station**
1099 S. Pantano Rd.
Tucson, AZ 85710
800/297-5543
**Silverbell Station**
975 N. Silverbell Rd.
Tucson, AZ 85745
800/297-5543
**Sun Station**
2100 E. Speedway Blvd.
Tucson, AZ 85716
800/275-8777

## MULTICULTURAL RESOURCES

**Tucson Black Chamber of Commerce**
1690 N. Stone Ave., Suite 113
Tucson, AZ 85705
520/623-0099
**Tucson Hispanic Chamber of Commerce**
823 E. Speedway Blvd.
Tucson, AZ 85719
520/620-0005
**Tucson Indian Center**
131 E. Broadway Blvd.
Tucson, AZ 85705
520/884-7131
**Tucson Lesbian, Gay and Bisexual Community Center/Wingspan**
422 N. Fourth Ave.
Tucson, AZ 85705
520/624-1779

## BABYSITTING/CHILD CARE

**A Family Sitting Agency**
520/722-8407
**A Peace of Heart Babysitting Service**
520/882-3081
**A-1 Messner Sitter Service**
520/881-1578
**Choice Care Agency**
520/322-6966
**Sick Child Program**
520/795-2433

## RESOURCES FOR NEW RESIDENTS

**Bright Beginnings**
520/721-8625
**Welcome Newcomers**
520/290-9191
**Welcome Wagon International**
520/622-3492

## DISABLED ACCESS INFORMATION

**Information and Referral Service**
3130 N. Dodge Blvd.
Tucson, AZ 85716
520/881-1794

# Cater to Your Interests on Your Next Vacation

## ABOUT THE AUTHOR

James Reel, one of the few people born in Arizona who has stayed put, has lived in Tucson for a quarter-century. Since 1988 he has written about classical music, jazz, and offbeat people and issues for *The Arizona Daily Star*, where his last known title was Arts and Entertainment Editor. His more unusual features have included a survey of what sorts of pipelines, tunnels, animals, and corpses lie beneath Tucson's streets. Before joining the *Star*, Reel toiled 12 years at the University of Arizona's KUAT radio, beginning as a

Sarah Prall

lowly substitute announcer and rising to the post of music director. Besides music performance programs, Reel also produced and hosted TV segments on local history. He currently writes features for the record magazine *Fanfare* and an irreverent monthly column on literary matters for the online magazine *The Whole Wired Word* (www.pictograph.com). His music-appreciation screed, *The Timid Soul's Guide to Classical Music*, is also available online (www.azstarnet.com/public/packages/reelbook/contents.htm). A graduate of the University of Arizona, Reel holds degrees in French and library science.

**JOHN MUIR PUBLICATIONS**
and its City•Smart Guidebook
authors are dedicated to building
community awareness within
City•Smart cities.

**We are proud to work with the
Literacy Volunteers of Tucson as
we publish this guide to Tucson.**

**Literacy Volunteers of Tucson** is an affiliate of
Laubach Literacy Action and Literacy Volunteers
of America. Founded in 1961, Literacy Volunteers of
Tucson focuses on raising public awareness of literacy
issues and on uniting students and tutors in appropriate
learning centers, including public school systems, churches,
community centers, and libraries. Volunteers tutor one-on-one
and in small groups and teach English as a Second Language
(ESL), Adult Basic Education, GED, and Citizenship.

**For more information, please contact:**
Literacy Volunteers of Tucson
Phone: 520/882-8006
Fax: 520/882-4986
Note: At press time, Literacy Volunteers
of Tucson was in the process of moving.
Phone and fax numbers are subject
to change.

**Literacy Volunteers
of Tucson**

"EACH ONE TEACH ONE"